365 DAILY MEDITATIONS FOR WOMEN

365 Daily Meditations for Women

MARY RUTH HOWES, EDITOR

IRIS BELLAMY / BECKY DUROST FISH

MARGARET ANNE HUFFMAN / MAXINE DOWD JENSEN

ANNE K. KILLINGER / DEBRA K. KLINGSPORN

REBECCA LAIRD / NELL W. MOHNEY

MARILYN BROWN ODEN / DONNA SCHAPER

KATHLEEN F. TURNER / SHIRLEY POPE WAITE

DIMENSIONS
FOR LIVING
NASHVILLE

365 DAILY MEDITATIONS FOR WOMEN

Copyright © 1997 by Dimensions for Living

This book is printed on recycled, acid-free paper.

ISBN 0-687-01733-5

Scripture quotations noted JBP are from *The New Testament in Modern English*, Copyright © 1972 by J. B. Phillips.

Scripture quotations noted GNB are from *The Good News Bible*, Today's English Version, copyright © 1976 by American Bible Society. Used by permission.

Scripture quotations noted CEV are from the Contemporary English Version of the bible, copyright © American Bible Society, 1991, 1992. Used by permission.

Scripture quotations noted NKJV are from The New King James Version of the Bible, copyright © 1982 by Thomas Nelson, Inc. Used by permission.

Scripture quotations noted JB are from *The Jerusalem Bible*, copyright © 1966 by Darton, Longman & Todd, Ltd. and Doubleday & Company, Inc. Used by permission of the publishers.

Scripture quotations noted KJV are from the King James Version of the Bible.

Scripture quotations noted NIV are from the *Holy Bible: New International Version*. Copyright © 1973, 1978, 1984 by the International Bible Society. Used by permission of Zondervan Bible Publishers.

Scripture quotations noted NRSV are from the New Revised Standard Version of the Bible, copyright © 1989 by the Division of Education of the National Council of Churches of Christ in the United States of America. Used by permission.

Scripture quotations noted RSV are from the Revised Standard Version of the Bible, copyright © 1946, 1952, 1971 by the Division of Christian Education of the National Council of Churches of Christ in the USA. Used by permission.

Scripture quotations noted TLB are from *The Living Bible*, copyright © 1971 by Tyndale House Publishers, Wheaton, IL. Used by permission.

Scripture quotations noted NEB are from *The New English Bible*. © The Delegates of the Oxford University Press and The Syndics of the Cambridge University Press 1961, 1970. Reprinted by permission.

Scripture quotations noted NASB are from the New American Standard Bible, © The Lockman Foundation 1960, 1962, 1968, 1971, 1972, 1973, 1975, 1977. Used by permission.

The meditations for April 4 and April 12 are from *Delight in the Day*, by Shirley Pope Waite. Copyright 1993. Used by permission of Tyndale House Publishers, Inc. All rights reserved.

98 99 00 01 02 03 04 05 06 — 10 9 8 7 6 5 4 3 2

MANUFACTURED IN THE UNITED STATES OF AMERICA

CONTENTS

FOREWORD

*W*elcome to 365 *Daily Meditations for Women.* We invite you to spend the next twelve months with twelve women of faith who share what it means for them to have faith and to live out that faith in daily life. Each month a different woman writes about her trust in Jesus Christ, her belief that God loves us and, through his Spirit, goes with us through all the events of our lives, good times and bad. They write, first of all, as women, but also as mothers, stepmothers, godmothers, grandmothers, daughters, wives, neighbors, working women, pastors, pastors' wives, caregivers, encouragers—and as people who struggle with faith. They celebrate the joys and achievements of women and call us to follow the steps of our pioneering mothers. They rejoice in the beauty of the natural world, but they are also realistic and note its dangers. They call us to risk; to reach out beyond our comfortable worlds to the foreigner and the stranger; to share our love, our riches, and our faith; to make the whole world our family.

Though each woman writes from her own perspective in her own style, you will discover recurring themes and images from month to month:

- the healing power of laughter
- the artistry and comfort of quilts
- the trauma of a parent's illness and death
- the support and comfort of friends
- the pain of a child's death

- the outstretched arms of Christ
- the joy in the present moment
- the benefits of memorizing Scripture
- the shock of accident and illness
- the transforming power of gratitude
- the need to face our fears
- the risks of love
- the beauty of worship
- the ache of unanswered questions
- the light in the darkness
- and always, the presence of God.

Encouragment, comfort, joy, blessing—these and more are waiting for you in 365 *Daily Meditations for Women*.

—Mary Ruth Howes, Editor

ABOUT THE WRITERS

IRIS BELLAMY is an ordained minister who serves with her husband as co-coordinator of Sonship Recovery Ministries, Inc., which ministers to substance abusers. She manages the administrative arm of the ministry, as well as the women's counterpart ministry known as Hannah's House. Her latest venture is Sonship Wives, which caters to the spiritual and emotional needs of the wives of recovering addicts. In addition to these responsibilities, she also is an executive assistant and the mother of one son, Anatole T. Gboizo II.

BECKY DUROST FISH, former editor of *Virtue* magazine, is a freelance writer and editor who also speaks to singles' and women's groups. She and her husband, Bruce, live in Bend, Oregon.

MARGARET ANNE HUFFMAN, former family editor and award-winning reporter for *The Shelbyville* (Indiana) *News*, is the author of numerous books, including *Through the Valley*, *Second Wind*, and *Everyday Prayers for Grandmothers*, and a contributor to *Flights of Angels, 365 Meditations for Mothers of Young Children, 365 Meditations for Mothers of Teens,* and

365 Meditations for Grandmothers. In addition to writing, she enjoys speaking to and serving in various community organizations. She and her pastor husband live on the Big Blue River in Shelbyville, Indiana, and have three children and two grandchildren.

MAXINE DOWD JENSEN is a freelance writer and the author of four books, including *The Warming of Winter* and *Old Is Older Than Me.* She lives in Lee's Summit, Missouri.

ANNE K. KILLINGER, who was trained as a concert pianist and once taught piano at Georgetown College in Kentucky, is a gifted writer and the author of *An Inner Journey to Easter* and a contributor to *365 More Meditations for Women* and *365 Meditations for Mothers of Teens.* Recently she served as the organist for the Little Stone Church on Mackinac Island, Michigan. She and her husband, John, have two grown sons and make their home in Williamsburg, Virginia.

DEBRA K. KLINGSPORN is a freelance writer and the author or coauthor of six books, including *Shattering Our Assumptions: Breaking Free of Expectations—Others and Our Own.* Before moving to Minnesota nine years ago, she was vice-president of Carol DeChant & Associates, a public relations firm based in Chicago. Prior to that, she worked for Word Publishing for nearly ten years as director of marketing and public relations.

REBECCA LAIRD is the editor of *Fellowship in Prayer,* a journal of spiritual experience in Princeton, New Jersey. She is an ordained minister, retreat leader, and author of five books, including *Leslie Weatherhead's The Will of God: A Workbook.* She and her husband have two daughters and make their home in Madison, New Jersey.

NELL W. MOHNEY is a popular motivational author and speaker who leads seminars for business groups, professional organizations, and church gatherings nationwide, including the Women's Conference at the Crystal Cathedral in Garden

Grove, California. She is the author of several books, including *Don't Put a Period Where God Put a Comma* and *How to Be Up on Down Days,* and is a regular columnist for the *Chattanooga Free Press* and *Kingsport Times-News Press.* Nell and her husband, Ralph, are the proud grandparents of Ellen, age fifteen, and Wesley, age twelve. They live in Chattanooga, Tennessee.

MARILYN BROWN ODEN is a seminar and retreat leader and the author of five books, including *Wilderness Wanderings* and *Land of Sickles and Crosses,* a contributor to *365 Meditations for Grandmothers,* and the writer of *Advent, A Calendar of Devotions* (1993, 1994, 1995). She also has been an elementary school counselor and has taught writing at two universities. She lives in Dallas, Texas.

DONNA SCHAPER is a minister, a writer, a mother, a wife, and a gardener. Her latest book is *Sabbath: A Way to Have Enough Time.* She lives in Amherst, Massachusetts.

KATHLEEN F. TURNER is a writer whose articles have appeared in numerous periodicals such as *Guideposts, Christian Herald,* and *Virtue* magazine. She also is a contributor to *365 Meditations for Mothers of Young Children.* She and her husband, Darrell, lead the singles' Bible fellowship at their church and edit and write the church's monthly newsletter. They have two daughters and make their home in Fort Wayne, Indiana.

SHIRLEY POPE WAITE is a freelance writer, speaker, and instructor who teaches writing courses through area community colleges and conducts workshops at numerous writers conferences. She also leads women's retreats and is co-founder of a local retreat now in its twenty-first year. She lives in Walla Walla, Washington.

January

In the Bleak Midwinter

Kathleen F. Turner

JANUARY 1   MY NEW CALENDAR

*You will keep in perfect peace him whose mind is steadfast,
because he trusts in you.*   —*Isaiah 26:3 NIV*

N o! Today I will not do it—make New Year's resolutions that I know I'll break within three weeks. I will, however, go through my old calendar and mark dates in my new one. While others plan diets, exercise programs, and revised sleeping schedules on New Year's Day, I enjoy my new calendar. Whether decorated with majestic photos, wacky sayings, or something inspirational, it launches me into the new year. And since no two years are the same, I never want the same style of calendar.

In the new calendar I write birthdays, anniversaries, and my daughter's always-scheduled-way-in-advance appointment with the orthodontist. I also wander through the previous year's calendar, reliving its events. "Remember when _____ happened?" I call out to my husband. "Can you believe that _____ was that long ago?" Some things are pleasant memories; others I want to forget. I wonder what the new year will hold and what I'll be thinking a year from now.

It would be good to know what is ahead, I find myself thinking. I could avoid certain situations, people, or places

11

and be prepared for every emergency. Then I think, *no*. I'd be spending so much time preparing that I wouldn't live in the precious present. I'd be living in the future. Worse than that, I wouldn't give God the opportunity to be everything to me. I would lose the exercise of my faith as it grows strong when hanging on to him in the face of uncertainty. One day at a time with God is good.

Father, as I close one calendar and lay open another one, I lay the days of this new year before you. Help me to walk in peace because my faith is steadfastly fixed in you.

JANUARY 2   THE TREES

. . . like a tree planted.   —*Psalm 1:3 KJV*

The wind shrieked through our backyard and wailed across the front. I watched from my window as millions of snowflakes were driven mercilessly by the relentless, bitter air. Garbage cans thudded over and rolled in the street. Leaves cartwheeled madly away.

The trees groaned and swayed like dry skeletons. The hickories, oaks, and maples that towered over our house and the houses nearby seemed helpless. One enormous oak, which had grown in an arc leaning toward the house across the street, looked as though it might be the first to snap and crash onto a rooftop. I cringed, waiting for the cracking to begin. *This is why you buy homeowner's insurance,* I reminded myself.

But the snapping and ensuing thud never happened. Then I remembered a fact about healthy, normal trees. For as much of the tree that exists above the ground, there is an equal amount of tree under the ground. These trees are huge. No wonder the wind was ineffective!

Like a tree, every Christian starts the new life as a sapling. As we grow in Christ, our roots inch deeper into him. Our faith grows, and we are less shaken by events and circumstances. Temptation's winds have decreasing sway in our lives, for we are trees planted solidly in Christ. Even though we may groan in the wind, we are unmovable, not because of who we are but because of where our roots are placed.

God, help me grow deeper in you so that when the winds of adversity and trial come, I am solidly rooted in you, swayed by nothing.

JANUARY 3   **ONE TREE**

"I will not," he answered, but later he changed his mind.
—Matthew 21:29 NIV

It wasn't that much of a storm—windy, some sleet. When I drove into the parking lot, I saw the fatality. The pine lay on the ground, soil-encased roots ripped from the earth. The roots didn't resemble the top of the tree. They looked more like a big dirty button sewn on the bottom of the trunk. That was all that had anchored the pine to the earth. It wasn't enough. The tree was top-heavy. Laden with ice, it pulled itself out of the ground.

I can give a good Christian performance. Can you? I know the clichés, the verses to quote. I can skip devotions and prayer and fake it. You too? But I get caught. The sharpness in answering the questions my kids ask. The annoyance at interruptions that I fail to see as God-sent. The worry that doesn't have to exist. The shame and sham I feel. The loss of intimacy I forfeit with God. Shortcuts never work. I cheat myself.

The son in Jesus' parable (Matthew 21) initially refused to obey his father. Did he have second thoughts? Whatever happened, he changed his mind and did what his father asked. Obedience strengthened the relationship and the character of the son. His roots grew deeper.

The pine tree never had a chance to grow its roots deeper. The city workers took it away. Today we have a chance to live God's way, to set our roots down deeper.

Lord, today please help me answer, "Yes, Lord!" immediately when I hear your voice.

JANUARY 4   I'M FREEZING

Let us throw off . . . the sin that so easily entangles.
—Hebrews 12:1 NIV

I was freezing to death. At least that's what my feet kept telling me every time I stood at the kitchen counter preparing a meal. Arctic drafts whistled around my shoes from the base of the cabinets, and I had ice cubes for toes.

How could the former owner have been comfortable with such cold? My heart sank as I thought maybe we had bought a "lemon." As the weeks crawled, I grumbled through one of the bitterest and longest winters in years. Constantly cold, especially in the kitchen, I kept trying to find ways to keep the house warmer.

Finally April arrived. As I circled the house one day, I noticed a vent under the kitchen window. Upon further inspection I realized that it was wide open and exactly in line with where I stood to cook! We knew about and had closed the vents on the end of the house but had missed that one. All winter the wind had whistled into the crawl space under the house. No wonder the house was cold!

Is there a sin that blows and settles into your life? One that takes the edge off your relationship with God? One that nips at your effectiveness in serving him? God is as eager to help us close those vents as I was when I found the one open under the kitchen window. From now on, every fall I'll make sure all the vents are closed. What do you need to close off today in your life?

God, today, with your help, I secure my life by closing myself off to _____ . Grant me victory over this sin throughout the hours that lie ahead.

14

JANUARY 5   ON MY KNEES

Just as you trusted Christ to save you, trust him, too, for each day's problems; live in vital union with him.
— *Colossians 2:6 TLB*

We tidied up after insulating the attic. My brother left. An hour later he called. "Did you happen to find my wallet?" After a thorough and increasingly frantic search, we realized the cellulose had to be searched!

Kneeling on a crossboard over the narrow rafters, I inched my way systematically through the fluff, alternating between "What if I can't find it?" and "Lord, *please* help me find it." My knees ached; my back hurt. It was like looking for a dime in a sand dune. Actually, it was more like $140, a driver's license, and credit cards. It was a tough place to be—the semidarkness, the cramped position, but a great place to ask God for help.

Three feet from the finishing point I submerged my hands. "I found it!" I announced.

I think God was glad to answer my prayer, but the vital union I had with him, the sense of dependence on him, was more important. A lost wallet, a troubled relation, a worn-out washing machine, an illness, a torn-up transmission—whatever our problem—can give us the chance to get closer to God.

Lord, I don't like to be in tight spots, and I sometimes get tired of being on my knees, but these are the places that keep me in vital union with you, which is really where I want to be.

JANUARY 6   THE MAILBOX

Martha was distracted.   — *Luke 10:40 NIV*

Not long after we moved into our home, my husband came in with the top half of the red mailbox flag.

"It snapped off," he explained. "Guess I'll throw it away."
You have to understand that sending and receiving mail at our house is right up there with eating. We complain less about food than the letter carrier being late. And, after buying a house, the last thing we wanted to do was run out and spend money on anything.

"Wait a minute," I countered. "I'll fix it."
They say duct tape fixes anything, and I believe it. That flag flew all winter. At times it looked like a wounded soldier, leaning precariously to the left. Still the indestructible gray tape worked.

I felt frugal and embarrassed by the tacky repair until one day I looked away from our wounded box and discovered that all the boxes on the beam displayed damage. Dented, gouged, rusting, they too looked pitiful. The boxes matched!

Sometimes I look at myself and see all the weaknesses, the failures. I'm embarrassed or discouraged. I think everyone else has it all together. Then God gives me a peek at someone else's struggles, and I am ashamed of my self-absorption.

Father, please forgive me for being so focused on myself that I fail to see the dents and scrapes others have received. Help me to balance my view inward and outward and to remember that we are all groaning and growing toward the likeness of Christ.

JANUARY 7   THE POPCORN POT

The LORD does not look at the things man looks at.
—1 Samuel 16:7 NIV

It's an awful-looking pot—faded banana yellow with nicks and chips in the passé paint. Grease, burned on from repeated use, permanently clings to the base. The inside is no improvement. The nonstick black coating looks like a bad paint job. Grease permeates the metal even when the pot is clean.

No, it doesn't look like much, but it's not going to any

16

garage sale soon. This plebeian pot makes the best popcorn. The thick bottom provides even heat. The lid lets just the right amount of steam escape so the popcorn is crunchy. The pot keeps the corn from ever burning.

I never use my shiny cookware for popcorn, only this old pot that I got at a garage sale. As I recall, the woman who sold it to me said, "It makes the best popcorn." So this pan has a reputation. It does something well.

I am so glad God looks at us differently from the way we do. I often feel like an old-fashioned pot when I compare myself with other people. *Look what she can do,* I sometimes think. *I wish I could be more like her. Why didn't I make the choices that would have taken me where she is?* Then I am reminded that God's viewpoint is different. To God I have a special purpose. So do you. Perhaps I am a spiritual popcorn pot. Maybe you are a "pie tin" or a "roaster," or "fine crystal." All are necessary in God's kitchen.

I am thankful, God, that you have a different way of looking at us. Help me remember that I am special and have a unique purpose to fulfill in your service.

JANUARY 8　　　　　　　　　　　　　　**WHO AM I?**

The LORD would speak to Moses face to face, as a man speaks with his friend. —*Exodus 33:11 NIV*

By modern standards Moses had an identity crisis, or, to be politically correct, he was personally challenged. As an infant he was cross-culturally and cross-economically adopted from a Hebrew home into the home of the Pharaoh of Egypt. He grew up as high in society as someone could. Then he ended up on the back side of the desert watching sheep instead of cutting political deals.

When God spoke to him out of the burning bush about leading millions of people across a sea into freedom, Moses was still trying to figure it all out. "Who am I?" (Exodus

17

3:11) he asked. He almost seems to say, "Why doesn't everyone leave me alone!" Left to himself, he would have walked away from the bush, whimpering, dragging his sandals in the desert grit with every step.

But God didn't let him get away with it. He saw what Moses could be. By Exodus 33, Moses is bold and direct with God. What was his secret? No secret. The more time he spent with God, the farther down the road they went together, the more Moses knew and depended on God. He no longer asked, "Who am I?" He was getting to the center of life with God.

Who are you? Who am I? The more time we spend in God's presence, the more we will understand who God is and who God wants us to be. Today pray like Moses:

Father, if you are pleased with me, teach me your ways so I may know you and continue to find favor with you (Exodus 33:13 NIV).

JANUARY 9   SNUGGLING

Come to me, all you who are weary and burdened, and I will give you rest. Take my yoke upon you and learn from me, for I am gentle and humble in heart, and you will find rest for your souls. For my yoke is easy and my burden is light.
—Matthew 11:28-30 NIV

My youngest daughter loves to take a warm shower, put on fresh, cuddly pajamas, and jump into bed between clean sheets. She wiggles into a comfortable position. "Oh, this feels so good," she says. She grabs a stuffed animal and tucks it in the crook of her arm. "Read me a story," she requests. After story and prayers, she is ready. "I'm going to go right to sleep."

She does. The warmth, relaxation, and soft, clean clothing comfort her physically and emotionally. They create an environment for rest.

18

God has made a similar environment for us—his presence. "Don't stand far away," God says. "Come to me." The arms are waiting and the lap is ready for us to snuggle up close to him, so that the weariness and burdensomeness of life may be eased from our shoulders. Then rest can wash over us.

Sometimes resting in God's presence is the last thing we think we have time to do. But it's really the first place we need to stop off when life presses. A promise goes with God's offer: "You will find rest for your souls."

Thank you, God, for the rest I can find in you. Help me to come to you quickly when I am tired and worn.

JANUARY 10   HEELS ON ICE

Now unto him that is able to keep you from falling, and to present you faultless before the presence of his glory with exceeding joy.   *—Jude 24 KJV*

My sister and I had been to a play and happened to be the first to leave the building. As we crossed the icy parking lot, I felt foolish about my shoes. Strappy and plastic-soled, they were useless for traction.

Suddenly I was looking up at the navy velvet sky sprinkled with stars. I lifted my head and realized I was lying flat on my back, in the parking lot. Oblivious, my sister was still walking toward our car.

Seconds later, she turned and saw me in my unladylike sprawl. "Are you okay?" she asked as she came back to help. Then she burst out laughing.

Unbelievably, I was okay, and the story has become a family classic. But I do not wear ridiculous shoes anymore, especially in the winter.

My shoes were useless to help prevent a fall. So is everything in my life except Christ. He is able to keep me from falling. No precipice daunts him. No icy patch baffles him. Nothing confounds him. He is able to keep all of us from falling.

19

Of course, there are times when we prefer to wear spiritually ridiculous shoes, and we fall. Singing in the choir isn't going to keep us from sinning. Reading a popular author's latest book isn't going to help us understand Scripture like studying it on our own. Reading these meditations won't, either.

Jesus can help us, when we put ourselves in his hands. His plan is to present us—the ones who choose to mess up—faultless before the throne of God! What an incredible Savior!

O God, no one is like Jesus. Thank you that he is able to keep me and present me to you faultless with great joy.

JANUARY 11   SOCKS

Trust in the LORD, and do good;
Dwell in the land and cultivate faithfulness.
                                        —Psalm 37:3 NASB

When you think of it, is there any other piece of clothing more thankless or abused than socks? What item of clothing takes more abuse from people than socks?

Babies chew them. (Yuck!) Children wear them like shoes. After a while they look as if they have soles and uppers—sometimes only uppers. I've never yet seen a sock belonging to a man that eventually didn't have at least one toe hole. We women fall somewhere in between the men and the kids.

Socks. We smell them up, throw them in corners, lose them in the dryer (no one knows how or where they go), make puppets out of them, use them for dust rags, and stuff things in them at Christmastime. They are useful, faithful things. We'd be rather lost without them, especially in the winter.

Being a faithful Christian is sometimes about as exciting as a pair of socks. We notice the joyful, exuberant, loving,

20

kind, generous Christians, but faithfulness is often a quiet thing, there for others to build on and use. God tells us to cultivate faithfulness—day in and day out—so that we may do the job set before us, like faithful, dependable socks. Faithfulness is following in the steps of Jesus, and a flock of faithful "socks" accomplishes the work of the kingdom. Let's put our feet into it!

God, faithfulness is built one step at a time. Help me walk faithfully in you today.

JANUARY 12   DAUGHTERS OF SARAH

You are her [Sarah's] daughters if you do what is right and do not give way to fear.   *—1 Peter 3:6 NIV*

I've always been a scaredy-cat about adventure or taking a dare. Sensible—that's what I am. Or, in today's psychology, the responsible firstborn. I want to know how everything will turn out before I do it, or at least I explore every possibility.

That's why I shocked myself and others when I chose to marry someone from New York City and to move there with him. What a change from a small rural town in the Midwest! For months after the move I lived in unacknowledged fear.

When I think of Sarah, I wonder how much fear she felt following Abraham through desert lands from Ur to Palestine and in and out of Egypt. Plenty, I imagine. However much fear seized her and whatever adrenaline coursed through her, she didn't let it dominate her life or render her ineffective. She chose to do what was right. Peter honors her strength of character and spirit by calling all who live in this manner the "daughters of Sarah."

Sometimes we confuse feeling fear with being cowards. Fear may grip us at any time; courage exists when we do right in the face of our fears.

21

Father, help me be a daughter of Sarah by choosing to do right in the face of fear.

JANUARY 13   FOR RUTH

She is clothed with strength and dignity;
she can laugh at the days to come.
—Proverbs 31:25 NIV

Whenever I start attending a new church, I begin looking for an older woman, someone who has raised kids, made it through midlife, and is coming into the homestretch with Christ by her side. Some would call them "old," and maybe they are. I prefer thinking of them as models—not Madison Avenue style, but God's style. They are dear, saintly women who have grown Christlike with the years.

Ruth was one of these women. Somehow she had wonderful radar for sensing when someone was having a hard time. She knew that it was difficult for me, a small-town girl, to live in New York City. As a transplant to the city years before, she knew the feeling.

Ruth often slipped up beside me and, in her gentle German accent, encouraged me with her understanding words or by listening to the frustrations of a new mother. Her kindness and sincere care boosted my morale and helped me keep going.

In 1996, Ruth went home to be with Christ. I cherish my memories of her and thank God for the blessing she was and is in my life. Her model of kindness challenges me to Christlikeness.

Would some people consider you old? Don't think that you are useless. Someone is probably watching you, looking for some inspiration, staying power, or kindness that will make all the difference in helping her get along on her path with Christ.

God, help me model the Savior so that anyone watching will see Jesus and copy him.

22

JANUARY 14   SNOW—FUN OR FRUSTRATION?

... "I will be your God through all your lifetime, yes, even when your hair is white with age. I made you and I will care for you. I will carry you along and be your Savior."
—Isaiah 46:4 TLB

When I was a child, I loved lots of snow. The more snow, the greater the chances of school being canceled. Of course, snow also meant sledding, snow forts, "Fox and Geese," and snow angels. How could life be better?

My father didn't like snow. To him it was pretty as long as he didn't have to be out in it—or if it only fell alongside and not on the streets and sidewalks. As a child I couldn't understand his viewpoint. But now that I'm older, I've adopted his opinion as I have had to drive through and shovel snow.

Growing older is like my attitude toward the snow. When I was younger, another year was a milestone. Now my birthdays are a mix of feelings. As my hair changes colors (to shades of silver rather than darker hues from a bottle) and wrinkles set more deeply, I struggle with the inevitable aging.

As with most things in life, we face aging individually; no one does it for us. We are not, however, alone in the process. God does not check out on us when the skin bags and the waistline bulges. He is not repulsed by a new pair of glasses or age spots. God goes the distance with us. He is a lifetime God who is aware of our physical frame and promises to carry us even through the ending years of our lives.

Thank you, God, for the promise of your presence throughout my life.

JANUARY 15   GETTING HOME

This certain hope of being saved is a strong and trustworthy anchor for our souls, connecting us with God himself.
—Hebrews 6:19 TLB

23

In 1978, a blizzard blew through much of the Midwest, dumping mountains of snow. Wind whirled the white stuff into drifts, making roads impassable and causing schools and businesses to close.

Our family business shut down for the day, but my father, brother, and I went to the office because we lived just across the field. As we walked home, I started laughing because the drifts were up to my thighs and walking was a joke. "Quit laughing," my father said sharply. Then he and my brother came alongside me and, linking arms, we finished the walk home safely.

I realized later that my father's sharpness came from his concern about the energy it would take to get home in the deep snow and the seriousness of being out in the bitter cold, struggling to cross the field. The situation was not funny, and laughter took away energy from the more important work of getting home.

Our arrival home was not necessarily a certainty. The familiar path had become an ordeal to travel rather than the usual quick walk. Our arrival at our heavenly home, on the other hand, has no such uncertainty once we have accepted what Christ has done for us. When that has been settled, the connection with God is unbreakable. At times we may spiritually walk in snow up to our hips or stumble on the pathway, but the absolute surety of reaching home is guaranteed.

Father, thank you for the certain hope of reaching my heavenly home because you are the anchor of my soul.

JANUARY 16   NO

Yet the news about him spread all the more, so that crowds of people came to hear him and to be healed of their sicknesses. But Jesus often withdrew to lonely places and prayed.
—*Luke 5:15-16 NIV*

Yes, I'll help in the nursery. Yes, I'll sing in the choir. Yes, I'll make cookies for the kids' class. Yes, I'll teach while you

24

are gone. Yes, I'll send a card for the group. Yes, I'll bring a casserole. Yes, I'll pray for this list of missionaries. Yes, I'll open up my home for that activity. Yes, yes, yes, yes . . . YES!

No. Not loud. Not guilt-ridden. Not angrily. Simply and clearly: No. That's what Jesus said. He was choosing his disciples and doing miraculous things. The crowds swelled as the news traveled the Galilee grapevine. This guy could do something for them. So they came to be healed. "But Jesus often withdrew" (Luke 5:16 NIV). He went away; not everyone was healed. He did this *often.*

What would it take to put "no" back into your vocabulary? Perhaps changing "yes" into "maybe" or "I'll think about it."

Jesus took time away from genuinely needy people to pray, to recharge, and to spend time with his Father. If Jesus Christ took a break often, shouldn't we say "no" even more often than he did?

God, help me today to say the appropriate "no's" so that I may say "yes" to you.

JANUARY 17   NO BURGERS NOW, THANKS

"My food," said Jesus, "is to do the will of him who sent me and to finish his work."   *—John 4:34 NIV*

Food. We buy, chop, cook, serve, eat, and clean it up. Sometimes our days seem to revolve around food.

There is one kind of food Jesus talked about that intrigues me—the food he ate when he talked with the woman at the well.

The disciples had gone into town for Ultra Burgers, and Jesus sat by the well. It's no surprise that soon he was talking to someone about spiritual things. Quickly he got down to the heart of the matter, and the woman got the point. Big things started to happen in town. When the disciples

25

returned and Jesus talked about having eaten, they wondered whether someone had gotten him a Super-Burger from "the other place"!

Jesus told them that the sustenance of his life was doing God's work. At that point I think Jesus wasn't hungry anymore. Reaching that woman was all-consuming; hunger vanished.

Sometimes God gives us a taste of that food as we serve him—leading someone to Christ, tearing down one more barrier to salvation, helping someone grow spiritually. It's like spiritual adrenaline that takes away our appetite for anything physical. It's a hint of what is to come.

Lord, help me today to hunger after doing your will.

JANUARY 18   LEAVES

Do not learn the ways of the nations. . . .
For the customs of the peoples are worthless. . . .
Who should not revere you,
  O King of the nations?
                                        —*Jeremiah 10:2, 3, 7 NIV*

In summer they shield our house from the grueling sun. In fall they splash color against the sky, and we rake them by the bagful. In winter they are ugly; they are also sneaky.

There are always some leaves left after we call it quits on raking the yard. Some are transplants from other property; some merely elude the rake. They seem to form a conspiracy. Scurrying up to the front wall of the house, they mass recruits for ambushes. A few at a time they skitter along, roll down the incline to the garage, and whiz around the corner to join the cars. From there it's a piece of cake—along the garage wall, right up to the doorway. As soon as someone comes into the house, the suction invites them into the family room. We vacuum, pick them up, then tolerate them. It's tiresome to keep at it.

26

It's one thing to tolerate leaves. It's another to allow insidious thinking to sneak into our lives. Things like: "Jesus is the Savior, but it's embarrassing to be so narrow. Couldn't there be a lot of ways to God after all?" or, "Who cares about issues of morality anymore? I'm too tired to stand up—I don't want to stand up." Sneaky thoughts we'd rather not admit.

When it comes down to it, we have to stand fast. There is truth. Our Christ embodies truth, and he is intolerant of falsehood. We must stand with him fearlessly. Swallowing the philosophies of humanity is not like harmlessly living with crunchy leaves. It's more like allowing sin into the heart of our homes.

God, in a world of so much relativism, help me stand for your truth.

JANUARY 19   BIRDS ON THE CHIMNEY

Are not two sparrows sold for a penny? Yet not one of them will fall to the ground apart from the will of your Father. . . . So don't be afraid; you are worth more than many sparrows.
—*Matthew 10:29, 31 NIV*

It is common in the winter to see birds sitting on the edge of a chimney to get warm. The only quirk in this clever idea is that for some reason, perhaps being overcome by fumes, the creatures can tumble down into the chimney and die.

In speaking about God's knowledge of the fallen sparrow, someone once said, "A lot of good it did the sparrow!" Do you feel like that today? Like the hurting psalmist who said, "I lie awake; I have become like a bird alone on a roof" (Psalm 102:7 NIV)? Do you feel abandoned up there on the chimney, desperately trying to stay warm, half asphyxiated by the fumes, swaying and almost ready to topple? Everyone ends up on the rooftop at some time, and most of us end up there more than once.

Feelings may tell us we are alone, but the truth is that God is up there with us in the wind and fumes. Wherever we are—on the roof, down the chimney, reveling in the warmth of spring—we can be at home with God. We are not alone or forgotten:

> Even the sparrow has found a home . . .
> a place near your altar,
>   O LORD Almighty, my King and my God.
> Blessed are those who dwell in your house.
>   (Psalm 84:3-4 NIV)

Thank you, God, for your abiding presence, whatever my circumstances or my feelings. The truth is that you are with me. Help me live today in that truth.

JANUARY 20   SOPHIE

Jesus withdrew to the region of Tyre and Sidon. A Canaanite woman from that vicinity came to him.
                                    —Matthew 15:21-22 NIV

Sophie, my name for this unmonikered woman, is identified by the place where she lives. Where we live tells people something about us. We might speak with a drawl, have to shovel lots of snow, live with the fear of flooding, or breathe smog. Sophie's locale meant that she, at least at this time, was part of a group of people outside the immediate ministry of Christ. She was not a Jew.

Are you "out of the country" spiritually? Do you want God to help you, but you aren't a citizen of his kingdom? Have you tried everything including church to fill the vacuum in your life? Does your hollowness haunt you in the quiet moments?

Jesus welcomes all who wish to enter his kingdom. He delights in new citizens. Like Sophie, an alien needs only to come and ask for mercy (15:22) and help (15:25). Forgiveness is for the asking; citizenship for the taking.

Sophie knew to whom she came. She would not let go until she received. Will you pass up this opportunity to change your citizenship? Sophie's experience with Christ changed her life. Will you allow him to change yours?

Lord, I've been in a faraway country. Now I want to live in your land. Help me to turn my life over to you now and forever.

JANUARY 21   A LESSON IN PRAYER

Then came she and worshipped him, saying, Lord, help me.
—Matthew 15:25 KJV

Do you ever get frustrated with all the articles, books, sermons, and lessons on prayer? I do. The acrostics, the codes, the patterns—the suggestions go on and on. After a while I want to throw my hands up and scream, "Can't I just *talk* to God?"

Sophie didn't read a manual on prayer in order to talk to Jesus. You can tell. She doesn't say: "O great Creator of the universe, everything is at your disposal and obeys your command. I bow in submission before your throne . . . blah, blah, blah." No. She worshiped him, asking for help. She recognized in her heart that Jesus Christ was the only One who could help. Not one more medical referral, not one more psychiatrist, not another counseling session. Isn't this true worship anyway—recognizing the supremacy of God and submitting ourselves to him?

I suppose flowery language can be used to worship God. Simple, direct language brings us into God's presence just as quickly. Sophie's request, "Lord, help me," is not flowery. It comes from the heart of her life. Jesus heard her, and they talked. That's what Jesus wants from each of us—honest talk. If even the thought of prayer makes you cringe, remember Sophie. She and Jesus talked together very directly. We have the same open invitation.

Lord, sometimes it is hard to talk with you because I've read and heard too much. Help me, as you helped this woman, to speak honestly and openly to you.

JANUARY 22   SAYING TOO MUCH

Jesus did not answer a word. So his disciples came to him and urged him, "Send her away, for she keeps crying out after us."   *—Matthew 15:23 NIV*

Isn't it strange that Jesus didn't answer Sophie? Don't we say to ourselves down deep inside, "That was a rude way to respond"? Of course, we'd never say it out loud. But we wonder why the Savior seemed to ignore this woman in great need. If he wasn't heartless, what was going on?

A friend of mine counseled distressed individuals. Often they listened but didn't follow her sound advice. Once, when her counsel was rejected, her mental response was, "Come back and see me when your life falls apart." She wasn't hardhearted, she simply knew that people are more apt to change when they have no other choice.

Perhaps Jesus allowed Sophie to follow and call after him to test her perseverance and faith. Maybe she needed to know how much this meant to her and how much her faith needed to be anchored unequivocally to this Jew.

Sometimes in our witness we say too much. We share the gospel and blab on and on. Jesus gave people time to think, grow, and consider what they were doing and what they needed to do. We need to share the words of the gospel, but there are times when, like Jesus, we do "not answer a word."

God, help me not to get in the way of the gospel by speaking too much. Reveal to me the times when I need to be silent.

JANUARY 23   BOLDNESS

Then Jesus answered, "Woman, you have great faith!"
                    —Matthew 15:28 NIV

30

Sophie had nerve! Imagine debating with Jesus over whether or not he should help her. But Sophie also knew who Jesus was. She repeatedly calls him "Lord" and asks of him what no one else could do.

What we need to do is reverse these ideas. Sophie understood who Jesus was, and because of that she had boldness. One leads to the other. Abraham knew this when he asked God to spare Sodom and Gomorrah (Genesis 18:16-33), just as Jacob did when he wrestled with God (Genesis 32:22-32). Understanding our God and Savior brings boldness into our lives.

Boldness like this is something we are encouraged to exercise. "Let us then approach the throne of grace with confidence, so that we may receive mercy and find grace to help us in our time of need" (Hebrews 4:16 NIV). Sophie's knowledge of God and boldness helped her ask aggressively and receive. Her faith was intact. I think if Jesus had turned her down, she would have said, "When, Lord? When will the crumbs fall off the table for those outside the house of Israel?" She wouldn't have given in. Her faith was absolutely unmovable.

Sophie wasn't her name. Jesus knew what her name was. He chose to call her "Woman." Today put your name in that verse. "_____, you have great faith!"

Lord, help me know who you are so I may come to you boldly, my faith anchored solidly in you.

JANUARY 24   **SNOW ANGELS**

The Son is the radiance of God's glory and the exact representation of his being. . . . Are not all angels ministering spirits sent to serve those who will inherit salvation?
—Hebrews 1:3, 14 NIV

Making the perfect snow angel has something to do with the kind of snow you flop into, but probably the real crux of making the ultimate snow angel is the matter of getting down and then up again. If you wallow too much either time, you have more of a snow pig than a snow angel. But when you have the perfect snow and the perfect technique, a snow angel is beautiful, rather like outdoor art. In fact, it's easy to get so enchanted with the perfection of the form that you forget the intensely sparkling brilliance of the snow that made the snow angel possible.

We are in the era of the angel. Pins, cards, buttons, statues, TV shows—angel paraphernalia are everywhere. I'm not really sure what all this stuff is supposed to do for us except reassure us that there really is someone divine out there who cares about us. Or maybe it's a distraction from the One who does care. Perhaps a moneymaking fad?

Whatever the intent, Jesus should be our focal point, not the angels. He perfectly represented a caring God and died so that we might have eternal life. Let's focus our worship on our Savior.

Triune God, I marvel at the supernatural, but I worship you exclusively. You alone are worthy to be worshiped.

JANUARY 25   CHILI POWDER

Your beauty . . . should be that of your inner self, the unfading beauty of a gentle and quiet spirit, which is of great worth in God's sight. For this is the way the holy women of the past who put their hope in God used to make themselves beautiful.　　　　　　　　　　　　　*—1 Peter 3:3-5 NIV*

What could taste better on a bitterly cold day than a spicy, hot pot of chili? Yum! When I make it for my family, I have to cut the chili powder in half. The younger people in the household don't have the same affection for the spice as the older ones. "Too spicy," they say. So we add cheese or cornbread on the side to cut the zing.

Sometimes we get too spicy in our daily living. Sharp with

the kids, touchy with husbands, snippy with colleagues. A tape recording of our words and inflections might shock us. We're like too much chili powder. Even the most expensive makeup applied to a perfect face can't take the edge off zingy words.

Wouldn't it be great if we could buy a tube of "Gentle and Quiet Spirit" to slick on each morning, so that our words would come out perfectly all day? The good news is that there is such a product—but we don't have to buy it; we ask God for it. God knows, however, that we need to develop these qualities with practice.

I tend to be a lot like chili powder, but I'd rather be sweeter, more like cinnamon. Where are you in the spice rack? Our spiritual sisters made themselves beautiful within. We can ask God to create the same beauty within us.

God, continue today to season me into the beautiful woman you want me to be.

JANUARY 26   GOD'S COCOA

We are able to hold our heads high no matter what happens and know that all is well, for we know how dearly God loves us, and we feel this warm love everywhere within us because God has given us the Holy Spirit to fill our hearts with his love.   —Romans 5:5 TLB

Stupid! Twice in one week I had made gross errors in presenting material in two different college courses. It didn't help that both classes were in my major field and the second presentation was before a class taught by my faculty adviser. I stared out the window and fought back tears of frustration and humiliation.

Although it has been almost twenty-five years since the events of that week, I remember it vividly. Memories like this one come back to me in the evening when I am tired and vulnerable. The Adversary slips alongside and whispers how worthless I am. When this happens, I first make myself a cup of cocoa. Then I take up "God's cocoa."

A mug of God's cocoa is truth that warms my soul—words about how much God loves me, failures and all. In the midst of what I consider stupidities, God is not embarrassed to claim me for his special prize. The truth washes over me like warm cocoa, and the Adversary slips away. I realize what unspeakable joy there is in being loved intensely by God.

Is something from the past or present banging you around and screaming "stupid" at you? Grab a mug of God's cocoa.

O God, for your constant and unchangeable love for me, I give you thanks.

JANUARY 27   OATMEAL LIVING

Well done, good and faithful servant! You have been faithful with a few things.   —*Matthew 25:21 NIV*

Gray, gloppy, and gluey, it glared up at me. A huge bowlful. You aren't supposed to go to Grandma's house and get oatmeal. Puffy, pink, yellow, green sugary things with a special toy surprise—yes. But not oatmeal. This was definitely against the Grandma Code.

Nevertheless, there it sat, as appetizing as wallpaper paste. There were no side dishes of eggs or bacon to rescue me. Aah, but there was a slice of toast.

Oatmeal is bearable with toast. A little bit of oatmeal, a big bite of toast. The oatmeal disappeared slowly, the toast, quickly. At last I was toastless and back to tasteless oatmeal. By then, Grandma had figured I wasn't an oatmeal fan, and she forgave me for my half-eaten bowl. I still am not wild about oatmeal. Now, though, a little bit of oatmeal tastes great with a lot of brown sugar!

I am no different spiritually. The blah—oatmeal—of life, the day in and day out of being faithful, is not very appealing. When God sends the toast or brown sugar along, that's great. I thrill in playing a part when someone comes to Christ, sharing truth about God's love, or encouraging someone and seeing her respond. But when God dishes up plain oatmeal, I'm not excited. My heart is less apt to pound when I keep on extending invitations and no one responds, when I pray and see no visible results, when I continue to train my children and feel as if the journey is perpetually uphill.

People say oatmeal "sticks to your ribs." It's healthy and useful. So are the oatmeal days of our lives. They allow us to prove ourselves and grow in the less glamorous ways that keep us humble and spiritually healthy. Oatmeal living—faithful with a few things—is some of the best living we can do.

Lord, help me come to your breakfast table and receive what you have for me today.

JANUARY 28   FRENCH CHEWING

Consider it pure joy, my brothers, whenever you face trials of many kinds, because you know that the testing of your faith develops perseverance.   —*James 1:2-3 NIV*

Years ago my aunt gave me a family recipe called "French Chewing." Like taffy, the ingredients have to be cooked to a certain consistency, cooled, and pulled out. Unlike taffy, French Chewing has an added ingredient—gelatin—that makes it more elastic than taffy.

Stretching the candy takes at least two people or, as my aunt suggested, one person could attach the Chewing to a hook on the wall and pull. However the cook manages, the Chewing has to be stretched to be what it is supposed to be.

As Christians, we don't amount to much until we are stretched. It would be wonderful if only the good experiences brought growth in our lives. The truth is that it's the hard times that make us grow. The Trinity gets together and stretches us. Sometimes it seems as though we will snap. There are times we feel as if we've been dropped on the floor in the stretching process or have been stuck like the candy on the hook—or even sampled prematurely.

We, like French Chewing, have more elasticity than we imagine, and God is aware of how far to pull us. When the candy lies on the waxed paper, stretched to perfection, it is far more desirable than the glob stuck on the hook or lying unpulled in a bowl. In a way, God lets us choose how we want to turn out—stretched, like French Chewing, or just a sticky blob.

God, help me respond to your stretching process in a way that will help me be molded into the mature woman you want me to be.

JANUARY 29   SOUP

. . . but have not love.   *—1 Corinthians 13:1 NIV*

What is January without soup? Flat. No soup is as good as my mother's world-class vegetable beef. So when I got my own kitchen and family, I wanted to make soup exactly like hers. There is no recipe. Neither one of us has ever made it precisely the same way twice. Nevertheless, it is the most delicious soup.

It has a tomato base with a combination of potatoes, carrots, green beans, corn, peas, celery, and a few limas (baby limas, please). I suppose it would also be tasty with onions and an okra (for that good, southern flavor). A bit of savory stock and some chunks of beef enrich the goodness.

I've made the soup with all these ingredients—but it tasted as good as a simmered rug. Everything was there. Well, not everything. Not the half teaspoon of sweet basil. When I realized what was missing and added it, the soup was delicious.

We can do all kinds of things for God, but unless we have God's love filling us, all we do and say is as savory to God as the soup that tasted like cooked rug.

I could have kept cooking the soup, hoping for a better taste, but without the basil it would have been useless. Likewise, we can't rev ourselves up to love. We need to ask God to add the transforming ingredient of his love to our lives today, the love that will permeate all we do.

God, I can't truly love anyone or do anything without the gift of your love in my life. Please give me the measure of love I need to serve you throughout this day.

JANUARY 30   STAYING ON THE ROAD

I will instruct thee and teach thee in the way which thou shalt go: I will guide thee with mine eye. —*Psalm 32:8 KJV*

I had finished my evening class. As I went to the parking lot, I knew it wasn't going to be a good trip home. I had twenty miles to drive, and big flakes of snow were quickly accumulating. As I headed out of town on the interstate, traffic thinned to nothing, and the road was blanketed in white. The darkness overhead was a solid black velvet curtain.

My hands tensed on the wheel. Suddenly lightning ripped across the sky followed by a crash of thunder. Snow, lightning, thunder. What a bizarre and intimidating display of elements! The lightning helped illuminate the road, but still I could only guess at where the pavement was. It was going to be a long, slow trip home.

A pickup truck caught up to me and passed. The red taillights encouraged me as they glowed in the blackness, but the ribbon of tire marks in the snow cheered me even more. They gave me a point of reference, a way to go. The lightning, the taillights, the tire marks—they all led me the twenty miles home.

I'm convinced that God sent all those things to help me find my way home. God does the same thing as we travel through our spiritual lives. God convinced me through a verse in Joshua that we were going to move. A few months later we did. Words of godly friends, rebuke from hymns, questions from my children, love from my husband, even unexpected opportunities— all have been ways God has kept me on the road. Sometimes the signs of direction are as dramatic as lightning; other times they are as steady and encouraging as the glowing taillights. But always they guide us. That is God's promise.

37

God, thank you for the guidance you provide, even in the darkest of times.

JANUARY 31   QUILTS

That the trial of your faith, being much more precious than of gold that perisheth, though it be tried with fire, might be found unto praise and honour and glory at the appearing of Jesus Christ. —*1 Peter 1:7 KJV*

I love quilts. I love looking at photos of quilts, studying patterns, envisioning the possibilities from a pile of scraps. Some of my favorite quilts are ones my mother has made for family members. In them I can see fabrics used to make a skirt I wore decades ago, a jumper my sister had, my brother's bathrobe.

The squares of material take me back to the past. Most of the patches recall bright, happy times. Sometimes, however, the memories are hurtful—growing pains, difficult years in school, cruel things people said. The memories cloud the beauty of the squares as I focus on the negative.

When a friend and I rummaged through an odd assortment of scraps to make a quilt, we groaned at some of the 1960ish colors. "Remember, though," she said positively, "there's no such thing as an ugly quilt!" I remained skeptical. But my friend was right. The finished quilt blended all the pieces together in an artistic pattern.

Our lives are like quilts. When God gives us an "ugly" square, we can focus on it and rebel at its being included in our lives. Or we can choose to look at how God is going to make something exquisite when all the blocks are in place. God knows precisely where to position things. God makes no mistakes with the fabric of our lives.

Lord, I do not always understand why you allow certain things into my life. Help me to trust you and put complete confidence in your plan for my life.

February
Celebrating Change

Anne Kathryn Killinger

FEBRUARY 1   THE COMFORT OF DARKNESS

Commune with your own hearts on your beds.
—Psalm 4:4 RSV

*L*ife sometimes seems to be an endless process of change. Just when you think you have successfully nailed everything down and breathe a sigh of relief, something invariably pops loose and takes you off in an entirely new direction.

I find this very unsettling, for I am the sort of person who likes everything to be orderly and predictable. If I have been meeting someone for tea every Tuesday for two years, I don't like to reset my inner computer to adjust to a Friday meeting.

But I have learned a secret for dealing with life's unexpected turns. I have discovered that there is nothing more comforting at the end of the day than lying on a bed in a dark room, perhaps with a bit of moonlight filtering through a crack in the drapes, and feeling the closeness of God in the silence. In this quiet setting I mentally begin my litany of prayers, asking God's blessings on my family and friends, on the ill, on the needy, and so on until my mental list has been exhausted. Then I confess to God my fears and frustrations about all the changes taking place in and around my life. Sometimes, if I am feeling particularly overwhelmed, I lift up my hand and ask God to hold it.

I never do this without feeling a sense of peace flowing over me. It is a very simple thing to do, I know. But as my mother used to say, "The proof is in the pudding"—it works.

Thank you, God, for being my peace and stability in a world of threatening change. I really couldn't cope without you.

FEBRUARY 2   DIFFICULTIES AND HOPE

I consider that the sufferings of this present time are not worth comparing with the glory about to be revealed to us.
—*Romans 8:18 NRSV*

Life can sometimes be so difficult! Work piles up, and we think we'll never get out from under it. The people around us get so caught up in their own agendas that we feel neglected and unloved. A member of the family has an accident. Tempers flare and thoughtless words are spoken. There may even be an illness or a financial setback. We get so frustrated that we wonder if life makes any sense at all.

I confess that I was feeling that way one day recently when I walked into a little church. I went in because I thought I would sit there quietly and let some of my confusion subside. I wasn't prepared for the treat that waited for me.

A young man from Jamaica was in the chancel quietly playing his guitar and singing about the love of God and what it meant to him. He had a beautiful voice, and there was an angelic look about his face as he sang.

I learned afterward that he had a wife and three small children back home in Jamaica. He was working in our country to earn some money to give them a better life. I felt ashamed of myself for thinking I had troubles, for his were

40

far greater than mine. Yet he smiled broadly, and hope seemed to radiate from his heart. He had something so wonderful to look forward to, and talking with him made me realize I did too.

Forgive me, dear God, when I become self-absorbed and forget what the future holds for all of us who trust you and look forward to the glory of the life to come. When I remember, nothing in the world can trouble me.

FEBRUARY 3   DON'T SHUT THE DOOR

Look, I have set before you an open door, which no one is able to shut.   *—Revelation 3:8 NRSV*

Sometimes in life it is difficult to keep a door open. It would be so much easier to slam it shut and never have to deal with what is on the other side.

When we were in school and became disenchanted with a course, we were often tempted to toss our heads and turn our backs on it, dismissing it because we found it hard or unsettling.

When tensions build up in our work, we want to walk away and not face up to them.

When love seems to have disappeared from our relationships, it is easy to dismiss them and say, "Who cares?"

When our lives are out of tune with God, we have a tendency to close the door and turn the key in the lock as if it doesn't really matter.

What a pity it is that these things happen every day of our lives, and we miss the rewards that lie just the other side of the door. Wouldn't it be better to keep the door ajar and see if we can't make it through?

Dear Lord, don't ever let us refuse the open door of your love and hospitality. What great compassion it must take to keep it always wide open for us blind, struggling mortals!

So do not worry about tomorrow, for tomorrow will bring worries of its own. Today's trouble is enough for today.
—Matthew 6:34 NRSV

When our second child was small, he loved to play in the sandbox. I don't know why, but what he loved most was to stand in the middle of the sandbox and pour a bucket of sand over his head. By the end of a morning in the sand, his little shoes were always scratched and discolored. One day as an older friend who was visiting watched him reveling in the sand, she became very upset by what he was doing. "You should tell him not to do that," she said, "and you should polish his shoes immediately to teach him to be neat." I'm afraid I didn't react as she wished. My first thought was: *In ten years, who cares?*

I suppose I feel that way about a lot of things in life. What is the point of becoming anxious about trivial matters? My dear mother could worry the warts off of frogs, but in the end it only brought her anguish and poor health. We spend a lot of time worrying about things that aren't worth distressing ourselves about.

Even in church people tend to become disturbed by little things that others do or say, or by some change in the liturgy or the traditional way of doing things. It ought to amaze us that the building doesn't collapse after all our fretting.

In ten years, who cares?

God, wouldn't it be simpler to ask ourselves what the point is before we get ourselves so exercised about things? Better yet, why don't we ask what your point is!

FEBRUARY 5   LEARNING AND HEALING

Keep alert, stand firm in your faith, be courageous, be strong. Let all that you do be done in love.
—1 Corinthians 16:13-14 NRSV

I have been learning to play an electronic organ. I carefully watched the instructor demonstrating the many choices and blends that could be produced by this button or that. After mastering the procedures, I demonstrated them for someone else. She watched me as intently as I had watched the instructor. This made me nervous. What a responsibility it is when someone watches us and copies our actions!

But isn't this what people do all the time? Children invariably mimic our actions. Friends are influenced by our opinions and behavior. Even our spouses are affected by watching us and following our lead.

I am overwhelmed to realize how important my thoughts and actions are, and how they may direct the behavior of others. I'm not sure I'm ready for such responsibility. I will have to be very careful not to give anyone else the wrong signals!

I'm awestruck, O God, to think that anyone would want to follow my steps. Watch me and make me an example of your love, lest I lead anyone astray.

FEBRUARY 6   FINDING FAULT

Good people have kind thoughts.   —Proverbs 12:5 CEV

In the small town where I grew up, everyone knew everyone else's business. It was easy to pick out the town complainers, the folks who made criticism their life's vocation. On the whole, most of them were fairly nice people. They simply couldn't refrain from finding fault with everything and everybody.

One day I had lunch with one of these self-appointed condemners. Soon I began to count the objects of her grumbling. The bread was sliced too thickly. The turkey was dry. The lettuce was tough. The tomato was old. The coffee was lukewarm. The service was sloven. Then I lost count because I tuned her out when she embarked upon criticisms of the church, the minister, the organist, the choir, the officers, and so on.

It's too bad that some people are so dissatisfied with life that they try to infect others with their disdain for everything. Don't they realize that negativity is unattractive? Maybe not. At least my friend didn't. She droned on and on, until I was glad to get away from her and find a place where the mental atmosphere was less polluted.

The world is a huge place, Lord. Can't these little ones of yours find an oasis for complainers and all move there so the rest of us won't have to listen? Oh dear! Am I falling into her pattern of criticizing?

FEBRUARY 7   THE MIRACLE OF MINDS

Let the same mind be in you that was in Christ Jesus.
—Philippians 2:5 NRSV

I have heard minds described in so many ways. Some people have agile minds, minds that appear to be continually in motion. Good students are described as possessing intelligent minds. Artists and musicians are often said to have especially creative minds. Persons with a head for mathematics and physics are given credit for scientific minds.

The one who sees the hilarity in things is said to have a comic mind. A person seeking new territories to explore has an adventurous mind. The child who erects complex constructions with Legos or Tinker Toys possesses an engineering mind.

The human mind is truly a marvel, because it is capable of so many fascinating directions and incredible feats. One might even say it is a miracle given by God!

How diverse our minds are, O God. I only ask that mine may not be closed, but will always be open to learning more about you and the world you have made. I really want it to be Christlike, for his was the greatest mind that ever was.

But take care and watch yourselves closely, so as neither to forget the things that your eyes have seen nor to let them slip from your mind all the days of your life; make them known to your children and your children's children.
—Deuteronomy 4:9 NRSV

When I was a child, our teachers demanded a certain amount of memory work from us. We learned poems and took turns reciting them in front of the class. As a group, we memorized the opening of the Declaration of Independence and portions of Lincoln's Gettysburg Address. And then, like little sheep, we obeyed the call to quote them.

In church classes, children were taught to memorize Scripture, the names of the books of the Bible, and the Lord's Prayer. We had Bible drills to locate particular scriptures, and we used biblical recitations to answer the roll call in various youth organizations. The purpose of this memory work wasn't merely to keep our minds stimulated. Our teachers knew that our hearts and lives were being formed by the passages we committed to memory.

So many difficult situations in my life have been eased by recalling some helpful verse or poem from those early years. It has happened over and over, and I am always grateful for the memory of something, some treasure tucked away in my youth, that has come to my rescue as an adult.

Maybe we should be more insistent about our children's memorizing things, God, especially the things that will make them wise in your ways and will turn their hearts toward you.

FEBRUARY 9   LESS IS MORE

It doesn't matter how much you have.
—2 Corinthians 8:12 CEV

For years I felt that my husband and I tended to overbuy for special occasions. Birthdays were always times for big and often expensive gifts. So were Valentine's Day, Mother's Day, Father's Day, and a host of other significant times. At Christmas, our living room looked as if someone had brought in half a department store and dumped it around our tree.

Shopping during those years was a tremendous burden. We began during the after-Christmas sales to prepare for the next round of giving, and the entire year was filled with anxiety about what we had bought for whom and whether it was as good as what we had given the year before.

One day we decided to call a halt to this escalating pattern and see if it was really true that "less is more." It was. As we simplified our giving, looking for one or two small, choice items instead of dozens of awe-inspiring presents, we found that the occasions themselves mattered more. Birthdays and holidays became important in themselves. And Christmas became far more spiritual than it had ever seemed in the days of the great present extravaganzas.

William Soutar was right when he wrote, "So much can wither away from the human spirit, and yet the great gift of the ordinary day remains; the stability of the small things of life, which yet in their constancy are the greatest."

Dear God, thank you for the simple and unassuming gifts that enable us to enjoy life to its fullest, and even to its brimming over.

FEBRUARY 10   THE JOYFUL CHALLENGE

We know that all things work together for good for those who love God, who are called according to his purpose.
—Romans 8:28 NRSV

My husband was invited to spend the summer in a resort town as the minister of a small church. We had visited the area a couple of times in the past and liked it, so the decision to accept the offer didn't take very much effort.

Somehow, during the course of preparing for the transition, my services were offered as organist for the little church. I am not a trained organist; my musical abilities have always been focused on the piano. But I allowed myself to be convinced that the church needed my services and that I could make the necessary adaptation.

The nearer the time drew for us to go and for me to play the organ, the more impossible the task appeared to me. I really had the jitters. But my husband kept saying, "Try to do it. Please give it a chance."

Thank goodness I did! It turned out to be one of the most joyful challenges I had had in years. I practiced long hours and learned amazing things about the harmonizing of pipes and flutes and strings. How beautifully the tones blended together in the magnificent instrument. I almost felt as if I were in heaven when I was playing, and I hated to see the summer end.

I learned a lot about the organ, God. But the most important thing I learned is that nothing is impossible if I can only stay in tune with you.

FEBRUARY 11   **LIGHT IN THE DARKNESS**

For this reason I bow my knees before the Father, from whom every family in heaven and on earth takes its name.
—Ephesians 3:14 NRSV

I have always tried not to think about bad things, on the premise that if I was lucky they would not happen until tomorrow and if I was very lucky they would not happen at all. But what a Pollyanna, unrealistic way to live!

Recently I came face to face with an ugly possibility. One of the tests from my annual physical checkup came back questionable. The doctor assured me that it was probably a benign situation, even though the results of the test suggested that it might be cancerous. Still, I had to wait three months before other tests could be made.

47

For once, I couldn't really put off worrying. My yesterday's road became today's road with a vengeance, and I faced reality as I had never faced it before.

But I was amazed to discover, in the midst of all my anxiety, what peace God can give for living with ugly possibilities. I found a light in the darkness that was as bright and beautiful as any sunrise I have ever seen. I learned, through prayer, that God

> will lead the blind
> by a road they do not know . . .
> I will turn the darkness before them into light.
> (Isaiah 42:16 NRSV)

On my knees, O God, I humbly thank you for the light along the way. Don't let me ever forget that there can be fear and darkness in my life, but enable me always to look beyond them to your peace.

FEBRUARY 12   TALKING TOO MUCH?

When words are many, transgression is not lacking, but the prudent are restrained in speech.
—Proverbs 10:19 NRSV

My husband was on a trip and, as is his custom, he called home every night. One evening when the phone rang, I picked it up and could barely whisper hello. I had a bad case of laryngitis. His joking remark was, "Why do I have to be away from home when you can't talk?"

That casual remark made me think about how much we do talk during an average day. In the work most of us do, talking is necessary. The schoolteacher can't be mute. Lawyers must present their cases orally. A doctor has to ask questions. Ministers have to preach. Almost every profession requires an enormous amount of talking.

Then I thought about those who are spokespersons for

Christianity. What does their talk sound like? I hear an awful lot of talk from them about condemnation, anger, fear, and exclusion—words that don't really reflect the love of God. Maybe we Christians talk too much—about the wrong things!

Father, isn't love the basis of all belief? If we can't stop criticizing one another and instead speak freely of your generous nature, perhaps it is time to send a plague of laryngitis!

FEBRUARY 13   FRIENDSHIP IS A DUET

A friend is always a friend.   —*Proverbs 17:17 CEV*

I think we sometimes forget how much friends really depend on one another—and in how many ways. If my car won't start and it's my morning to drive the car pool, I call and ask a friend to drive. If I need a recipe I can't find, I telephone a friend. If I have a troubling report from my doctor, I phone a friend to confess my anxiety. If I receive a call from the doctor relieving my fears, I call the friend to share the good news.

My friends call me for the same reasons. Friendship is a two-way street. It is never a solo act but always a duet.

This was brought home to me recently when a friend told me about visiting a Hopi reservation in the West. My friend collects baskets, and she was admiring an exquisite basket made by an ancient Hopi man. As she studied it, she asked him what the design meant. He smiled and said, "You tell me." She was at a loss. Finally, he asked her if the design on the basket was even on both sides. She replied that it was. He smiled again and said, "It's a friendship basket."

What a special friend you have been to me, dear God. Forgive me when I cause the design to be uneven.

FEBRUARY 14   SUSTAINING POWER

The greatest of these is love. —1 Corinthians 13:13 NRSV

At a large dinner party we attended, everyone seemed to be chattering away about the usual things. Then the conversation took a turn as someone shared a particularly personal story. That was followed by another personal narrative, and then another. Everyone seemed to have a story to tell. One couple told how their teenage daughter was killed in an automobile accident, and how their faith sustained them through the time of grief and readjustment. A woman told about her two sons who contracted Hodgkin's disease; one had survived and the other had died. Then her husband suffered a heart attack and died quite prematurely. One of her grandchildren was born with a serious physical impairment. Despite all these troubles, her face was radiant with the love of God as she talked. Another couple's child had blown her mind on drugs and had been hospitalized for years. But they managed to talk about it with equanimity and courage because of their enormous faith in God.

It seemed to be the same with everyone who told a story: Human life can be tragic and almost unbearable, but faith in God makes an incredible difference in the way people accept their troubles. The words *God* and *love* kept recurring in their speech. I went home and reread Paul's letter to the Corinthians, especially the chapter where he talked so beautifully about love. He was right: Love is the most sustaining power in the universe, because it is the gift of God!

Thank you, dear Lord, for your gift of love. Let it run like a river in our souls, so that it sustains us even in the times of greatest drought and peril.

FEBRUARY 15   WE STILL NEED CHICKEN
EVERY SUNDAY

Whatever you bind on earth will be bound in heaven.
—Matthew 18:18 NRSV

When I was a child, Sunday was always the best day of the week. My family attended Sunday school and morning worship, which was always as much a social gathering as it was a spiritual occasion. Then came our Sunday dinner, which was almost always a delicious fried-chicken feast. The chicken, purchased the day before and freshly dressed, was cooked to perfection by my mother. How wonderfully warm and safe I felt with my family on Sundays!

After I married and had children, Sunday was still the happiest day of my week. Our young family attended church, and we carried on the tradition of the fried chicken—though I'm afraid the chicken wasn't on foot the day before. In a busy week, Sunday was the one day when the family could be together to visit, laugh, and share our lives. What great security we experienced just being together!

Now things seem to be different. Many parents have to work or travel on the weekend. If the parent is a single parent, he or she is likely to be too worn out to enjoy a special day. Children are involved in many activities and have to be transported here and there. Few families seem to have the time for real togetherness and connectedness. What a loss!

It is important for our families to have at least one day a week together, isn't it, God? Couldn't our hyperactive families enjoy at least a couple of hours together—maybe with a little help from KFC?

FEBRUARY 16   PRUDENT SPEECH

When words are many, transgression is not lacking, but the prudent are restrained in speech.
—Proverbs 10:19 NRSV

One evening my husband and I were strolling through the streets of a resort town. At one point we had to walk off the sidewalk to avoid a couple and their three children, who were trying to rearrange their luggage so that the parents could carry it and still keep a hand on the children. They looked like any normal family struggling to get from one location to another. Suddenly the woman exploded at the man, saying he wasn't packing the luggage correctly. The man retorted, and a battle of obscenities ensued. The three small children sat on the sidewalk, watching and listening, fear and confusion written on their faces.

We felt an impulse to stop but decided we shouldn't become involved; so we walked on down the street. Later, we saw them again. Now, the battle over and their travels resumed, they looked tired and beaten. No one had won. The children's consciousness was scarred, and the parents had probably said some unforgettable things to each other. We were saddened by the whole episode and thought how useless it had been. If only the parents had heeded the words of the writer of Proverbs, they would have avoided the argument and their children would have been happier. Even God, I think, would have been happier.

Let the words of my mouth and the actions of my life always be acceptable to you, dear Lord—you who gave us the perfect example of speech and behavior.

FEBRUARY 17   NO PICKET FENCES

There is no longer Jew or Greek, there is no longer slave or free, there is no longer male and female; for all of you are one in Christ Jesus.   *—Galatians 3:28 NRSV*

When my husband and I married many years ago, I dreamed of owning a little brick home with a white picket fence around it. The fence wasn't to keep anybody out. It merely represented my fantasy of a perfect home. Unfortunately, a lot of fences aren't erected with such a happy dream in mind.

There are fences that divide families. Anger and disagreement between parents or siblings, or between parents and children, can split a home so badly that no one is happy in it.

There are fences that divide races and people with different lifestyles. Hatred of those who are unlike ourselves can raise these fences to such heights that they seem virtually unscalable.

There are fences that divide religions. Isn't it ironic that people can become so violently separated by the ways in which they understand God, who wants so badly for all of us to become one?

Jesus came to tear down fences, not erect them. Wouldn't it be wonderful, for a start, if all of us who call upon him were to start demolishing barriers instead of protecting them?

Dear God, I'm grateful that you don't build fences with big NO ENTRY signs on them. Please help me never to be guilty of maintaining any fences you don't want to be there, even if my church encourages me to do it.

FEBRUARY 18   CONQUERING FEAR

Lord, you have been our dwelling place
*   in all generations.*
Before the mountains were brought forth,
*   or ever you had formed the earth and the world,*
*   from everlasting to everlasting you are God.*
*   —Psalm 90:1-2 NRSV*

Last September my husband and I took a ferry cruise on the Great Lakes. I must confess that I do not enjoy viewing the sea from a boat. My idea of maritime enjoyment is to admire the various sailing vessels on the water while my feet are firmly planted on dry ground. But this was a special occasion with friends, and it was a calm, Indian-summer day. My goal was to put aside my fear of water and enjoy the beauty around me. In other words, I was going to grin and bear it!

But an uneasy feeling crept over me every time we hit a big wave, and pretty soon the palms of my hands were dripping wet. When a voice suddenly boomed over the loud-speaker, I was sure we were doomed. The owner of the voice, however, was only telling us that we were arriving at Mackinac Bridge, one of the world's longest suspension bridges. When we were directly under the bridge, I marveled at the majesty of that gigantic five-mile-long structure. The voice on the loudspeaker mesmerized me with statistics, and I agreed that it was possibly "the safest and most beautiful span ever built."

To my amazement, I realized I was no longer afraid of the water. I was so caught up in the beauty and grandeur of the bridge that something had happened to my fear.

God, I know that although my boat is so small and the sea is so very, very wide, you will always loom over me like that mighty bridge. How could I ever be afraid with all that greatness watching over me?

FEBRUARY 19   TURNING ON THE LIGHT

I urge you to put yourselves at the service of such people.
— 1 Corinthians 16:16 NRSV

One cold, rainy day I went into our church to practice the organ for a Sunday service. Our church was open daily so that visitors could view the beautiful stained-glass windows. When I arrived, I found a couple of women from other countries standing in the sanctuary. I stopped to chat with them and answer their questions about the windows. They wanted some printed information, but I couldn't find any. I invited them to return on Sunday, when I was sure someone could provide what they were looking for.

As I walked toward the organ, I thought about the light behind the chancel window and said, "I'll turn on the light behind this window for you." But when I turned, they were out of earshot. I ran up the aisle to catch them, but they had left the building and were headed out into the rain. I felt sad as I walked back toward the organ; they had missed the glory of that lighted window on a bleak day. It made me wonder how often I have turned away too soon and missed doing something that would have given someone pleasure or encouragement.

O God, please don't ever let me be lazy or indifferent in dealing with others. And don't let me fail to do whatever I can to make others' days brighter or happier, because I find that I miss a blessing when they miss theirs.

FEBRUARY 20   **"I DO MYSELF"**

Let the LORD lead you and trust him to help.
                                   —Psalm 37:5 CEV

During all his growing-up years, our youngest son was extremely independent. Whenever I offered to help him with anything, even when he was only two years old, he always said, "I do myself." Sometimes, standing by as he struggled to master some new task, I felt completely superfluous and unnecessary.

On reflection, I realize that my son is a lot like me. I often try to do things by myself. When life's responsibilities begin to crush me or the unhappiness of a situation is taking a terrible toll, I find myself trying to make it uphill all by myself. I pant and strain and fret and struggle, thinking I have to make everything work without help from anyone else.

Only when I finally realize that I'm beaten, or have gotten myself into a corner where I can't get out, do I finally turn to God. And there God is, quietly watching me struggle the way my son once struggled, even though God is infinitely ready to help me. Why is it so difficult to let a parent come to our assistance?

Dear Lord, life is too big and complicated for me to handle all by myself. You know it goes against my grain to ask, but would you please help me?

FEBRUARY 21   THE GIFT OF LAUGHTER

Make a joyful noise to God.   —*Psalm 66:1 NRSV*

I grew up in a church where people didn't laugh. Everything that went on in the brick-and-stained-glass edifice was supposed to be in dead earnest. That was unfortunate for me, because I have always been prone to laughter. I remember the time at a funeral when a woman tripped and fell headfirst into the open coffin. I thought I would burst at the humor of it! And I nearly died the time the organist dropped her bottle of tranquilizers among the pedals and dived after them without turning off the organ!

I'm happy to say that times have changed and laughter is now acceptable in church—in most churches, at least. I heard about one church where the minister preached about Jesus being a clown, emphasizing his sense of humor in dealing with people. Several church members were offended by this characterization and left the service. Some were overheard accusing the minister of blasphemy.

I don't understand such touchiness. To me, laughter is healthy and good. I keep a picture of the Laughing Jesus on my refrigerator door, and I feel a giggle well up in my heart every time I look at it. I don't think Jesus called any of us to be sourpusses!

Laughter is good, isn't it, Lord? Doesn't it help us to serve you cheerfully? And don't you sometimes laugh at the things we do?

FEBRUARY 22   SAY SOMETHING NICE

Do not judge, so that you may not be judged. For with the judgment you make you will be judged, and the measure you give will be the measure you get.   —*Matthew 7:1-2 NRSV*

I don't like criticism. Does anyone? My mother used to say, "If you can't think of anything nice to say, don't speak."

It was a nice sentiment, but I'm afraid not many people practice it. At least, we hear a lot of criticism.

Some people preface their critical remarks with, "I'm telling you this for your own good." Yeah, sure. Why do they think you need to hear all the bad things about yourself? And why do they think they have to remind you of your mistakes for the rest of your life?

One time I was taking some members of my family on an outing and we ran out of gas. It really wasn't too bad, because we weren't very far from a gas station. But one member of the family has never let me forget it. Even though it happened years ago, she never gets in the car without reminding me of it. I feel as if I ought to be wearing scarlet letters spelling "OOG"—Out of Gas!

Mom was right. I'll try not to speak if I can't think of anything nice to say.

Dear God, help me to have a positive spirit toward others and always try to find the best in them, because that's the way I want you to look at me.

FEBRUARY 23   A COMMAND, NOT A SUGGESTION

Honor your father and your mother, as the LORD your God commanded you.   *—Deuteronomy 5:16 NRSV*

What has happened to the fourth commandment in recent years? I have seen small children practically withering their parents with abusive language and demands. Teenagers often hurl disrespectful epithets at their elders. Some young people marry and turn upon their parents as if the parents had never done anything for them. I've even seen adult children belittle their elderly parents, humiliating them because they are forgetful or no longer able to perform certain acts.

There are few things more bewildering to parents than to be shown unkindness or scorn by children they have reared and cared for. Shakespeare's King Lear was right: a child's mistreatment of his or her father or mother is "sharper than a serpent's tooth." Such mistreatment is always biting and hurtful, releasing poison into the human system.

My parents didn't always do everything right, and I'm sure there were times when I resented them. But I hope I'll always remember that I wouldn't be here if it weren't for them, and continue to be properly grateful for everything they've done for me. Besides, God gave us a commandment, not a suggestion.

Dear God, you've been a wonderful parent to me. Help me to be the sort of person you'll always be pleased to call your child.

FEBRUARY 24   NO PRICE TAG ON LOVE

See what love the Father has given us. —*1 John 3:1 NRSV*

Is there such a thing as unconditional love? I have tried to practice it, but I always realize how hard it is and how impossible it is to sustain. Still, I'm not going to give up on it, because it's an important goal.

My husband and I recently attended a memorial service for the stepson of a man we barely knew. The man and his stepson had not been close. In fact, they had had major differences in recent years. So the father didn't dress up for the service to show respect for his stepson. Nor did he buy any flowers for the service. Nor did he buy a nice urn for the boy's ashes. Instead, the ashes lay in a plastic bag inside a drab plastic box provided by the crematorium. My husband and I felt awful. It was as if the man were still judging the stepson so harshly that, even in death, he couldn't be gracious and forgiving toward the boy.

The father couldn't practice unconditional love. The boy's behavior may have been too much for him, but what an ugly person the father's inflexible and unforgiving nature made of him. I probably won't ever achieve unconditional love, either. But seeing the father behaving in that manner made me want to try even harder, lest I someday prove as unloving as he.

O God, please don't ever let me put a price tag on love, for I know that you will never put a price tag on your love for me.

FEBRUARY 25   SLOW DOWN

Therefore I tell you, do not worry about your life.
—Matthew 6:25 NRSV

Everywhere I look today, people seem to be worrying and scurrying, trying to make their lives better. Little children are pushed toward the ambitions their parents once had and failed at. Young people rush through adolescence, hardly able to wait until they can get away from home and have lives of their own. Women compete in the marketplace for jobs and status, living under the tension of trying to get ahead, be the best, and have the most. Men shorten their lives by taking on too much responsibility, spending too much time on the road, and worrying about how to climb the corporate ladder.

What a pity it is that we can't see the futility of such a fevered existence before it's too late. God didn't set us down at a starting line, fire a gun, and say, "You're not a success in my book if you don't finish first." The Bible pictures God making the first man and woman and putting them in a garden. There wasn't any hurry or bother. Life happened in slow motion, without anxiety. It was Adam and Eve's sin that introduced anxiety. And I suspect that sin and anxiety are still related to each other.

Help me not to hurry and worry, God. Let me take the time to wait before you until I know what real life is all about.

FEBRUARY 26   CELEBRATE OUR LIMITATIONS

And the one with the two talents also came forward, saying, "Master, you handed over to me two talents; see, I have made two more talents." His master said to him, "Well done, good and trustworthy slave; you have been trustworthy in a few things, I will put you in charge of many things; enter into the joy of your master."
—Matthew 25:22-23 NRSV

Most of our lives we have heard, "You can do better than that." We heard it from our parents, because they wanted us to strive to do our best. Our teachers hounded us with those words to make us develop to our full potential. Even church leaders said the words, so that we would give 100 percent of our time and talents.

As I have grown older, I have discovered that sometimes those people can be wrong. Our best might not always appear so to others. When you're told you can do better and you become frustrated because you think you're already doing your best, it may be helpful to pull back and review the situation.

There are, after all, a great many things we can't do. How many of us will become renowned artists, musical composers, authors, or scientists? Very few indeed. But doing our best doesn't mean we have to be outstanding. It may mean accepting our limitations and making the most of life as it is.

I like to think of life as a patchwork quilt. The big pieces form a colorful design. But the smaller pieces are just as important, for they complete the design and hold everything together. Wise people realize their capabilities and limitations and make the best of both.

O God, help us to understand that the things we can't do are not important to you, as long as we're honestly doing our best; and give us the common sense to learn how to celebrate our limitations!

So those in the west shall fear the name of the LORD,
and those in the east, his glory;
for he will come like a pent-up stream
that the wind of the LORD drives on.
                             —Isaiah 59:19 NRSV

My husband and I live on an island in the summertime. One day last summer a wind came up that lasted twenty-four hours. It didn't come in little gusts. It came as a fierce wind, beating against the house and whipping the trees mercilessly. At night, I lay awake listening, thinking I could not tolerate another minute of the battering sound.

To while away the fretful time, I began thinking of the wind as a healing spirit that brought freshness into the world. Then I thought of my own life and how much I could use a fresh breeze to clear out the mental cobwebs and help me to begin thinking of creative ways to deal with my daily existence. There were relationships that needed attention, and ways of looking at things that needed changing. Maybe God was letting me know that a storm isn't a bad thing, especially if it blows away the staleness and makes us see the world in new ways.

When I finally dropped off to sleep, I felt peaceful and secure. Life was going to be better because of the wind.

Lord, how humdrum life can become when we do things and look at things the same old way all the time. Thank you for the periods of storm and stress, when the winds of your Spirit blow away the stagnant air and propel us in new directions!

FEBRUARY 28   **SPRING REVIVAL**

O LORD, how manifold are your works!
In wisdom you have made them all;
the earth is full of your creatures. . . .
when you take away their breath, they die. . . .

When you send forth your spirit, they are created;
and you renew the face of the ground.
—Psalm 104:24, 29-30 NRSV

There is a Chinese proverb that says:

The thunder sounds and wakes the hibernating
creatures.
That which seemed dead revives, and pursues
its destiny.

I remember it today, when spring seems to be bursting forth with all the daffodils, hyacinths, redbud, and forsythia in our neighborhood. The season is very early this year, but not unwanted, for the winter has been severe.

Life itself is like the seasons, isn't it? It is a combination of winter and springtime, the rough and the smooth, the dark and the light. There are times when we feel like hibernating, and other times when we want to emerge and shout for the sheer joy of being alive.

But for all the diversity of the seasons of life, there is one constant: God, in divine love and kindness, keeps everything in order.

Why, O God, do you always revive us after our worst winters and make everything work together for good? It must be because of our excellent destinies as your children.

March

Bloom Where You Are Planted

Nell W. Mohney

And in the vine were three branches: and it was as though it budded, and her blossoms shot forth.   —*Genesis 40:10 KJV*

*U*pon retirement, my husband and I moved into a house where the landscaping had not been completed, and we were able to choose most of the plants. Having grown up in the South, I knew that spring wouldn't be complete without some pink azaleas.

Shaking his head, the landscape architect declared: "Azaleas won't grow in this soil. Several families living in this complex tried it, only to find that the plants never budded or bloomed and died within a year or so." Though our neighbors confirmed his statement, I didn't want to give up my dream of pink azaleas. With a little research, I found there was a sturdy variety that, with a little cultivation, would grow in almost any soil. The landscape architect agreed to try, and for ten years now we have had healthy plants that bloom prolifically.

Sometimes we are like that. We are not happy with the place where we live or the people with whom we work. Rather than blooming, we whine and complain. If we allow

Christ to enrich our soil, we can become Christians who are sturdy enough to bloom where we are planted.

O God, forgive us for seeing only problems in our circumstances. Let us be willing to allow Christ to cultivate our hearts, minds, and spirits, so that we can bloom where we are planted.

MARCH 2 "I AM THE VINE"

I am the vine, you are the branches. Those who abide in me and I in them bear much fruit, because apart from me you can do nothing. —*John 15:5 NRSV*

As a young mother, I had a neighbor named Helen, who was only three years older than I but was light-years ahead of me in ordered living. Whereas I was often fragmented and overwhelmed, she seemed unflappable. She was healthy and well organized, and she seemed to truly enjoy her three boisterous but happy children.

One day when my four-year-old son had spilled finger paint on the kitchen floor and the baby was screaming from the playpen, my doorbell rang. Harried and hurried, I rushed to open the door. There stood Helen—cool, calm, and collected—surrounded by three squeaky clean and smiling children. I wanted to slam the door and tell her to go away.

Instead, I invited her in, an invitation that she thankfully declined. She simply said, "I made some chocolate chip cookies and thought that you and the boys might enjoy some." After thanking her, I went inside, sat at the kitchen table, buried my head in my hands, and wept for my out-of-control life.

The prayer wrung from the deep places of my heart went something like this:

God, I feel like a wilted, cut flower on a branch that has pulled away from the vine. Empower me with your presence so that my ordered life can bring forth your fruit. In the name of Christ, I pray.

Abide in me as I abide in you. Just as the branch cannot bear fruit by itself unless it abides in the vine, neither can you unless you abide in me.   —*John 15:4 NRSV*

"Helen, I know you are a Christian, but so am I. Yet you seem to have it all together, and I live in a state of perpetual frustration. What is your secret?" I asked my neighbor when I finally summoned up courage enough to talk about my feelings of inadequacy.

That day she introduced me to what she called "the vine life" as recorded in the fifteenth chapter of John. It has served as the north star of my spiritual journey, my anchor in the storms of life. In fact, if I were shipwrecked and could have only one section of the Bible with me, I would choose that wonderful fifteenth chapter of John. It is filled with assurances of the love of Christ, and specific directions about how to live our faith—how to bloom where we are planted.

Helen first told me that I was seeing her life through rose-colored glasses; I was comparing my worst days with her best days. When I saw her neatly dressed and looking "spiffy," most often she was en route to a meeting; when I was invited to her house, it was clean for company. Her children squabbled, got dirty, and spilled finger paint as often as mine. So what was the difference? At a time of real crisis, she had discovered "the vine life" and its resultant applications for everyday living. She had connected to the Source.

O Lord, help me to remember that I am never alone. If I stay connected to you, I can grow and blossom and bloom.

MARCH 4   "YOU ARE THE BRANCHES"

I am the vine, you are the branches.   —*John 15:5 NRSV*

Why is it so hard to relinquish control? This tendency can be seen in retirees who don't want to turn loose of their jobs; in parents who refuse to see their children as young adults, capable of making independent decisions; in a club member who seeks to manipulate and control meetings. More important, the tendency can be seen in each of us as we seek to control the circumstances of our lives. We take on more and more and feel responsible for other people's reactions. Life becomes a treadmill.

It is to this tendency that Jesus speaks when he reminds us that he is the Vine and can free us from carrying the weight of the world on our shoulders. If, as branches, we stay connected to him, we become energized to meet life's situations with calmness rather than panic. In the words of the apostle Paul: "I can do all things through Christ who strengthens me" (Philippians 4:13 NKJV).

This is not a one-time connection, as in the gift of salvation. Instead, it is a day-by-day living in his presence. For me, the connection is best made in the early morning. Bishop Ralph Cushman verbalized this in the words of his poem "I Met God in the Morning." He ends the poem with these words:

> So I think I know the secret, learned from many
> a troubled way.
> You must seek Him in the morning, if you want
> Him through the day.

Lord, let me "set my sails" in your direction each morning as I connect with you.

MARCH 5   "THIS IS THE DAY"

This is the day that the LORD has made;
let us rejoice and be glad in it.
—Psalm 118:24 NRSV

Someone has said: "Yesterday is history; tomorrow is a mystery; today is a gift. That's why we call it 'the present.'"

To live fully in today and to stay connected to Christ, the Vine, we need to begin each day with him.

The book *The First Four Minutes* suggests that the climate of any endeavor is determined by its first four minutes. The first four minutes after we meet someone, we decide whether or not we want to continue the relationship; the first four minutes in which family members are together after work and school determine the climate of the evening; the first four minutes each morning set the direction of the day.

In these minutes we cultivate the soil of our minds and spirits for whatever we wish to produce. Just as I cultivated the soil for my pink azaleas, so also the early morning conditioning prepares us for the growth of the fruit of the Spirit.

There are two things that I like to put into my mind upon awakening. First I focus on biblical affirmations such as Psalm 118:24, Philippians 4:13, and Colossians 1:27, which says, "The secret is simply this—Christ *in you*! Yes, Christ *in you* bringing with him the hope of all the glorious things to come" (JBP). Then I pray prayers of gratitude. When I follow this with a quiet time of devotional reading, prayer, and silence, I know I have claimed the day for God.

Loving God, remind me to condition my thinking each morning so that I can claim the day for you.

MARCH 6   ALLOW FOR CUTTING AND PRUNING

Every branch in Me that does not bear fruit, He takes away; and every branch that bears fruit, He prunes it, that it may bear more fruit.   —*John 15:2 NASB*

One day when the landscape architect drove through our residential development, he stopped at our house and suggested that our azaleas needed pruning. I had been aware that some of the branches looked straggly and that the plants were getting out of proportion to the space they occupied. The thought of cutting my plants, however, frightened me. I was so afraid they would die.

67

The gardener knew his business. Though the pruning seemed drastic, I rejoiced in the healthy, luxuriant growth that resulted. In the same way, Jesus says there are certain things in our lives that need pruning if we are to stay spiritually healthy, to grow and bloom where we are planted.

What needs pruning will vary from person to person, but if we sincerely ask, Christ will show us what to eliminate and what to prune. In my life, these have included bad habits such as procrastination and lethargy, and negative emotions such as fear, resentment, uncontrolled anger, and jealousy.

Pruning can be painful. For example, it's hard to give up resentment, and to forgive. But if we want to bear the fruit of the Spirit, we have to yield these recalcitrant branches to the Pruner's shears.

Loving God, grant me the courage to give up my straggly and recalcitrant branches, so that I may have the beauty of your peace.

MARCH 7   PRUNE UNHEALTHY FEAR

For God did not give us a spirit of cowardice, but rather a spirit of power and of love and of self-discipline.
                                        —2 Timothy 1:7 NRSV

A favorite story of mine concerns the pilot of a 747 jetliner. As the plane taxied down the runway, the pilot's voice could be heard over the loudspeaker: "Good morning, ladies and gentlemen. Welcome aboard Flight 827 en route to London's Heathrow Airport. We will reach a cruising altitude of 38,000 feet and will be traveling at a speed of 550 miles an hour. We will fly over Canada, Greenland, Iceland, and the tip of Ireland. As we reach our cruising altitude, the flight attendants will serve you breakfast. We will take off . . . as soon as I get up my nerve."

Haven't we all felt that way at times? Only fools are completely fearless. There are healthy fears. The healthy fear of water will motivate you to learn to swim and practice water safety. Abnormal fears, however, will paralyze you, making it impossible to take needed action.

Fears can be pruned by changing our thoughts. Fears, after all, are thoughts. They can be pruned by prayerful affirmation, such as "Perfect love casts out fear" (1 John 4:18 NRSV). Also, you can act courageously. "Do the thing you fear, and the death of fear is certain," said Ralph Waldo Emerson. The strongest way to eliminate unhealthy fear is to build up faith.

Eternal God, help me to remember that the power of the presence of Christ will keep me from being motivated by fear.

MARCH 8   PRUNE WORRY

For we walk by faith, not by sight.
—2 Corinthians 5:7 NRSV

The word *worry* comes from an Anglo-Saxon word meaning "to strangle," or "to throttle." If you have ever been really worried about something, you know how right on target that meaning is. You feel as if you can't breathe. "I am worried sick" is another apt description. Worry is misuse of imagination.

I had an aunt who was the worst worrier I have ever encountered. To be around her was to be robbed of any vestige of joy. She was always worried about getting some dread disease. When she came to visit us, the windows couldn't be opened because she might be in a draft and catch a cold. She couldn't go with us to the church picnic because people and flies would be there, and both carried germs. When she died at an old age of natural causes, I'm sure she would have liked her epitaph to be "I told you I was sick!"

Mark Twain said that he had known a lot of troubles in his life, and most of them had never happened. Take time to analyze your worries and see if you are using your energies on past events or on imagined future events.

Worry is like a broken record. Your thoughts go round and round in the same groove and can't get unstuck for action. Concern, on the other hand, is seeing the same problem from a clear perspective and taking positive action to correct it.

Eternal God, forgive me for wasting time in endless worry. Enable me to see my problems clearly, to take positive action, and to walk in faith.

MARCH 9   PRUNE UNCONTROLLED ANGER

One who is slow to anger is better than the mighty, and one whose temper is controlled than one who captures a city.
—Proverbs 16:32 NRSV

Anger is like steam: If it is to have constructive value, it must be controlled. Steam can be used to blow a horn and make a lot of noise, or it can be used to turn the wheels of a steam locomotive.

People are like that. It is easy to use your anger over any little thing that happens: when you are inconvenienced, when your feelings are hurt, when you aren't recognized often enough. As a result, you have no anger left to put under God's control for changing the evils of the world. When Jesus became angry and drove the money changers out of the temple (Luke 19:45-46), he was not acting out of personal hurt but out of a desire to change an evil system.

The feelings of anger may be the motivation you need to make a difference in the world. If Abraham Lincoln hadn't become incensed about the evil of slavery, we might never have had the Emancipation Proclamation. If Robert Raikes hadn't felt anger about the children of England who had no opportunity to learn, we might never have had Sunday schools or public schools.

Destructive anger often stems from perfectionism, self-centeredness, and paralyzing fear. Keeping a spiritual journal and having a disciplined prayer life can help you see destructive patterns and channel this emotion under God's direction.

Eternal God, thank you for the dynamic gift of emotions, which can motivate our actions. Help me to channel them through your love and purposes.

MARCH 10   PRUNE NEGATIVISM

Whatever is true, whatever is honorable, whatever is just, whatever is pure, whatever is pleasing, whatever is commendable, if there is any excellence and if there is anything worthy of praise, think about these things. —*Philippians 4:8 NRSV*

We are bombarded daily by news of unrest, terrorism, and violence. If we choose to fill our minds with these thoughts, we fall prey to negativism. We become pessimistic, unhappy people. For many people, negativism is a thought pattern that has become habitual.

You may have been reared in a negative environment, but you can interrupt the pattern. It will take time and effort and prayer, but you can rid your mind of the pollutant of negativism. You can become a thermostat rather than a thermometer. There is a "more so" philosophy at work in life. Whatever you are now, you will, through the power of habit, become more so as you grow older—unless you interrupt the pattern.

In addition to praying and interrupting negative thought patterns, there is another technique that helped me as I struggled with negative conditioning. I wore a rubber band on my wrist, and when I said something negative, I would snap it. If you do that often enough, you get the message!

If you want to think clearly, creatively, and concisely about a problem, you need to prepare your mind with calm serenity. Centuries ago, Paul understood this when he wrote, "Let this mind be in you which was also in Christ Jesus" (Philippians 2:5 NKJV).

71

O God, enable me to live with positive hope and joy, because I live in the sure knowledge of your great love and power.

MARCH 11   PRUNE RESENTMENT

Whenever you stand praying, forgive, if you have anything against anyone; so that your Father in heaven may also forgive you your trespasses.   —*Mark 11:25 NRSV*

Following a seminar I presented, a thirty-nine-year-old secretary stayed to talk with me. Ostensibly, she came to talk about feeling left out of office camaraderie. She spoke of recurring headaches, insomnia, and stomach problems. Learning that a complete physical checkup that very week had uncovered no serious problems, I began to probe about what was really bothering her.

It turned out that she was harboring a grudge against a sister who had received a little more of the family inheritance than she. The incident had happened twenty years earlier, and the accumulated weight of carrying such a grudge was evident in her bitter spirit, her physical symptoms, and her bad personal relationships. She was not hurting her sister, but she was destroying herself. Her only way out was to forgive her sister, but she was resistant to the idea. She chose to hold on to the grudge, either because it was habitual or because she felt justified.

It is easy and comfortable to hold on to a grudge, but it is deadly. Just as a splinter under the skin of your finger causes infection, so also resentment can cause anger, cynicism, and loss of joy. The only way out is through the forgiveness that Christ offers.

O God, free me from any resentment that embitters my spirit and clouds my witness.

MARCH 12   YOU REAP WHAT YOU SOW

Do not be deceived; God is not mocked, for you reap whatever you sow.   —*Galatians 6:7 NRSV*

Sow a thought and you reap an act;
Sow an act and you reap a habit;
Sow a habit and you reap a character;
Sow a character and you reap a destiny.*

Philosophers, psychologists, teachers, and religious leaders have disagreed about many things through the years, but they all seem to be in agreement about the importance of thoughts.

Many individuals have eloquently expressed the power of a person's thoughts. The Roman emperor Marcus Aurelius said: "The world in which we live is determined by our thoughts." American author and philosopher Ralph Waldo Emerson said: "A person is what he or she thinks about all day long." The Harvard sociologist and psychologist William James declared: "The greatest discovery in my generation is that human beings can alter their lives by altering their attitude of mind." The Bible tells us: "As he [a person] thinketh in his heart, so is he" (Proverbs 23:7 KJV), and "You reap whatever you sow" (Galatians 6:7 NRSV).

Thoughts are living entities, which, when consistently held, become attitudes. We need to guard our thoughts so that our attitudes, our habits, and lives reflect the presence of Christ.

Eternal God, help me to remember that I am fearfully and wonderfully made. What I sow in my mind, I will reap in my relationships.

*Anonymous quatrain quoted by Samuel Smiles (1887).

MARCH 13   PRUNE BAD ATTITUDES

*Keep your heart with all vigilance,
for from it flow the springs of life.*
—*Proverbs 4:23 NRSV*

Charles Swindoll, Christian author and speaker, has said that attitude is more important than facts. In fact, he is so

73

convinced of the importance of attitude that he believes life is 10 percent what happens to us and 90 percent how we react to it. In other words, we are in control of our thoughts —and therefore of our attitudes.

Let me list three attitudes that I consider deadly. The first is playing the blame game. When bad things happen to some people, they look for others to blame—parents, boss, spouse, government leaders, even God. The attitude of blame lowers self-esteem and leads to bitterness and cynicism. It should be foreign to the Christian.

The second deadly attitude is self-pity. It is akin to the blame game in that it makes victims of its owners. Whereas blaming is aggressive, self-pity is passive. Both, however, are deadly. Self-pity causes you to withdraw, internalize your hurts, and feel sorry for yourself.

The third deadly attitude is distrust and doubt. Honest doubt can be good if it leads to knowledge and faith. If, however, it stems from distrust, it will separate you from others, close your mind to opportunities, and keep you from the resources you need.

God of love, help me to prune from my life the attitudes that separate me from you and others.

MARCH 14   CULTIVATE AN ATTITUDE OF GRATITUDE

Give thanks in all circumstances; for this is the will of God in Christ Jesus for you.   —1 Thessalonians 5:18 NRSV

Soil, enriched with nutrients, made it possible for my azaleas to grow. Likewise, in order for us to grow, we must enrich the soil of our minds and spirits if we are to bloom as Christians. One such nutrient is the attitude of gratitude.

I learned something of the power of gratitude following the death of our oldest son, Rick, who had just turned twenty and was a student at a local university. Rick was critically injured in an accident and died ten days later. It was such a traumatic experience that I had a difficult time overcoming my grief.

One of the things that helped me was to reread Paul's words to the Thessalonians (1 Thessalonians 5:18). He was not suggesting that I give thanks that our son had died, but that in the midst of tragedy, I should give thanks.

That simple statement transformed my perspective. For example, in my prayers I would say something like this: "Thank you, God, for your love made evident in Jesus Christ. Thank you for a husband who loves me. Thank you that we have another son. Thank you that we had Rick for twenty years, and for our happy memories. Thank you for the church, which is truly the body of Christ." Each day I could feel my grief lifting.

That act of gratitude so revolutionized my life that I continue it to this day. On the rare occasions when I oversleep and don't do it, I find myself irritable and impatient. Gratitude opens your heart to God and life; ingratitude snaps it shut.

Eternal God, call to my remembrance your many blessings in my life so that I may express my gratitude.

MARCH 15   CULTIVATE COMPASSION

Finally, all of you, be of one mind, having compassion for one another.   —*1 Peter 3:8 NKJV*

Compassion, the ability to feel with others, was an attribute that our Lord modeled so beautifully during his earthly existence. It was also modeled for me by a nine-year-old girl on the Sunday following our son's funeral service.

Rick's service had been on a Sunday. By the following Sunday, our family members had returned home, our younger son had returned to college, and my husband was in the pulpit. I had to walk into church alone on that Sunday. It was one of the hardest things I've ever had to do, but I knew that postponing it would only make it harder.

That morning, when I walked to the pew where Rick and I usually sat, there was a vacant seat beside me. Almost before I was seated, a little girl left her pew, sat down beside me, and with the most disarming smile, simply patted my hand and said, "Mrs Mohney, I love you." I knew what she was saying: "I know how you must be feeling this morning, and I am sorry." All of my carefully mustered control melted like ice in the sun, but I shall never forget that act of compassion and the touch of her small hand.

Eternal God, help us to share with each other the compassionate caring that was modeled by Jesus.

MARCH 16   CULTIVATE A POSITIVE ATTITUDE

If God be for us, who can be against us? —Romans 8:31 KJV

Do you know someone who is so negative that you hope you don't see him or her in the morning before you have had a good strong cup of coffee? Could there be those who hope they don't see you until they have had one?

One of the most positive people I have ever known was Dr. E. Stanley Jones, whose books have had a powerful impact on the spiritual lives of millions of Christians around the world. As a young person, I considered Dr. Jones to be my spiritual mentor through his books. Later in life I had the opportunity to meet him when he accepted an invitation to speak in our church and be a guest in our home. That experience was a shining hour in my spiritual journey.

Dr. Jones truly believed that "Jesus is Lord," and he lived his life under the lordship of Christ. His positive faith affected every area of his life: his mental acumen, his time management, his relationships, and his availability to Christ. His final book, titled *The Divine Yes,* was written while he recuperated from a crippling stroke at age eighty-nine. He believed that his positive attitude enhanced his healing. He not only walked again, but he also preached victoriously until he moved from the earthly to the heavenly dimension of life.

Help me, O God, to live my life under your divine "Yes."

MARCH 17   CULTIVATE MAGNANIMITY

What God has made clean, you must not call profane.
—Acts 10:15 NRSV

Webster's *New World Dictionary* defines *magnanimity* as a quality of rising above pettiness and prejudice. To me, this means seeing everyone as a person of worth, even if you don't like or agree with him or her.

As a young person, I attended a World Conference of Christian Youth in Oslo, Norway. My roommates were from several European and Asian countries. Though English was the common language, we were different in many ways. We didn't look alike; we didn't wear the same kind of clothes; even our toothbrushes were different! But we all laughed about the same things and were deeply moved by the same things. In addition, we all were Christians.

On the last night of the conference, we were asked to wear our native dress and sit under our national flag. The Bishop of Oslo led our worship by having us stand and pray aloud the Lord's Prayer, using our own language or dialect. Later it was announced that we had used 122 languages and dialects as we prayed, "Our Father who art in heaven."

I think I joined the human race that night. I had been a white American from a very provincial section of North Carolina. That night I began to see all persons as people of worth, as God's people.

O loving Christ, help me to stay so focused on your powerful and loving presence that I may rise above petty differences and see others as you see them.

*In the world you face persecution. But take courage; I have
conquered the world.*   —*John 16:33 NRSV*

The great French Christian Teilhard de Chardin once
wrote that the two unmistakable attributes of a Christian are
positive hope (optimism) and joy. As Christians, we can have
these qualities even in a world full of tragedy and even as we
struggle against evil. The reasons: We are not alone—God is
with us; and we have read the Bible and know how it all
turns out.

We have only to look at how Jesus faced life's tragedies,
even death on the cross, and used them for the glory of God.
Likewise, Paul took difficulties and defeats and turned them
into vital victories because his hope, his trust, and his very life
were rooted in faith in Christ. Only then could he write: "All
things work together for good for those who love God, who
are called according to his purpose" (Romans 8:28 NRSV).

Optimism for the Christian is based on the faith that nothing can happen that we and God together cannot handle.
This doesn't mean being unrealistic or putting our heads in
the sand or expecting no difficulties. Rather, because of our
belief in God, in Christ, and in the power of the Holy Spirit,
we can feel competent to face life. We know that difficulties
will come, but we see them as temporary challenges rather
than as permanent problems.

*Enable me, O God, to be so rooted in faith that I may live
with positive hope and joy.*

MARCH 19   OPTIMISM HELPS WHEN YOU ARE ILL

*Nevertheless My lovingkindness I will not utterly take
    from him,
Nor allow My faithfulness to fail.*
                                    —*Psalm 89:33 NKJV*

Optimism is an important outlook for everyday life, but it is especially helpful in times of illness. I learned this in a very personal way several years ago. As I dressed to go to church one evening, I felt something hard in my abdomen.Though it caused me slight concern, I decided it was a hardened muscle resulting from increased abdominal exercises.

Around 2:00 A.M., however, I awakened with my fears as thick as flies at a summer picnic. *What if this is a tumor? What if it's malignant? What if I die?* Those paralyzing thoughts gave me a panic attack. Then Psalm 89:33 brought me back to the source of my optimism—God's love and grace as seen in his promises and made evident in the person of Jesus Christ.

There was a malignancy. Then there was surgery, followed by long months of chemotherapy. But because I believe that joys lie hidden in problems, when I awakened in ICU, I found myself thinking: *OK, Nell, what are the joys in this situation?* I found them in abundance: the support of friends through prayers, flowers, visits, food; the increased closeness of our family, especially my husband, who became my "head nurse," providing cold cloths and soothing words during my bouts with nausea. Most of all, God's presence gave me power to "hang in there."

Eternal God, let me claim the promise that your faithfulness will never fail.

MARCH 20 CULTIVATE CONFIDENCE

I came that they may have life, and have it abundantly.
—John 10:10 NRSV

From Jesus' words in John 10:10, it seems obvious that Jesus does not want us to be weak, ineffective, lethargic, and fearful persons. He implied that we are to live with confidence and power.

After you have accepted your Christian heritage, there are

many things you can do to facilitate growth and self-confidence. Dr. Norman Vincent Peale was a good example of this. Growing up a minister's son in a small town, he was painfully shy and had a self-image of inadequacy. In an interview several years ago, Dr. Peale told me that he might have remained shy without the intervention of a college professor.

One day after Norman had performed miserably in an oral exam, the professor asked him to stay after class. Without tact or concern for the student's feelings, the professor blurted out: "How long are you going to act like a scared rabbit? You had better change the way you think about yourself, Peale, before it is too late."

Dr. Peale told me that stronger than anger was his desire to be confidently whole. His plan of action, which included daily affirmations, not only enabled him to become one of America's most popular preachers and authors, but also inspired millions to cultivate confidence.

Eternal God, help me to live confidently in the knowledge that I am empowered by your Holy Spirit.

MARCH 21   CONFIDENCE COMES THROUGH
                                          SURRENDER

Those who find their life will lose it, and those who lose their life for my sake will find it. —*Matthew 10:39 NRSV*

As paradoxical as it may seem, we have to surrender our lives to the lordship of Christ in order to be free, whole, and confident. Jesus gave us the paradox when he said that in order to find our lives, we must lose them for his sake.

In surrender, the self doesn't die or become diminished. In fact, it is only in surrender that the self becomes fulfilled. When the self is of primary importance, it becomes what William James, Harvard sociologist, called "the convulsive little ego." This is true even when the self is dressed up to look like healthy ambition, righteous anger, or strong commitment. Instead of being integrated, the self-centered person becomes fragmented.

Only under the lordship of Christ can the self be fully realized. It is then that we tame the wild horses of passion and negative emotion, so that they work as servants rather than as master. In a strange way that we do not fully understand, the surrendered self becomes more aware of others, lives more harmoniously with others, and lives in deep communion with God. It is then that we truly find life.

Eternal God, help me to be willing to find my life by losing it for the sake of Christ.

MARCH 22   CULTIVATE LAUGHTER

A merry heart doeth good like a medicine.
                                        —Proverbs 17:22 KJV

From the beginning to the end, the Bible encourages laughter. I've always enjoyed the biblical story of aged Abraham and Sarah doubled up with laughter on being told they were to have a baby. Can't you almost hear Sarah saying, "Lord, have you checked with my gynecologist lately?" But God had the last laugh because their miracle child was born, and his name, Isaac, means "laughter."

Often I have wondered if the Creator laughs when we strut around with feelings of imperial self-importance and self-sufficiency. God must, however, be more saddened than amused when we forget our dependence upon him or forget that we, like Abraham and Sarah, can accomplish unbelievable things when we claim his promises and seek to fulfill his purposes. Solomon reminded us that even in laughter, the heart may ache (Proverbs 14:13), but humor gives us a needed break from the pain of heartache.

In his book *The Humor of Christ,* Elton Trueblood reminds us that Jesus said we must become like little children if we are to enter the kingdom of heaven. He points out that a part of childlikeness is the ability to laugh. How childlike are you?

81

Eternal God, help me to keep your perspective as I develop my ability to laugh.

MARCH 23   LAUGHTER IS HEALTHY

A merry heart doeth good like a medicine: but a broken spirit drieth the bones. —*Proverbs 17:22 KJV*

From the Bible to Aristotle to Kant and Locke, the power of laughter has been taught through the years. In recent years, the physical benefits of laughter have received much attention. The late Norman Cousins, who served for years as editor of *Saturday Review,* laughed himself back to health and wrote about it in *The Anatomy of an Illness.* He experienced the curative power of laughter in his life-threatening illness.

Part of his rehabilitation regimen was to rent Laurel and Hardy movies and watch them for several hours each day. Not only was this a distraction from pain and a spirit lifter, but it actually helped strengthen his immune system. Later he joined the staff of a medical school where he helped patients understand the role of positive attitudes and laughter in their recovery.

Laughter can even help to ease the pain of grief. I know a woman whose husband, age forty, was killed in an automobile accident. They had three children, ages ten, eight, and four. Both parents were persons of steadfast faith who practiced joy and laughter in their lives. Though they went through a period of grieving after his death, the mother was able to continue some of the fun things they had done as a family as a means of remembering him and coping with their grief.

Thank you, God, that in your plan, laughter is a means of keeping me whole and healthy.

MARCH 24   CULTIVATE JOY

The joy of the LORD is your strength.
—*Nehemiah 8:10 KJV*

Knowing that he is in daily, excruciating pain from injuries sustained in a fall while mountain climbing, I asked Tim Hansel, "How can you be so joyful?"

The tall, articulate, joyful man who was speaking in our church replied, "Every day I choose joy. You can choose to be joyous or you can choose to be miserable. The choice is yours." Immediately there flashed into my mind a sentence from Barbara Johnson's book *Splashes of Joy in the Cesspools of Life:* "Pain is inevitable but misery is a choice."

There are many things joy is not. Some people think that joy is dependent upon circumstances—good health, material possessions, good family, happy temperament. Yet we all know joyless people who are healthy and have a comfortable lifestyle, a good job, a happy marriage, and children who are doing well.

The root of the word *happiness* is "happenstance," implying that happiness is often dependent upon circumstances— a promotion, a wedding, a new baby, a new house, a new car. All of these can give you a feeling of pleasure, but joy is a far deeper quality. Joy is not a human achievement. It is a gift from God.

Eternal God, help me remember that life is often difficult and unpleasant, but it can be joyful when your Spirit lives in me.

MARCH 25   JOY IS A GIFT FROM GOD

The fruit of the Spirit is love, joy, peace, patience, kindness, generosity, faithfulness, gentleness, and self-control.
—Galatians 5:22-23 NRSV

Joy is a gift from God. But a gift is not a gift until you receive it. On Broadway, Mary Martin used to sing: "A song is not a song 'til you sing it; Love is not love 'til you give it away." I'd like to add that a gift is not a gift until you receive it.

Actually, the gift of joy is the miracle of a life in whom

Christ lives. That miracle was so visible in the life of the apostle Paul. That brilliant man had many deep and important things to say in his thirteen letters found in the New Testament, but one thing he said over and over again: "In Christ! In Christ!" The eminent German scholar Adolph Deissman reported that Paul used that phrase, or a similar one, such as "in him" or "in the Lord," 164 times.

As I read Paul's letters, it seems to me that he means a simple daily surrender of our wills to Christ. Paul speaks of this as "I die every day" (1 Corinthians 15:31 NRSV). To die every day is simple but not easy, because our lives are so ego-centered. Surrender is symbolized by a daily question: "Lord, what are *we* going to do today?"

Come into my heart, Lord Jesus, so that I may receive your gift of joy.

MARCH 26   RECEIVE THE GIFT

I have said these things to you so that my joy may be in you, and that your joy may be complete.
                                            —John 15:11 NRSV

Receiving the eternally significant gift of joy is somewhat analogous to swimming. After the techniques of swimming have been explained and demonstrated, then you have to get into the water and trust yourself to its supporting power.

For many years I lived in an all-male family—one husband, two sons, even a male dog. I had to do lots of "masculine" things—fishing, hiking, camping, and swimming. Now, I could swim in shallow water, but I was terrified of deep water. When our youngest son graduated from the shallow end to the deep end of the pool, I took my pride in hand and joined an adult beginner's class.

I did well in the class until the instructor said, "Today we are going to the deep end of the pool." I was very "Christian." I let everybody go ahead of me! At the other end of the pool she said to each swimmer, "Jump in." I looked at all that deep water, and everything in me rebelled. "I can't. I just can't do it," I said.

She asked me this simple question: "Do you believe this water will hold you up?"

"Yes," I replied hesitantly.

"Then act like you do. Jump in." She was calling my bluff. Either I believed it or I didn't, and the test was action. I jumped.

Either we believe that the waters of faith will hold us up, or we don't.

Eternal God, let me know the joy of Christ living in my life.

MARCH 27   CULTIVATE STILLNESS

Be still, and know that I am God.   *—Psalm 46:10 KJV*

Air Force Captain Scott O'Grady was rescued after being shot down in Bosnia. When he arrived at the Aviano Air Base in Italy, he said that after parachuting to the ground, his first impulse was to run. Instead, he became very still, prayed, assessed the situation, and remembered his training. He survived the six days before his rescue by drinking rainwater, eating bugs, and staying quiet so that enemy forces couldn't detect his position. He said that during that time, he also trusted God and the ability of the American Air Force to come to his rescue. He had developed the ability to focus.

We too need to focus on the power of God to quiet and renew our minds. In a fast-moving world, it is easy to be fragmented. We try to sit quietly, but our minds move in a million directions. This is evident even in church. Though we may be engrossed in the choir's anthem or the minister's sermon, we are quickly distracted by a late arrival who walks to the front pew.

For me, cultivating stillness has been made easier by affirming verses of Scripture that quiet my spirit and allow me to be focused. Among my favorites are Isaiah 30:15, "In quietness and in confidence shall be your strength," and Isaiah 40:31, "They that wait upon the LORD shall renew their strength" (KJV).

Eternal God, help me to find the peace of God that passes all understanding (Philippians 4:7).

MARCH 28   CULTIVATE PEACE

My peace I give unto you.   *—John 14:27 KJV*

Christ's peace is the harmony within that keeps us calm and confident in every situation. This was true for Chicago businessman Horatio Spafford in 1857. He was taking his wife, Anna, and their four daughters to Europe. A last-minute business crisis caused him to delay his trip, though he expected to take a later ship and join his family in England.

Tragically, near Newfoundland, the ship on which his family traveled collided with another vessel and sank in twelve minutes. A falling mast stunned Anna, and when she regained consciousness, she learned that all four of their children had gone down with 474 other passengers. She was one of 22 persons who survived to reach Cardiff, Wales, after long weeks on the crowded vessel that plucked them from the icy ocean. She cabled her husband only two words: "Saved. Alone."

Horatio sailed immediately to Wales. When his ship reached the spot where his children had drowned, he expressed both his grief and his faith in a poem.

> When peace like a river attendeth my way,
> When sorrows like sea billows roll.
> Whatever my lot, Thou hast taught me to say,
> "It is well, it is well, with my soul."

His words have blessed millions and helped them to find God's peace in the midst of their tragedies.

Eternal God, allow your peace to fill me and flow through me to others.

MARCH 29   CULTIVATE PEACEFUL THOUGHTS

Peace I leave with you; my peace I give to you. I do not give to you as the world gives. Do not let your hearts be troubled, and do not let them be afraid.   —*John 14:27 NRSV*

When I feel stressful or panicked, I try to see in my mind's eye a peaceful scene until its quietness envelopes me. I like to imagine a summer camp in North Carolina where I went as a teenager. It holds for me happy memories of fun and spiritual growth. I see myself seated alone on Vesper Hill, looking down on a very placid lake. Soon my mind is quiet enough to be open to God's creative thoughts. As energy begins to flow again, I can feel myself moving from fragmentation to focused, orderly thinking.

I have a friend who envisions a symphony hall filled with beautiful music for her peaceful scene. Another friend becomes peaceful by "seeing" a big fire burning in the fireplace of her den on a cold, winter evening. Her husband is seated in an easy chair, reading, and their children are quietly doing their homework.

We live in a fragmented, noisy, and high-pressure world. One of the most needed survival skills for Christians is learning to relax our bodies and minds. One step toward that goal is cultivating peaceful thoughts. Choose your own peaceful scene sometime today, and let God's love and peace fill you.

Eternal God, enable me to move from chaos to your deep and abiding peace that passes understanding.

MARCH 30   STAY CONNECTED TO THE VINE

I am the vine, you are the branches. Those who abide in me and I in them bear much fruit, because apart from me you can do nothing.   —*John 15:5 NRSV*

Though you may prune and cultivate the branch representing your life, you won't bear lasting fruit until you are connected to the Vine—the Source of spiritual vitality. At times, I get busy and allow pressures to mount in my life. One extra thing to do can send me crashing downward. It means I have been doing everything in my own strength, and my spiritual batteries are no longer charged. I need to allow my parched spirit to be refreshed by the living water. Yet sometimes I don't take the time or have the motivation to do it.

The story is told of a young salesman who gave what he thought was a convincing sales pitch to an elderly farmer. Declaring that the book he was selling would double the farmer's productivity in two years, the salesman asked, "Would you like your farm to be more productive?"

"Yep," said the farmer.

"Then you'll buy the book?" asked the young man as he pulled out a sales sheet.

"Nope," replied the farmer.

"Why not?" asked the surprised salesman.

The reply: "I already know more to do than I'm doing!"

Isn't that our problem? Our motivation comes when we remember Jesus' words: "Without Me you can do nothing" (John 15:5 NKJV).

O God, help me to stay closely connected to Christ, the Vine.

MARCH 31   BLOOM WHERE YOU ARE PLANTED

And in the vine were three branches: and it was as though it budded, and her blossoms shot forth. — Genesis 40:10 KJV

Is it hard to be a Christian in your circumstance? Are you in an office filled with nonbelievers? Bloom where you are planted! Are you a young homemaker, stuck with the routine responsibilities of small children? Bloom where you are planted! Are you dealing with a teenage rebel? Bloom where you are planted! Are you living alone and surrounded by lonely people? Bloom where you are planted!

This is easy to say but difficult to do. We can easily grow discouraged unless we walk in daily fellowship with Christ and continue to cultivate and enrich the soil of our minds and spirits and to prune their weeds.

One more thing: Don't quit. Years ago, Margaret Johnson wrote a book titled *When God Says No*. The message of three stories from that book encourages me when I feel like quitting. I pass the message on to you in the hope that it will bring you encouragement too.

Based on experiences of her mother, Margaret repeated these three admonitions to enable her to keep on keeping on: "Hold on." "Don't run." "Take one step more." So, when it is difficult to bloom in your garden, put your faith in Christ and follow those admonitions.

Eternal God, in this one chance I have at life, don't let me wilt like a cut flower, but help me bloom for you.

April

Of Fools' Days, Due Days, and Birthdays

Shirley Pope Waite

APRIL 1   APRIL FOOLS' DAY

She's nobody's fool!" I've often heard that description of a shrewd or wise woman. Recently it set me to wondering about the origin of April Fools' Day.

As early as A.D. 1000, jesters, called "court fools," were employed by kings and noblemen as part of their retinue. Performing clownlike antics to help a ruler forget his troubles, jesters had to be clever, and many even gave advice to their superiors.

April Fools' Day originated in France in 1564, after the adoption of a new calendar changed New Year's Day from April 1 to January 1. Those who forgot or were slow to make the change were called "April fools." The custom of fooling friends on that day, especially dispatching them on fruitless errands, became popular and soon spread from France to other countries. (I was fascinated to learn that the fruitless errand fooling may have come from the trial of Christ when he was needlessly sent from Annas to Caiaphas and from Pilate to Herod.)

Like court jesters, Christians may sometimes be regarded

as weak-minded, illogical, and lacking good judgment—in other words, as fools. We shouldn't let it bother us. We know where our true wisdom is—in Christ (1 Corinthians 1:30). If we err on the side of foolishness, may it always be for Christ. Still, the apostle Paul reminds us, "Be careful how you act. . . . Don't be fools; be wise: make the most of every opportunity you have for doing good" (Ephesians 5:15-16 TLB).

APRIL 2   FOOLS FOR CHRIST

"Won't you please help us out?" Dani begged my husband and me a few years ago. She was a director for Vacation Bible School, and she was having difficulty recruiting helpers. Most young women in our church worked full-time. The few stay-at-home moms couldn't do all the work. Dani herself had two small children and another on the way.

I could help behind the scenes, in the kitchen, or as registrar, I reasoned. Kyle could set up props and move furniture. But Dani wanted us to be "pilots" in one of the biblical "ports" (the theme was "Seaside with the Savior").

We reluctantly agreed, decorated our classroom to look as much like Caesarea as possible, and obtained authentic costumes. (Kyle was a dead ringer for Yassir Arafat—even growing a beard!)

The first day of VBS arrived. We both felt foolish. How would these little ones relate to a couple of old folks? As one mother brought her child into our room, the little boy looked at Kyle and did a double take. In an awe-filled voice, he exclaimed, "Mommy, look! There's Jesus!"

We became "Rhoda" and "Jonathan" to over one hundred children. Then came the final event—a potluck in our church parking lot. We were asked to wear our costumes. Again, we felt foolish. Then five-year-old Cassi ran to us, grabbed us around the legs, and said, "Oh, Rhoda and Jonathan, I'm so glad you're here!"

If the apostle Paul could be a fool for Christ (1 Corinthians 4:10), so could we!

91

*He had no form or comeliness that we should look at him,
and no beauty that we should desire him.*
—Isaiah 53:2 RSV

My friend was participating in a Lenten Bible study at her church. The leader suggested they read the Messianic prophecies in Isaiah 53, and record their thoughts.

Helen sent me what she wrote after reading the above verse. With her permission, I share the following:

No beauty? No beauty in the eyes that looked upon the crowd beneath his feet for whom, at that very moment, he poured out his life?

No beauty? No beauty in those shattered, bloody hands that once touched a blind man's eyes, causing them to see? Those hands that stroked a dead girl's brow, so life coursed strong again? Those hands that blessed the bread and fish to satisfy the emptiness of hungry men?

No beauty? No beauty in the bloodied head or side, torn and scarred, so *my* life could be one of wholeness and joy?

No beauty? No beauty in those tortured feet that walked many dusty miles, bringing him to those whose own feet could not walk . . . then at his touch, could run again?

No beauty? Ah, friends, since time began, no artist's brush, no writer's pen, no sermon, has ever shown me such beauty as I see when I behold the figure of that man upon the cross.

Thank you, Helen, for adding a new dimension to my Lenten season.

APRIL 4   WHAT DO WE SAVE?

I've often wondered how people from bygone days managed their daylight hours. Would they laugh at our daylight saving time?

There is just so much daylight in any given twenty-four hours. I'm not sure what we *save*, but there are some things we *lose* from this time manipulation.

Tempers, for instance. My kids equated bedtime with darkness. I would often lose my temper trying to get the kids to bed at a decent hour.

"But, Mom, all the other kids stay outside until dark."

It wasn't so bad after the school year ended, except that nobody wanted to eat supper until 8:00 P.M. Any diet-conscious person knows it's difficult to lose those extra pounds eating a heavy meal that late.

I lose precious hours of reading. Curling up with a book is my after-dark pastime. When it's daylight, I feel obliged to continue my labor. People who work all day appreciate the extra hour for yard work. Since I don't enjoy that task, the sooner it gets dark, the sooner I lose sight of those noxious weeds.

There are also initial mix-ups as we "spring ahead" and "fall back." Our oldest daughter was married on the Sunday that daylight saving time began one year. Some folks arrived at the church in time for a glass of punch and a piece of wedding cake. The process is reversed in the fall. We get to church an hour early and wonder where everybody else is.

"Fast" time or "slow" time, spring or fall, the psalmist hit the nail on the head when he said, "My times are in your hands" (Psalm 31:15 TLB).

APRIL 5   PALM SUNDAY

For several years, Palm Sunday was reenacted in our church parking lot. A local farmer provided a donkey, and one of our bearded parishioners dressed in a long garment and appropriate headdress. He was a dead ringer for Jesus.

As he slowly rode around the parking area, children and their teachers called out "Hosanna" and laid leafy branches as well as coats and jackets in the donkey's pathway.

One year the donkey refused to tread on any clothing.

While trying to sidestep, the beast moved closer to the crowd. One child called out, "Oh, it isn't Jesus after all! It's Mr. B——!" Another child added, "But he acts like Jesus!"

Those words caught me up short. Could I act more like Jesus—not in outward appearance, or by riding a donkey on Palm Sunday, but by my actions?

I vowed to practice more of the Lord's attributes: showing compassion toward the new widower in our church; running errands for my neighbor who has two-year-old twins; providing transportation for my nondriving friend; showing tolerance toward the church member who doesn't agree with me theologically. Most of all, I could love unconditionally.

Lord Jesus, help me to be more like you.

APRIL 6   SLEEPLESS NIGHTS

On my bed I remember you;
I think of you through the watches of the night.
—Psalm 63:6 NIV

David wrote Psalm 63 while in the desert in Judah. Most likely he was seeking refuge during Absalom's rebellion, a time when worry and concern must have kept him awake through all three of the night watches. Yet he deliberately focused his mind on God.

Although I'm normally a good sleeper, I occasionally have insomnia—usually when I have something exciting or stressful on my mind. So I've learned to play mental games on such nights.

I pray through the alphabet for people. I may start with first names—Alice (my sister-in-law), Betty (my neighbor who suffers from chronic neuralgia), Charlie (whose mother is dying), Dale (who will begin serving a new church), and so on.

For variety, I recall last names: "Lord, bless the Aosveds (a newly married couple), Mrs. Barrett (a shut-in from our congregation), the Coles (who've had a death in the family), Tony Davis (my grandson)."

94

Of course, I skip some letters. I don't know anyone with a first or last name beginning with "X."

When light finally streams through my window, the time spent in intercessory prayer somehow makes up for the lack of sleep. I'm thankful that the Lord helps me to take my mind off myself and pray for others throughout the night watches.

APRIL 7   THE NAMES OF GOD

Another game I play during the "night watches" takes me through the alphabet naming the attributes of God. My list is by no means exhaustive, and it is not original. Worshipers throughout the centuries have tried to describe and give names to the great "I AM."

I've also used this mental game when I'm stuck in traffic while commuting, or when I'm in the dentist's office where magazines are outdated.

Here is a sample list:

A	Almighty		M	Miraculous
B	Beautiful		N	Nearby
C	Creator		O	Omnipotent
D	Divine		P	Powerful
E	Everlasting		Q	Quieting
F	Faithful		R	Ruler
G	Great		S	Satisfying
H	Holy		T	True
I	I Am		U	Understanding
J	Jealous (Yes!		V	Valuable
	Check the Ten		W	Wonderful
	Commandments		X	Exalted (This is
	—Exod. 20:5			cheating a little.)
	and Deut. 5:9.		Y	Yahweh
	See also		Z	Zealous
	Exod. 34:14.)			
K	King			
L	Love			

Now come up with your own list!

95

"What's that vine coming up in my flower bed?" I wondered. With a delicate lavender hue, it looked familiar. But I hadn't planted it. Then I remembered the trellis by the back door in one of my childhood homes. Sweet peas!

Poet John Keats wrote about sweet peas of a different color:

> Here are sweet peas on tip-toe for flight,
> With wings of gentle flush o'er delicate white.

Keats wasn't the only Englishman who found much to be admired in April's flower. After it was introduced into the country in the early 1700s, the English fell in love with the hardy climbing plant.

The sweet pea apparently descended from an annual that grew wild in Sicily, Sardinia, and southern Italy. Originally, it was referred to as a "weedy little plant." However, English botanists and growers experimented with the flower, and by a 1900 Bicentennial Show in London, 264 different kinds of sweet peas were exhibited. Now there are more than a thousand varieties. Such hues! White, shades of pink and lavender, red, blue, and purple. Such sizes! Some are dwarfs; others attain heights of seven feet. Such shapes! In some varieties, the petals are smooth and velvety, while others are crinkled and wavy.

And what a tremendous variety of shapes, sizes, and hues we humans come in. Many of us start out as "weedy little plants," growing wild, needing cultivation. But when we get into the hands of the Master Grower, we are changed "into his likeness with ever-increasing glory" (2 Corinthians 3:18 NIV).

APRIL 9   THE LAST SUPPER

No artist has depicted the Last Supper as dramatically and poignantly as Leonardo da Vinci, born in April 1452.

"I am innocent!" Philip seems to plead. "There's a traitor here!" Thaddaeus is perhaps telling Simon. Impatient Peter holds tightly to a knife. John bows in silent grief. Judas, in shadow, clutches a money bag. With the possible exception of his *Mona Lisa*, the *The Last Supper* mural is considered one of the greatest paintings in the world, and has inspired more books, articles, poems, and lectures than any other work of art.

Painting was only one of da Vinci's talents. He is described as the most gifted person who ever lived. He was an engineer, architect, mathematician, astronomer, botanist, zoologist, geologist . . . the list goes on! He improvised songs, accompanying himself on a lyre he made. He is attributed with inventing the helicopter, even the automobile, but he lacked the necessary sources of power to pursue these inventions further. However, Leonardo is best remembered during Holy Week for his painting *The Last Supper*.

I was privileged to see a wood carving of this masterpiece in Nashville, Tennessee. The awesome reproduction, 17 feet wide and 8 feet high, is carved in lime wood and walnut. No less awesome is my 5 inch by 12 inch olive wood replica of *The Last Supper*. The intricate facial expressions on this carving from the Holy Land amaze me.

I'm even more amazed and awestruck when I remember that after Jesus' last meeting with his disciples, he suffered death on the cross for humankind. His glorious resurrection puts human achievement—even da Vinci's—into proper perspective.

APRIL 10   IT HAPPENED ON GOOD FRIDAY

On that first Good Friday, a seemingly tragic event occurred that changed the history of the world. Nothing can compare to our Lord's crucifixion—or to the victory that took place Sunday morning.

On a Good Friday more than eighteen hundred years later, another tragic event occurred that changed the history of our country.

The day began as any other in the life of our sixteenth president. He rose early and started to work in his office. He had an egg and a cup of coffee for breakfast; then he returned to his office, where he read the newspapers, signed documents, and talked with a legislator. He welcomed a friend from Maryland: "Old fellow, everything is bright this morning. It has been a tough time, but we have lived it out—or some of us have."

After the Friday staff conference and lunch, he and his wife went for a ride. She told him, "Dear husband, you almost startle me by your great cheerfulness."

He talked of the future, a possible trip to Europe, settling on a farm, practicing law again. He commented, "I never felt so happy in my life."

Yet, before that Good Friday was over on April 14, 1865, President Lincoln lay fighting for his life, which ended the next morning at 7:22.

Lincoln had earlier made a statement: "I do the very best I know how; the very best I can; and I mean to keep doing so until the end." How prophetic were his words!

I don't know when or how my life will end. But I would like to be remembered, not only as a woman who tried to do my best in a cheerful and happy spirit, but also as one who followed the Lord until the end.

APRIL 11   JABEZ! WHO'S HE?

A fellow writer once suggested a certain biblical prayer to use in my writing efforts. I posted it next to my computer screen and then forgot it. Like many things we see daily, it went unnoticed for years.

Recently I used a question-and-answer book designed to accompany daily Bible reading. While studying 1 Chronicles, I read the question, "Who was Jabez?"

Who knows? I thought, before I read the passage. Jabez, I learned, is mentioned only once in the Bible. He is remembered, not for some heroic act, but for his prayer. Suddenly I recognized it as the one posted on my computer.

Jabez asked God for four things:

1. Oh, that you would wonderfully bless me
2. and help me in my work;
3. please be with me in all that I do,
4. and keep me from all evil and disaster!

Then the Bible states, "And God granted him his request" (1 Chronicles 4:10 TLB).

No wonder my friend suggested Jabez's prayer. I certainly pray for God's blessing. I ask God to help me with my writing as well as other things in my life. And I certainly ask the Lord for divine protection.

Perhaps the prayer of Jabez can become your prayer too.

APRIL 12   THE EASTER CANTATA

Our son was eager to have us watch a video of the Easter Cantata performed by his church. Unfortunately, the taping was done by someone who knew little about lighting; consequently, the quality of the video was very poor.

As family members gathered around the TV, Mark gave a running commentary of the performance.

At one point, our granddaughter Jessica ran to the screen and pointed to herself. "This is where the children sing for Jesus," she said.

The young man who portrayed the Christ was a former biker with long hair who resembled the mental image most of us have of Jesus. The video was powerful, despite the poor quality.

The lighting in the living room didn't help either, and the shadows of those of us watching were superimposed on the screen. I sat on the floor at my husband's feet. From my vantage point, I was suddenly struck by a scene that will be forever etched in my mind.

Jesus had been crucified (cleverly done with his back to the audience) and the cantata reached its climax. There on the TV stood the triumphant Lord, with outstretched hands as if to receive the whole world. The silhouettes of family members scattered around the room were reflected onto the screen in such a way that Jesus seemed to be embracing us all—both the saved and the unsaved!

Tears filled my eyes as the cantata drew to a conclusion and the scene disappeared before my eyes. Yet it was a message from God himself—one I so desperately needed for reassurance.

I silently prayed, "Lord, give me patience as I await your perfect timing in the lives of my precious loved ones."

APRIL 13   PEACE! BE STILL!

A great windstorm arose, and the waves beat into the boat, so that the boat was already being swamped. . . . He woke up and rebuked the wind, and said to the sea, "Peace! Be still!" Then the wind ceased, and there was a dead calm.
—*Mark 4:37, 39 NRSV*

I've often wondered why Jesus and the disciples left in the evening to cross the Sea of Galilee. Couldn't they tell by the weather that they should wait until morning? Why take chances?

Since I visited Israel, I understand the situation better. We had crossed the sea from Tiberias to Kibbutz Ginosar, enjoying onboard Sunday morning services and holy Communion on the calmest of waters. It was beautiful. We were then bused to the seaside ruins of Capernaum. Our guide referred to the erratic nature of this body of water. The pear-shaped Sea of Galilee, he told us, is actually a freshwater lake. "Cool air comes from the Mediterranean area through narrow mountain passes and clashes with hot air coming up from Saudi Arabia," he explained.

So much for scientific explanations, I thought. But as he spoke, to my astonishment, it began to rain. The wind came up, and before our very eyes the water, which an hour before had been smooth and placid, became a maelstrom of foam and high waves.

The guide shouted above the wind, "These waves are tame. They sometimes get as high as twenty feet." No wonder the disciples were frightened! And yet our Lord told the waves, "Be still," and the sea became completely calm.

The misery of the wind and rain that day in Capernaum not only showed me the truth of this incident; it showed me another truth as well. I've been like the disciples, sometimes calling out in troubled times, "Lord, do you not care that I am perishing?" But now that I've seen the kind of physical storm that Jesus calmed on the Sea of Galilee, I will trust him to calm the storms in my life.

APRIL 14   A GIFT FROM GOD

You made all the delicate, inner parts of my body, and knit them together in my mother's womb. Thank you for making me so wonderfully complex! It is amazing to think about. Your workmanship is marvelous. —Psalm 139:13, 14 TLB

During their early years of marriage, a child was out of the question. There were master's degrees to pursue, employment to seek, a home to buy.

After eight years, the time had come. But—nothing. Month after month, disappointment and frustration grew. They made doctor appointments, took medications, kept meticulous charts. Grandparents prayed, but still nothing.

Eventually the couple were referred to one of the country's leading infertility clinics. Specialists decided upon a procedure with a fancy name—gamete intrafallopian transfer (GIFT)—and within an amazingly short time, tests were positive. What elation! But there were complications, and she spent a week in the hospital.

Finally—in April—she let herself believe she was pregnant, as the child began to grow. The following thirty-two weeks were uneventful, except for the joy and fun of preparation—equipping and decorating a nursery, buying baby clothes, deciding on a name.

Then the child decided to put in an early appearance. Weighing over six pounds, he wasn't a "preemie"; however, he greeted the world in a breech position, resulting in a hairline fracture and a dislocated hip. (Both eventually healed.) But what a beautiful child! How do I know? He is my grandson!

In this season of new birth, I'm thankful for children, grandchildren, and all precious new life around us!

APRIL 15   **RENDER UNTO CAESAR**

April 15! Does the date make you cringe? I know the feeling. The post office makes every effort to see that our tax returns are postmarked by midnight, but the deadline can still give us a few more gray hairs.

During the first years of my marriage, taxes were due a month earlier. (April 15 became the deadline in 1955.) How we dreaded March 15! Sometimes a headline would read, "Beware the Ides of March." That was the warning given to Julius Caesar. On the old Roman calendar, the "ides" fell near the middle of a month, and Caesar was assassinated on March 15.

Have you noticed that in recent years, groups have sprung up advocating nonpayment of taxes, claiming we owe the government nothing?

Jesus would have disagreed. Each of the Synoptic Gospels records Jesus' reply when the Pharisees question paying taxes. He told them, "Give . . . to the emperor the things that are the emperor's, and to God the things that are God's" (Matthew 22:21 NRSV; see also Mark 12:17; and Luke 20:25).

We may feel taxes are unfair and begrudge every dollar we send to Uncle Sam or our states. Nevertheless, we pay "Caesar," knowing we'll receive services in return.

What about God? God doesn't threaten to fine or jail us for nonpayment, nor does God set a yearly deadline. In fact, God loves a cheerful giver, and in return promises to provide us with "every blessing in abundance" (2 Corinthians 9:8 NRSV).

That sounds like a pretty good trade-off.

102

Whenever I go to the mall, I'm armed with a shopping list. I'm not a browser, and usually I head directly to the store and department where I can find the specific things I'm looking for. I don't always find them. One item may be back-ordered and another item may be somehow different from the advertisement—or I may not recognize the new packaging. Occasionally I have needed something for a special occasion and have reluctantly settled for second best, only to discover that the substitute worked better than my original choice.

I also have a heavenly shopping list, to remind God that I have read the "advertisements" in his Word.

1. Salvation for my children

"He is patient . . . not wanting anyone to perish, but everyone to come to repentance" (2 Peter 3:9 NIV).

2. Healing of my aches and pains

"He welcomed them . . . and healed those who needed healing" (Luke 9:11 NIV).

3. Financial provision during the retirement years

"And my God will fully satisfy every need of yours according to his riches in glory in Christ Jesus" (Philippians 4:19 NRSV).

4. Energy to continue teaching

"There is nothing I cannot master with the help of the One who gives me strength" (Philippians 4:13 JB).

5. Protection while traveling

"The LORD will protect you from all danger; he/will keep you safe./He will protect you as you come and go/now and forever" (Psalm 121:7-8 GNB).

I may not always recognize God's answer if the packaging is different from what I expect. God may send a substitute answer, but because God is the Manufacturer, it will surely be better than the original.

My heavenly shopping list also may have items that must be back-ordered. God knows every circumstance surrounding my life, and God knows that my faith will grow as I wait for the answer.

Of one thing I can be certain: Unlike the items on my mall shopping list, God's "heavenly storehouse" will never be "out of stock" or "discontinued."

APRIL 17   BUCKLE UP

I stopped by a neighbor's house after running errands. As I got into the car to leave, I automatically reached for my seat belt. Then I thought, *I'm only two blocks from home. Why bother?*

But within that short distance, I experienced discomfort. I felt vulnerable and "loose"—the same way I feel when I attend a special event with my tummy pooching out, or when I let go of someone's arm while trying to cross a wobbly bridge.

As I pulled into my driveway, I recalled an incident during those "pre-seat-belt days" when my children were small. We were returning from a nearby city where we'd picked up my mother-in-law, who planned to spend some time with us. I was driving, she was beside me on the passenger's side, and my husband and children were in the back. One of the boys wanted to join us in the front seat. Taking my eyes off the road momentarily, I cautioned, "Don't kick Grandma."

In that split second, the car hit gravel along the shoulder. My body and the car weaved back and forth as I fought to regain control. Kyle kept shouting from the backseat, "Don't fight the wheel!" I loosened my grip and finally pulled to a stop. Fortunately, there were no cars in the opposite lane. One rear hubcap landed in an irrigation ditch, another in a field a few hundred yards away. None of us were seriously hurt, but both my wrists turned black with bruises from my desperate attempt to straighten the vehicle.

The Bible speaks of a belt of truth: "Stand firm then, with the belt of truth buckled around your waist" (Ephesians 6:14 NIV). When we wear this belt on life's highway, we no longer feel vulnerable or out of control spiritually. God has a firm grip on us, so we don't need to "fight the wheel." God

104

holds us back from danger. Just as a seat belt is useless if not used, so also we must "buckle up" by studying God's Word, if we would know the truth.

APRIL 18   TASTE GOD'S WORD

I was en route, reluctantly, to a small community about sixty miles away. I'd been invited to a wedding shower for my future daughter-in-law.

I'd only met her once when my stepson stopped by unexpectedly to introduce us. Since he rarely kept in touch, we were surprised to see him at our doorstep with a young lady. They were on their way to her hometown, where her family would meet him for the first time. *What is she really like?* we wondered. *Is she really the right girl for him?*

Now I was driving on this lovely spring day to attend the shower. I tried to think of Bible verses about peace, love, and joy. They flitted through my mind like swallows diving in and out of their holes in a cliff wall.

I pulled off the highway and prayed. My Bible lay beside me, and I opened it, hoping to find a word of advice. My eyes fell upon Jeremiah 15:16:

> Your words were found, and I ate them,
> and your words became to me a joy
> and the delight of my heart. (NRSV)

I began to sing the verse to a made-up tune. And I remembered what a friend had told me the day before: "Shirley, you must show this young woman love. She has had nothing to do with your son's past relationships. You will soon become her mother-in-law, so be the best mother-in-law possible."

I went to the shower, and with every bite of tea sandwiches, cookies, and mints, I hummed the tune to my newfound verse. I visualized myself eating the scripture's words, allowing them to become a joy and the delight of my heart, creating love in my heart for my new daughter.

That young woman has been the perfect mate for my stepson for twenty-five years now. And I have found that "tasting" God's Word makes a spiritually nutritious snack!

APRIL 19   THE SMILE OF GOD

I've always loved daisies. As a child, I lived near a field full of black-eyed Susans. We loved to pick them and make chains from the blossoms. I didn't know that the farmer who owned the field looked upon those daisies as an obnoxious weed. White daisies were used for my eighth-grade graduation exercises. And even into my teens, my friends and I emulated the heroine in the opera *Faust* by plucking daisy petals, saying, "He loves me, he loves me not."

The daisy, one of the oldest and best known of English blossoms, is April's other flower. It bears the Anglo-Saxon name "the day's eye" because of its appearance and the fact that the petals close at night.

Besides wild varieties such as the black-eyed Susan, there are cultivated varieties, ranging from the common white daisy to the Shasta daisy, a hybrid developed by Luther Burbank.

The English daisy arrived in America many years ago. One account suggests it came over as a "stowaway" in the horses' hay with General Burgoyne's army at the end of the eighteenth century. In fact, the daisy has "escaped" from its original place of growth so often that it has been said that it must have been one of the first flowers to stray outside the Garden of Eden.

The poet James Montgomery called the daisy "the smile of God," and wrote,

> The rose has but a summer reign,
> The daisy never dies.

I like to think that when we accept the "smile of God" in Christ, we, like the daisy, will never really die. Of course, you and I don't have to play the "petal" game with God, because we know that God loves us at all times!

106

Elation, joy, and pride! These high emotions can plummet so quickly to deflation, hurt feelings, and sadness.

I was scheduled to teach a couple of classes at a writers workshop, the first ever to be held on the campus of our community college. Almost seventy people attended. I was fully confident about one class, having taught it at previous conferences. The second offering was a "first," and I was unsure of myself.

A week later, the college newspaper featured a lead article about the workshop. It read in part: "A local legend, Shirley Pope Waite, delighted a large audience with her presentation. . . ." Me—a local legend? I swelled with pride!

A few days later, I received a compilation of evaluation comments from the conferees. I couldn't believe what one person wrote: "S. Waite: Rambly, unorganized; . . . disappointing." *That said of a "local legend?"* I thought.

For several days I went around with a sinking feeling in the pit of my stomach, berating myself—*what business do I have teaching others about writing?*

But the more I thought about it, the calmer I got. I knew that individual students react differently to the same teacher, so not all students had the same opinion. At the same time, there might be some truth in that evaluation. Could I learn something from the negative comments? Well, for one thing, I would try to reorganize my notes for that one class.

Not even a "local legend" is a finished product beyond improvement. The apostle Paul was right. I'm one of those "works in progress" he talks about in Philippians 1:6: "He who began a good work in you will carry it on to completion until the day of Christ Jesus" (NIV). Because God has begun his good work in me, I know he will carry it to completion.

APRIL 21   DAUGHTERS OF THE KING

I feel a special kinship with Queen Elizabeth II. Perhaps it's because her birthday today is so close to mine, or that we are just a year apart in age. Maybe it's because we both had three sons and a daughter.

When I was growing up, my English grandparents subscribed to a London newspaper and kept me well informed about the two princesses, Elizabeth and Margaret. I wrote imaginary letters to Elizabeth and played "princess dress-up."

I especially remember a story I read or was told—whether true or not, I'm not sure—about the two princesses. When they were children and playing on the grounds of Buckingham Palace, they wandered away from their governess. A short time later, a newly employed guard saw them and gruffly wanted to know what they were doing there.

"We want to see the king!" Elizabeth told him.

The guard replied, "Why, that's impossible! Nobody can see the king, miss. He is a busy man. He doesn't have time to talk with little girls."

Elizabeth is said to have pulled herself up to her full height and replied, "He's not too busy to see us. We are the daughters of the king."

We too are daughters of a King—the "King of kings and Lord of lords, who alone is immortal" (1 Timothy 6:15-16 NIV). He is never too busy to grant us an audience.

APRIL 22   LAUGH YOUR WAY TO HEALTH

A popular children's book tells of a boy who had a terrible, horrible, no good, very bad day. During a children's sermon in our church, the boys and girls were asked if they'd ever had that kind of day. They nodded their heads in agreement.

Then the storyteller explained in simple language how endorphins—natural hormonelike substances with painkilling properties that are secreted by the brain—magnify feelings in ninety seconds. "So, when you're going through a bad time," she said, "just say, 'Endorphins, you can't make me have a bad day! I'm going to laugh so I can rejoice in the Lord!' "

108

That's good advice for all of us. Laughter is healing and healthful, a fact recognized by the medical profession. Some hospitals actually maintain a "humor lab," a room that's cheerful, brightly lit, devoid of medical equipment, and stocked with classic radio tapes such as Abbott and Costello and Amos 'n' Andy. Humorous videotapes such as Laurel and Hardy, W. C. Fields, Charlie Chaplin, "Candid Camera," and Bob Hope specials are also available, as well as joke and cartoon books.

On a more everyday level, I've been trying to take a daily ten-minute "humor break." From a humorous "first-aid" kit I've created—stocked with cartoons, jokes, funny greeting cards, and even comedy tapes—I pick something to make me laugh. Another suggestion I follow whenever I can is to play with a child and rediscover a sense of delight. In other words, dare to be silly! The humor break is a sure way to get rid of the terrible, horrible, no good, very bad days.

Remember, "A merry heart doeth good like a medicine" (Proverbs 17:22 KJV).

APRIL 23   SHAKESPEARE'S APRIL

Shakespeare's writings mention April and May more than any other months. He must have loved spring. Perhaps too April brought him special pleasure, as his birthday is thought to have been April 23. That's the day before mine. Since I'd always wanted to be a writer, I was impressed that I had been born under the same zodiacal sign as the great author.

Before I became a Christian, the zodiac fascinated me. Like many people, I was inclined to put my faith in the stars—God's creation—rather than the Creator. Today I no longer read my horoscope. Instead I turn to God's Word for daily direction.

I am thrilled to know I have been created to glorify and praise God. I read in the Old Testament, "All who claim me as their God will come, for I have made them for my glory;

I created them" (Isaiah 43:7 TLB). The New Testament states the same thought: "God's purpose . . . was that we should praise God and give glory to him" (Ephesians 1:12 TLB). Revelation also tells me that all things were created for God's pleasure (4:11 KJV).

Shakespeare wrote of the "uncertain glory of an April day," a fact about April most of us have experienced—balmy breezes that turn into windstorms, a gentle rain that becomes an unpredictable downpour, and the first blossoms of spring that bravely stand up against an occasional frost.

Come to think of it, however, these things have a *certain* glory, because they were fashioned for our pleasure by our Creator. But even more awesome is knowing that God created *me* for *his* pleasure! Wow!

APRIL 24   MORE SO

Today is my birthday. I can hardly believe I'm among the group society calls the elderly. But as an eighty-five-year-old friend says, "I still feel forty inside."

Someone once said, "You don't grow old—you grow more so." Hmm! What kind of person was I at forty? Fifty? Pleasant to be around? Set in my ways?

We now have a thirty-six-year-old pastor. He's the same age as my youngest son. Sometimes I close my eyes to listen to his strong voice and dynamic message. Upon opening my eyes, I am jolted back to reality, and I say to myself, "What's that kid doing up there?"

With Pastor David's arrival came changes—in worship, in music, in sermons. Some of the elderly members complained. That's when I began to feel forty again, even thirty. It's been a joy to see younger families attending. I clap my hands enthusiastically with the music during the "Rejoicing in Praise" times. When the "Young Disciples' Time" is announced, boys and girls seem to come out of the woodwork. I've even become one of the volunteers to lead this special time for children. Yes, I like the changes.

Instead of growing old, I want to grow more tolerant, more loving, and more understanding, so that "even in old age [I] will still produce fruit and be vital and green" (Psalm 92:14 TLB).

APRIL 25   ARBOR DAY

We have a humongous maple tree in our backyard. The man who sprays it each spring says it is one of the largest in town. As my gaze takes in its 157-foot height, I silently thank the people who first planted it as a seedling and nursed it through its early growth.

Perhaps you were involved in an Arbor Day tree planting ceremony when you were a child. If you've moved away from that area, do you ever wonder how "your" tree fared?

In April 1872, J. Sterling Morton, a Nebraska newspaper publisher, wanted to awaken people to the importance of trees. He pointed out the vital part trees play in nature's scheme—conserving soil and moisture, producing oxygen, providing shelter for wildlife and products for people. Thus was born the first Arbor Day.

A committee for National Arbor Day has been trying to revive interest in this special event. It recommends that Arbor Day be observed on the last Friday in April, a good planting date for many states. The committee would like all citizens to learn the importance of trees for our very existence. At this writing, more than half the states now observe Arbor Day on the proposed date. Perhaps you can promote tree planting in your community.

I, for one, am grateful to the unnamed folks who planted our tree. Squirrels use the branches as a playground, while birds find it a perfect rest stop. Oh yes, my husband complains (just a little!) in the fall as our yard is buried in leaves, but I remind him of the refreshing shade we enjoy all summer. As with *The Giving Tree* in Shel Silverstein's story, our maple tree offers many more benefits than burdens. And I remember with Joyce Kilmer that "only God can make a tree."

111

Whenever I buy my daughter or a friend jewelry accented by their birthstones, I tend to feel a little cheated as I enjoy the colors of their stones. My transparent birthstone doesn't seem all that special—I've worn it now for almost fifty years, from the time my husband first placed it on my finger—even though it's a diamond.

To better appreciate my birthstone/wedding ring, I read about diamonds. The best known of all precious gems, a diamond is a piece of carbon formed millions of years ago. In order to have a stone that can be cut and polished into a gem, miners need to blast, dig, crush, wash, and sort over 250 tons of ore.

The average person hears much about a diamond's weight, measured in carats, but I learned there are three equally important "Cs," each of which has a spiritual counterpart in my life.

Color—the ability to break light into all colors of the rainbow. "You are the light of the world," Jesus tells me, so "let your light shine" (Matthew 5:14, 16 NRSV).

Clarity—the presence or absence of flaws. "Keep yourself pure" (1 Timothy 5:22 NRSV).

Cut—a correct pattern of faceting to reveal the greatest beauty. "Be beautiful inside, in your hearts, with the lasting charm of a gentle and quiet spirit which is so precious to God" (1 Peter 3:4 TLB).

Like the diamond, I am merely "a piece of carbon." When God wants to fashion me into a precious gem, he needs to blast away misconceptions, dig deeply into my conscience, crush evil forces, sort through "tons" of sin, and wash me in his blood.

An unknown source said, "A diamond is the most precious of gems . . . costliest of jewels . . . associated with life's happier moments."

As a Christian I can say, "Jesus Christ is the most precious One . . . offering me the costliest gift of salvation . . . desiring to give me my happiest moments."

One of those happiest moments was when I said, "I do." So when I see advertisements for birthstones, I am reminded that mine is a pledge to my husband for life. And I am proud to wear this transparent stone that brilliantly refracts the light.

APRIL 27   WHAT HATH GOD WROUGHT

We may live in the computer age, with its instant communication, but for decades messages were sent via Morse code. Shortwave radio buffs still use Morse code extensively.

The code was named for Samuel F. B. Morse, who patented the telegraph in 1840. Few, however, are aware of his many failures.

Morse was born April 27, 1791, the son of a minister. After moderate success as an artist (his portrait of Marquis de Lafayette hangs in New York City Hall), he was denied a commission to do a painting for the Capitol.

Living in an attic room, he turned to his newest interest, the telegraph. After five years of work, a demonstration intended to bring financial backing was a failure. Many found the device amusing, but they would not invest.

After building a sturdier model, Morse tried to interest Congress. No luck. He made overseas contacts with no results. Years of further disappointment followed. He then readied an underwater demonstration, touted by New York papers, but a ship's anchor caught the wire. Folks claimed the invention was a hoax.

Morse must have remembered Thomas Palmer's quatrain:

'Tis a lesson you should heed,
Try, try again;
If at first you don't succeed,
Try, try again.

Morse made one last attempt to pique the interest of members of Congress. Finally they passed a bill appropriating money to test the telegraph.

113

Then came the big day! Morse tapped out a message via a telegraph line from the Capitol to Baltimore, words from Numbers 23:23: "What hath God wrought!" (KJV).

Even after years of failure, hardship, and disappointment, Samuel Morse gave God credit for the results.

In the face of defeat, adversity, and pain, may I have faith and courage to tap out the same message to the world: "See what God has done."

APRIL 28   YOU ARE THE SALT OF THE EARTH

Several hundred years before Christ, Job lamented, "What is food without salt?" (Job 6:6 CEV). Even though I have no sense of smell or taste, I can sympathize with that question, because I can still identify saltiness, which adds some enjoyment to eating.

Salt has had a bad rap in recent years. For some, it must be used in moderation. Yet when Jesus told his followers to be the salt of the earth (Matthew 5:13), they knew exactly what he meant.

Salt was the chief economic product of the ancient world, created for the most part by evaporating seawater. It was so precious that Caesar's soldiers received part of their pay in salt—known as *salarium,* hence our word *salary.*

Newborns were rubbed with salt to ensure good health (Ezekiel 16:4). This practice was found among Palestinians as late as 1918. Salt often was used as an antiseptic, even as a treatment for toothache. One of its major uses was to preserve food, as well as to flavor it. Salt also was sprinkled in oil to make lamps shine brighter. The use of salt in sacrificial offerings symbolized cleansing and purity. God called his covenant with the Israelites one of salt (Numbers 18:19).

As a Christian—the salt of the earth—I need to add brightness to life, work toward "cleansing" our society and preserving it from decay, and add flavor to life's routine.

As salt, I should cause others to thirst for God. I hope and pray that my actions and speech will always be gracious, seasoned with salt (Colossians 4:6).

APRIL 29   HIDING PLACE

When my grandson was two years old, he never tired of the "blanket game." He would cover his head and as much of his little body as he could with his blanket, and then call out, "Find me, Grandma!"

"Where's Tony? Is he behind the davenport?" I would ask. Giggles beneath the blanket.

"Where is that boy? Is he under the rocking chair?" Giggles, accompanied by wiggles.

After searching for Tony in such unlikely places as the bookcase, under a pillow, even in a vase of flowers, I would sneak up and suddenly pull the blanket off the hiding child.

"There's Tony!" Lots of giggles, followed by, "Let's play that again, Grandma!"

I once heard a speaker relate a similar anecdote. He, his wife, and young daughter went to visit Grandma in her apartment. After they knocked on the door, three-year-old Mary put her hands over her face.

Grandma asked, "Didn't Mary come with you?" After walking around the family and peering down the hallway, she added, "Oh, I'm so disappointed."

Then Mary withdrew her hands, saying, "Here I am, Grandma!" Of course, you know Grandma's response.

The speaker pointed out how we, as adults, do the same thing with God. We think we're hiding from God, failing to realize that he is present to us and that we are in his presence every moment of our lives.

Hide from God? Impossible! Even under our "blankets" of insecurity, fear, and worry, God is with us.

> You are my hiding place;
>   you will protect me from trouble
>   and surround me with songs of deliverance.
>   —Psalm 32:7 NIV

115

Deadlines! Most people dread them; others thrive on them. I fall somewhere in the middle, but I admit that a deadline motivates me as nothing else can.

Take writing, for example. I can receive an assignment six or eight months ahead of a deadline, but the final few weeks find me in a state of panic as the closing date looms on the horizon. Why the procrastination? Why submit myself to that kind of pressure? Too often I leave God out of the picture, forgetting to approach an assignment in prayer, asking God for help.

Earlier (April 11), I mentioned a verse I had posted next to my computer screen. I need only look at the bottom of the screen to read another verse. This one is David's advice to his son Solomon, regarding the completion of the temple: "Be strong and courageous and get to work. Don't be frightened by the size of the task, for the Lord my God is with you. . . . He will see to it that everything is finished correctly" (1 Chronicles 28:20 TLB).

That's pretty good advice, whether it's for writing something, planning a family vacation, or finishing a project at home or work. Rather than procrastinate, I seek God's help and "get to work"!

May
The Re-Creating Season

Margaret Anne Huffman

Read Song of Solomon 2:10-13.

Mother Nature is throwing her spring fling this month, and I've no idea what to wear—even less what to take for a hostess gift.

Winter dimmed my creativity with too many snowbound days, and spring on my wooded riverbank has been cold. April played the fool much too long, dropping trees in stormy tantrums and flooding basements. Body and soul, I'm ready for spring. Warmth, gardens, migrations, holidays.

Come with me as we see what this month has to offer. Just as today children are collecting items for May baskets, we'll gather, sort, and create. By month's end, we'll have found something special. Believing in a God of surprises, we will check in unexpected places and, from time to time, stop, be quiet, and simply know that God *is*.

Join hands with me and one another, as children around a maypole, as we celebrate with Solomon: "Winter is past" (Song of Solomon 2:11 NRSV).

Creator God, we marvel as you unfold your hand and reveal birds' nests, budding plants, first buzzing insects. We are grateful for spring, a sure sign of your re-creation. We know you are continually making all things new, even us. Guide us this month into making wise choices about what to find, what to keep, and what to fashion into something else. We will follow your example: creating, re-creating, honoring. Bless our efforts.

MAY 2   MOVE FURNITURE

Read Philippians 3:13-14.

Orphan Annie Cat is annoyed with me. I moved "her" chair from beside the fireplace to the window. As she was adjusting, I moved it again, trading its place with the couch. "Isn't that better?" I said to her as she spring-cleaned her white bib and paws in the new spot.

Spring-cleaning—or rather, spring-rearranging—is good for the soul.

It is my belief that furniture should be moved each faith season—Lent, Advent—and every other time we need to get ready for change. We need symbol and ritual to help us move on, move over, move along. We yearn to be replenished, to discover something new that can nourish, transform, uplift. We need winter's dust blown off our souls, and it's hard to do that while sitting in the same old place, expecting the same old things, doing it the same old ways.

Try it . . . move a chair, table, couch. Tomorrow, plan to go outdoors and say your prayers over a breakfast picnic— even if you have to wear a coat and get up a few minutes early. Start a journal, jotting down what you saw, heard, smelled, felt. At work—whether at home or an outside job— rearrange something, even if it's where you park.

A little huffing and puffing gets us in the mood to invite God's re-creating spring spirit. After all, "The more you do what you've always done. The more you'll get what you've always gotten," sings the Wiz in the musical by the same name. We don't want to stay in a wintry rut.

Keep us moving—open and expectant—God of surprises. We are ready for you to enter lives we've opened as wide as our windows.

MAY 3   COLOR ME BLUE

Read 1 Timothy 4:4.

Having pledged to seek change, I'm bumping into my deeply entrenched resistance to it! Take crayons. I find it difficult to color in the lines of life now that plain old blue and yellow are gone. It's out with the old, in with the new for crayon makers, who create dandelion, fuchsia, cerulean, and multiskin tones. To make room, they axed eight "ho-hum" crayons from the waxy rainbow. Color *me* blue, blue, blue.

When I bought the new crayons for the grandkids, the smell was all I recognized. Do kids, I worried, want to live in *fluorescently strawberry* worlds? Climb *jungle green* trees? Before I could launch into full-blown dismay, I spied the grandson's neon pink backpack. "Isn't it great?" he asked—his enthusiasm for school as bright as the pack. I was jolted from my dingy view by his eager acceptance of a world where trees saved by recycling *should* be colored a joyous green, and smiles to greet a new century beg to be drawn in wildly exuberant strawberry grins.

It is painful to do away with familiar props. Crayon smell is one of the aromas most readily recognized alongside coffee and peanut butter. Mess with my memory anchors, and I feel misplaced. Yet in this new array of colors, something *is* missing that I celebrate: prejudice. Prejudice against folks whose skins aren't peachy. In the hands of today's children, folks can at last be colored the tint they are—a picture of hope.

We are grateful, God, that you paint with love's paintbrush. Drawings on my refrigerator are about a rainbow assortment of people, holding hands beneath a cerulean sky and sharing vibrant possibilities for ecology, inclusion, peace, and sharing. Color me hopeful.

MAY 4   A SUNDAE ON MONDAY

*Read Psalm 101:2; Deuteronomy 30:19*b.

If we are what we eat, then I am a triple-fudge ice-cream cone with an order of fries on the side and pizza arriving any minute. And if our fantasies confess the real us, hear mine: When dream guys knock at my door, they woo me not with flowers and jewels but with peanut butter pie. They take me not to a tryst but to a fine restaurant. I swoon and devour it all.

Yet tucked inside this me is a fit, healthy, trim person. Tucked inside is the me I yearn to be—a me who yearns to be gorgeous. Okay, not gorgeous, but as cute and vigorous as I can be—a hiking, climbing, horseback riding, laughing, dancing, swimming, middle-aged child of God.

After repeated conversations with God about this new me, I believe with Jeremiah that God says to me "I have [plans] for you . . . for welfare and not for calamity to give you a future and a hope" (29:11 NASB). In that promise, nowadays Mother Huffman's cupboard is, if not exactly bare, different. Brown rice, spinach noodles, nine-grain breads, no-frills popcorn. Fruits, veggies, low-anything dressings, and no-nonsense yogurt grin from the fridge.

I've sworn off diets, replacing their *"can'ts"* with all that I *can* have: more time, bendable knees, a bathing suit, play. I've hit a brisk stride as I eat my way to a new me: a moving out, tossed-salad type of a person.

What new person lives in you, longing for release?

Are there graces for lettuce, Lord? And low-fat, no-fat, meat-free, fun-free meals? Send me words for blessing this paltry meal; help me find joy in making these healthy

120

choices. Hold up for me a mirror of the new creation you see
me to be, for I need a companion at this table.

MAY 5   EARLY MOTHER'S DAY

Read Psalm 33:20.

Mop in hand, I asked myself: *Am I catching up or getting
ahead?* A birthday, a graduation, and Mother's Day next
week meant I was doing both that year.

At last, the final task: spreading a new cloth on the dining
table. For years, I'd fought a losing battle about its clutter of
coats, mail, dolls, jars of fireflies, dirty gym clothes, bird
eggs, snake skins, books, and lunch boxes. It stood between
front door and refrigerator—flight pattern of the family—
until they grew up and away. Now it stays decorator-perfect,
bare and stylish. I gave it a final tweak and headed to bed.

Four hours later the phone stopped more than self-
congratulations; it stopped my heart. Bike accident, plastic
surgery, hospital.

Our environmentalist graduate-student son, who biked
instead of driving, had hit a parked car obscured by fog. A
fine seamstress of a surgeon quilted him together while we
paced the waiting room.

Waiting.

Can there be anything more symbolic of women? How did
Mary stand the waiting—for a son's birth, for him to leave the
temple, to persuade his detractors, to see if he would be
defeated by a cross? Waiting, waiting.

She was waiting with me for my son to come through the
surgery doors on his own two feet with a patchwork face too
beautiful to behold. Waiting to see if he wanted to come
"home" home. Waiting, there, to see if soup could quiet
tremors in his shaky body. Waiting to hear his humor,
unbruised, concoct a tale about his swashbuckling scar.
Waiting to see if he feels up to studying for finals. Waiting to
see where he dumps his books.

A homing instinct guided him to the dining table. Can there be a more wonderful early Mother's Day gift than a nosegay of clutter on the dining table? I think not.

I stand before my messy table and bow humbly in grati-tude for its beauty. This was a near miss, O God, and I felt your presence as we waited to find out how near. I was reminded of the day I crossed a railroad track, only to look in my rearview mirror and see a train framed there. I felt you then; I felt you today. It's the near misses that do me in. Almost as scary as the accident, Lord, is the danger I was in of preferring bare tables and neatly pressed lives. I couldn't have borne the tidiness.

MAY 6   TUG OF WAR

Read 1 Peter 4:10; Psalm 144:12.

I scramble to keep up with the puzzle of being "A woman for today." I flounder in a unisex world between old and new role expectations, and I sometimes envy the certainty of those who are convinced theirs is the only right way.

We long for "the good old days"—which weren't good for many except Hollywood—even as we strain for the future. On the heels of the first women who said, "Why?" came others who said, "Why not?" Now here we come, saying, "What now?" To my amazement, as we answer, a tug-of-war is polarizing us.

Instead of battling, doesn't it make more sense for us women to retrieve our natural traits: nurturing, arbitrating, relating, comforting, teaching, creating? We can love *and* use the other traits: the fighting, foraging, defending, dis-covering, building, and designing traits that settled frontiers, navigated migrations, advised kings in battle; that invented Liquid Paper, disposable diapers, drip coffee, chocolate chip cookies, penicillin, rabies and meningitis serums and vac-cines, voice-controlled wheelchairs, computer language, refrigeration, space helmets, cotton gins, and Apgar scores; that discovered radioactivity, nuclear fission, DNA molecules, and X and Y chromosomes.

Invention-making, homemaking, baby-making, corporate-merger-making, peacemaking. We women have always excelled at "doing" verbs.

Support those, O God, who bear the weight of social change needed to jolt us from smugness into equality and acceptance. Inspire us to bring positive change for women who are victims of economy, brutality, and discrimination. Keep us uneasy in our own hard-won successes as long as there are any who have no choices. Bless our diversity; may it flourish.

MAY 7   GIFT OF SILENCE

Read Isaiah 41:6; 1 John 3:16-18.

"Hello," I said sleepily into the phone. Due to a time change, my friend was up earlier than I. Or perhaps she'd never slept. Her husband, she cried, is leaving. Younger woman, fewer responsibilities. You can write the script yourself. Suddenly she is the woman left behind—butt of jokes, subject of conjecture, and target of her own finger-pointing blame.

What are we to do when one of our sisters is shamed and hurt?

Male bashing is out; advice giving, ditto.

We can sit and listen, send cards, call, invite her for visits, *go* visit. We can be a mirror that holds up to her an image of one who deserves better than being a "discard," a loser, a victim. We can be companions for her grief at the death of innocence, trust, dreams, and assumptions. Knowing safety lies in simple gestures, I will send this friend a cactus for her windowsill, reminding her that some things bloom even in arid and seemingly barren spots, and that she too can bloom again, and that, yes, it is okay to feel prickly.

My phone bills will mount; my headaches will increase. Yet I am glad and humbled to be part of my friend's support. May God place a loving hand over my mouth, lest I say too much.

Dear God, give us hands to extend, arms to hug, ears to hear, eyes to spot trouble, and, most of all, mouths that stay closed! Shattered friends need our presence, not our commentary.

MAY 8   BREAST-DISCOVERY

Read Psalm 22:11; Jeremiah 15:18-20.

I jump, startled—a bluebird hit my window. Dazed, it teeters on a branch. I know the feeling: A routine mammogram today revealed a mass so deep in breast tissue that it can't be felt and so large that it must be trouble.

O God, why? Why me, why now, why this?

Lumps, illnesses, relationship shifts, accidents—whatever—leave us suddenly vulnerable and, like the bluebird, out on precarious branches that can break at any moment.

We hadn't planned on this, but we will take what the month brings. Come with me to see how the bluebird fares.

Today's journal entry: "Like plucking petals from a daisy, I consider God's role in this: *loves me, loves me not.* Is it true that if God loved me, this wouldn't have happened? Nope. For if I believe God loves me only if life is okay, I cheat myself of an *always* God—*always* there, *always* loving, *always* dependable. No, this is not God's will; God is weeping too."

As I watch the bluebird valiantly try to keep flying, I decide that tragedy—this or any other—will not define me. Nor will a new doubt: Is God testing me? Nope again. God is a resource to help me deal with calamity, not the sender of it. What a silly idea, I tell my husband; for if God causes trouble, how can we ask the same God to deliver us from it?

In my fear, however, I will struggle to be honest and "not restrain my mouth" (Job 7:11 RSV), for I know God is sturdy and can handle—even welcomes—me as I pray to be kept as the apple of God's eye (Psalm 17:8 NIV).

Great Physician, forgive our easy blame of you.

MAY 9   STILL WATERS

Read Isaiah 30:15; Psalm 46:1-11.

Lightning, flash floods, downed trees and power lines. Three flickers and you're out. Spring storms leave me in the dark in more ways than one. My computer is useless; my restless spirit—even more restless with this added worry— equally so. Forced to curtail my mad dash deadline to deadline, I've spotted what it is that I'd lost long before today: peace.

I can't relax, can't focus, can't calm my wandering mind. Life is one endless list of *have to, ought,* and *should.* The tail is wagging the dog. There is no stillness in me to know God or anything else. I can't sit still.

Stillness is suspect. We fill time with activities, guaranteeing we won't have idle—wasted—moments. We worship at the feet of laborsaving devices to gain more time to fill with grim determination. I can't seem to learn this, though I've tried, adding "learn to relax" to my list of *have tos.*

Our dog, Nutmeg, loathes storms and begged me to sit with her today. I gathered her onto my lap and sat watching the storm from the porch. Gradually the rain stopped, but still I sat. The dog left. I sat. Electricity came back on. I sat. And sat some more. Like a dove after a storm, a solution to my restlessness had appeared: simply sitting.

Harder than it sounds, I plan to sit regularly on a log overhanging the river. If not there, on fences, steps, porches, swings, and rockers. Mostly I will sit by myself, although Nutmeg and the cats will likely tag along. Sitting places are excellent places for collecting thoughts, not to mention fragmented lives.

Bless me, Lord, with your gifts of silence and stillness. I talk and do too much.

MAY 10   A LITANY FOR MOTHERS

Read Proverbs 1:8; 31:28.

They come in all shapes and sizes, colors, temperaments, and styles. They shaped us before we were born, as they still do today—even if they're no longer around. They are Mother, Mom, Ma, Mommy. They are ours. And sometimes all we can do is kneel beside their love.

O God, hear us as:
We pray for mothers
    who bake chocolate chip cookies,
    who hum while they iron,
    who help find lost keys, mittens, and schoolbooks.
And we pray for those
    who steal crumbs and crusts,
    who cry while dividing them among the kids,
    who need no keys: cardboard houses don't lock.
We pray for mothers
    who lovingly tend and teach offspring,
    who create satisfying careers at the same time,
    who balance career/family/self choices with energy
        left over.
And we pray for mothers
    who work two and three jobs and need childcare,
    who would stay home and bake cookies if they could,
    who are tied to choices someone else made.
We pray for mothers
    who did the best they could for us, their daughters,
    who assured us we can be whatever we dream and now

126

who live what we learned at their knees, and,
who, passing it on, celebrate *our* offsprings' successes.
And we pray for mothers
who never clean house: bombs just blow them away,
who don't have to diet, poverty takes care of that,
who nurse dying babies at dried-up breasts,
who dream great dreams for their offspring, but
who measure success by just keeping them alive.
Amen.

MAY 11   SCRAP BASKET

Read Isaiah 43:1-2.

Life was so different before I became a mother. Then, I thought I knew what working full-time was. After kids, I understood that full-time doesn't mean your puny forty-hour weeks; it means perpetual vigilance. Even when they are in bed, at school, or out riding bikes, you are aware. Even when, like my trio—now 250–2,500 miles from home—you are aware.

I think of my mother, grandmother, great-great-greats. Centuries of awareness. I kneel before God's awareness of me, of all of us.

Being aware when the kids were little was tiring. It still is, as I prepare for my oldest child's thirty-third birthday and a family reunion. Each day I gather the kids in thought as I used to gather their small selves in the wicker swing.

Yet despite the enduring richness of those days, I lost awareness of me.

There's much ado about recycling and reclamation today. Can it also apply to people, to us who've lost ourselves? I've been gathering scattered bits of me in photo albums, scrapbooks of my career, folders of dreams, reams of book ideas.

I toss them, like dandelion fluff, into the air. They land, rearranged into a mosaic of quilt pieces. Hues of yesterday and today come together in this counterpane of self; my edges are stitched together with knowledge that I am a beloved child of God, named and known.

Each piece is needed: fancy scraps, worn scraps, and barely used scraps. Scraps stained by tears; scraps stiff from newness. Today's scrap is in the hands of grown-up kids, mates they bring, grandkids, and old and new friends.

The company is here. I hurry to the porch with my unfinished quilt draped over my shoulders—its warm embrace like that of a re-creating God.

God, I am aware of you guiding me as I gather myself. I am your colorful, unique child, and I dance in delight in that awareness.

MAY 12   WHAT TO DO WHILE WAITING

Read Psalm 4:8; Matthew 23:37; Psalm 138.

When in crisis, clean.

As I move between discovery and a planned biopsy, I am a whirlwind of activity: washing windows, playing from dawn to dusk with a visiting granddaughter, cooking, sorting drawers and closets. My "nest" is no longer adequate. It feels flimsy as I fill it to overflowing with doubt, anger, worry, "what if," facts, and figures. A breast lump now. Another time shock will come from something else. How vulnerable we are. How important to live a faith for all seasons. Easy to say, hard to do.

At first I prayed belligerently, *Why me?* Each day, though, the question changed. Today I woke asking, *Why me? What is there for me to do, say, be, learn, hear, share?* It's becoming a stewardship question!

Who will I become, I wonder, as I cling to the edges of my teetering nest in the limbs of a tall, tall tree beneath the wings of a broody hen God. Can I learn to be a more creative steward of my life no matter how many springs I have? Talking to God from this aerie, I learn that *wishing* is not the same as *hoping; courage* is *not* putting on a brave false face; and *faith* is *not* denying feelings. Rather, courage is honest;

128

the truth does set us free (John 8:32); faith is the "nest" where fears and feelings can be redeemed by God into tools of healing; and *hoping* is a verb. Not all the answers I want, but enough to console me. For now.

Stay near, loving Parent, for I feel I am falling from the nest.

MAY 13   SHORTCHANGED

Read Ezekiel 36:26; Ephesians 4:24, 29; Romans 12:1-2.

While cleaning a kitchen cupboard, I tried to lift a box of oatmeal. Didn't budge. It is my "piggy bank," full of coins; it's how I save for vacations. Burglars, I reason, don't look in oatmeal boxes.

One year, however, I felt as if one had. I'd carried a box of jingling promise to the bank to swap for cash to help pay for a long-planned beach vacation. My tally of the change would give us enough. The teller handed me the cash. It was a third less than expected. I'd been shortchanged.

How often we feel, believe, and act as if we've been shortchanged by God. We fret that we don't have enough money, power, time, position, personality, or energy; we suspect God of cheating and shortchanging us by giving others more of what we want. We secretly believe that life primarily takes from us, that there are "shortchangers" everywhere.

What will it take to create in us a new spirit? To be able to understand the difference between a bank teller overlooking two buckets of change, a breast lump, and a mean, cosmic shortchange? One is an error easily corrected; one is random; one is a crippling belief in which I shortchange myself. No robber could do a more thorough job.

With Ezekiel, dear God, we ask for the promise of the new heart and the new spirit, so that we quit looking over our shoulders, blaming others and remaining hostage to the belief that you are picking on us. Nothing could be farther from the truth.

129

Read Ecclesiastes 3:11; Philippians 3:13-14; Romans 8:28.

It's not just eating rhubarb pie that is so special; it is the making of it. My oldest daughter requested it for her birthday today. Rosy stalks in hand, I regretted the work involved and wished I'd bought a premade crust.

We aren't connected to results *or* roots in these *instant* days. I have a house full of antiques and rusty, dusty relics— apple peeler, nutmeg grater, yarn winder, spinning wheel, clothes wringer. All remind me that I need to live a more hands-on life now that I'm the family matriarch, one who's supposed to pass things on. An awesome responsibility! One of my favorite new items is a mug bearing the bold title "Keeper of the Family Tales." Would a woman bearing that title settle for premade crusts?

Sometimes. At other times, her life would be a place to learn by doing, mixing pie crusts with the tools of the old trade: sifter, rolling pin, lemon squeezer. She might drag out the hand-turned ice-cream freezer that made community as it made dessert. She would bridge then and now, as the writer of Proverbs says, "ways of pleasantness" and "paths [of] peace" (3:17 NRSV).

We have a calling to build foundations for future generations, to build paths of peace for those who live by the push of a button, by the zap of a micro-meal, and who buy premade everything—crusts to clothes to houses.

Storytellers, bridge builders, pie makers—a fine, divine calling from a God who entrusts such tasks only to those who are worthy. We are.

Bless our hands, God of past and future, as they remain firmly plunged into the essence of life. Keep us connected to our lives.

Read 1 Peter 3:8-12; Psalm 25:16-21; Romans 12:19.

Sighting down the barrel of a .357 magnum, I squeezed the trigger and blew the "man" away! Bull's-eye! I was writing a story on women and crime, so I'd enrolled in a police gun-safety course. The "man" was my bullet-riddled cardboard target; his mortal wounds earned me marksmanship scores. Having just covered a rape for a news story, I was considering buying a gun.

How could I reconcile being armed with being a peacemaker?

How can we reconcile faithful hospitality—being Samaritans—with reality? Defense with offense? How can we welcome the stranger and turn the other cheek, much less our back, on those who consider us objects, not people, and who often use their plea for "help" as bait for a trap?

Old, young, healthy, or halting, we wear bull's-eyes between our shoulders, caught in the crosshairs of random and domestic violence.

By the time you read this, one woman will have been raped. By the end of this week, one will have been murdered by her spouse. Before we turn away, let us prayerfully consider, *If we, O God, are safe, do we let our sisters tremble alone?* Like mud splattered from a puddle, violence touches us all. So, thank God, do interventions and solutions.

It's not enough to protest; we must aim higher—at minds that see women as possessions, objects. We must provide shelters and education and clothes and jobs for women with courage to leave dangerous couplings. We must provide sanctuary and belief for women with courage to name rapists, stalkers, harassers. We must praise our brothers who do value us; we must teach children how to respect and relate. We must not turn away.

We need a sturdy God for these violent times, Lord. Forgive us our thirst for violence as we entertain ourselves with it; forgive our quest for revenge, which makes us no better than those who hurt us. Bless and touch the victims who live in dread—and remembered nightmare. Assure us that senseless attacks can be redeemed and that healing will come. Guide us as we struggle with being armed peacemakers. Give us vision, courage, safety.

MAY 16   PLAID

Read Jeremiah 31:12-14; Matthew 24:32.

If you don't like Hoosier weather, wait a minute and it will change! So too does life. In the granddaughter's hands, the house has exploded into a wall-to-wall toy chest. Likewise, in God's hands, the yard has exploded into a coverlet of color: bloom and bud; cardinals; raspberry and gold of finches; blue-birds and indigo buntings; iridescent green of hummingbirds.

Toys, flowers, moods, and insights weave my favorite color of plaid, for who could choose one moment over another? At one with a Creator who designed us to adapt and flex, we do so. At a moment's notice, Mary gathered her infant son and climbed upon a donkey to move to safety. The woman at the well moved from stranger to friend.

With muddy knees and stained hands, I'm hurrying to plant my garden in anticipation of next week's surgery; who knows how laid up I'll be. Today, as I root around in life's very essence, I am comforted. I feel God in sunshine that melts like lemon drops on my face and soil that loses its chill in my hands. I see God in bulbs erupting, buds unfolding, and eggs hatching. On my knees in the dirt, I am surrounded by signs of God's care; it is scattered all around me like posies in an ever-changing garden of grace.

You color my days, Creator God, from love's palette.

MAY 17   CAPSIZED-BAPTIZED

Cleaning my way to the back of the closet where the sleep-ing bags are, I sling them over the railing to air them for a camping-canoeing trip in Maine. A camping-canoeing trip is a life-changing experience—especially the rapids on the Allagash Wilderness Waterway.

Our first trip, my husband and I were in the last canoe in the bunch. We finally paddled into the white water—and we were dumped! The moose by the edge of the river didn't even look up!

"Float feet first," our guide called from shore. He was there the second and the third times we were dumped, ready to help us back in. As we rounded the last bend, we heard the rest of the group before we saw them. Family, friends, and guides were cheering and applauding. We'd made it, soggy but valiant.

Capsized, baptized—closer connection than you might think. Both require moving into new waters, following a Guide you can't see, and finding support from those you can see. As I said, a life-changing experience.

Like the Ethiopian who suddenly stopped his chariot to be baptized (see Acts 8:26-40, especially v. 39), we can stop what we're doing—even worrying—leap into refreshing waters, and renew baptismal vows that may be as stale as last week's bagels. In the fine sprinkling of water or a deep-down dunking, we come into the family of God and are never again alone.

It's amazing to be named by a God who is present when we're born and when we die, and who promises that in between "the waters . . . shall not overwhelm you" (Isaiah 43:2 RSV). That's a promise to take into the "rapids" of life, knowing that a Guide is watching over us and that the "family" is cheering us on.

Great Guide and Companion, we hear you over the water's roar.

MAY 18   HUMOR IN STRESS

Read Proverbs 17:22.

133

You just have to laugh at the hospital gowns that scarcely cover bodies, much less terrified minds and questioning souls. Laughing helps "heal us" of whatever reality we face. Humor, as the writer of Proverbs reminds us, is good for the soul and its body. Did he imagine me in this getup while I wait for a high-tech core biopsy?

I had a good teacher: a Hoosier neighbor. While laid up with a rare form of leukemia on the eve of her national comedy debut, Clara Trusty practiced her comedy routine, welcomed grueling chemotherapy, and became informed about her disease. She used doctors and nurses as her audience and the IV pole as her microphone. In the next bed, another woman with a less serious form of the same disease pulled her curtain shut, summoned her family, and wouldn't bear treatments.

Their outcomes aren't as important as the process, for it comes to each of us in big and little ways: We must *choose* how to respond to life.

Faith is a storehouse of options, and our God is the greatest Creator, having given us the resource of humor. It grows from the "funny bone," which lies next to the heart. Prayer, medicine, support, humor—allies in our healing. Therefore, I've rented funny videos and I'm rereading books that uplift and amuse. I'm not taking this lying down in a skimpy gown. Too many jokes are yet to be enjoyed.

Thank you for belly laughs, Lord. They are good for souls and *bodies, pushing hope and oxygen through fear-frozen veins. Help me—help all of us—when disaster strikes, not to tighten up or give up. The punch line of our life is worth listening for.*

MAY 19   LOVE LETTERS

Read Matthew 18:3.

Dust bunnies should be voted national animal of our family and the magpie, that collector of sparkling junk, the

134

national bird. Through the years we have lived knee-deep in dust and stuff. No matter how diligently I tried, I never stayed ahead of either when the kids were young—also a time when there was never space just for me. The kitchen table hardly counted; ditto for the card table in the corner. I held to the dream of my own space like a barnacle clinging to a pier. It was with joy that I finally received my own space, and joy is still with me today as I write this.

A corner of our hillside home is my office, built by a spouse who'd seen my need. It has floor-to-ceiling bookshelves, windows overlooking the Big Blue River, and a family gallery on paisley walls. What fun we had hanging that wallpaper. I beheld my dream-space opened before me like a blank tablet.

And then I saw the scribbles on the wall—worse than shed hair from Annie Cat who curls naughtily in my chair; worse even than muddy paw prints from Nutmeg asleep on my feet.

I am on my knees, grateful that something shushed my angry voice, for my toddler granddaughter had wanted only to leave me a surprise. How proud she was; how lovingly she explained it to me; how humbled I was, for I had been given a love letter. *"I love you, Mammaw"* she said as she "read" it to me.

"The room *had* needed something," I remarked to Annie Cat after the little lady and her family left; it hadn't been quite perfect.

The flaw was its perfect emptiness—just like the rest of the house. Sometimes I would trade one spacious today for one yesterday of writing at card tables, pursuing dust bunnies, and scolding "the magpie."

Thank God it's never too late to read between the lines of interruptions and inconvenient interactions, for they are disguised invitations into the lives of our children, grandchildren and family; of friends; of one another.

Before she left that day, I gave my granddaughter her own writing tablet for future notes. I am leaving her note to me on my wall so she won't think I don't like it, because I do. Of all the treasures and trappings in this wonderful room, none are as valuable as the scribbles in the corner.

I got your message today, dear God, like handwriting on the wall of my soul: People, not places. Time, not things. Thought, not deed. *It is far better to chase kites on spring days, to chase balls on playgrounds, and to chase laughter rising from a baby's lips like bubbles on the wind than it is to chase dust bunnies beneath beds. Our history is best written on the dusty tabletops of overflowing days. Thank you for interruptions and imperfections. Give us wisdom to RSVP to their invitations with wisdom and joy.*

MAY 20   **IN A HEARTBEAT**

Read Hebrews 12:11-12.

I blew my diet—again—the same day a friend fell prey to her caffeine habit after being "clean" for a month. When it comes to changing habits, we've tried it all. We're dual-natured, "both/and" creatures. The aftertaste of our inconsistency is the rancid, roiling taste of a bad French fry.

We kick ourselves when we fall, obsess over our backsliding, and demand perfection. And what do we do when we blow it? We boomerang, give up, give in. My habit is food. What habit do you want to change?

Consider this: If we were on heart monitors, fluctuating squiggles would mean only that we are alive—wondrously, imperfectly alive! The worst image on a monitor is a flat line. Holding that thought, let's give ourselves a break and begin again.

Refine our ideas about being up-and-down people, Lord. Equip us with humor and plans for redeeming our backsliding. Motivate us to get "with it" again—and again, and again. Help us learn from our successes what works, so we can narrow the gap between ups and downs—not expecting or

136

demanding that either go forever away. They are simply chart-
ing the rhythm of living.

MAY 21   WOMAN'S INTUITION

Read James 3:13, 17-18.

The young woman, who was new in town, visited a group I attended. I immediately felt uncomfortable, but I didn't take time to pursue those vague, intuitive hints. With an "I dare you" look in her eye, she was easy to ignore, and she sat on the outskirts of conversation for weeks. I picked up her painful "vibes," but I continued ignoring her. It was months before I learned that her husband and two kids had died only one month before she'd moved to our town.

"Dear God," I later confessed, "why didn't I act on my gut feeling?"

It reminds me of a fish story I've told a gazillion times and will tell again, if only because I need to heed my own warning. It seems that one fish, Trudy, began darting about the pond, zigging and zagging. The other fish were disgusted. "Ignore her if that's how she's going to be," they said, doing just that until, finally, Trudy disappeared from their sight. What the other fish didn't know was that Trudy had been caught by a fisherman's hook.

Women "take it on the chin" about intuition. This God-given gift that needs no defense is useless until we act on it. As daughters who are cast in the image of a sturdy God, we are strongest when we listen with our soft hearts. With them, we can help those who are afflicted, those who are touched by poverty, those who are homeless, those who have HIV/AIDS—perhaps intuiting solutions, cures, and prevention.

Dear God, we ignore what our hearts tell us, especially when we fear that action might cost us something, even ridicule. It costs us far more to ignore your gift of insight, intuition, awareness, at-one-ness. We thank you for creating us so multidimensional.

MAY 22   HAPPY ANNIVERSARY

Read 1 Corinthians 13:7; Revelation 21:5; Song of Solomon 5:16 b.

Last week's storm felled a cherry tree in our woods. I wish it had finished the job because I can't get the roots out, no matter what I try.

Sitting hip to hip with my spouse on the stump, I watch our grandchildren playing in the branch-strewn yard and feel a kinship with the stump, for my husband and I are not really the roots of this family tree. Ours is a second marriage and stepfamily, which makes us more "stump" than "roots."

Either way, it is our gratitude to be together that makes milestones like this year's wedding anniversary all the more special. Even with my math ability, I can calculate we'll be golden oldies before the golden anniversary. As such, I hope we are an inspiration to those floundering in a youth-adoring world, where to be old is to be past love and loving; where casual, indifferent, and tentative relationships are often touted as the easiest; where negotiation and, yes, even teeth-gritting commitment are useless.

More than that, we are evidence, as the writer of Revelation said, that God is making all things new. Just as this tree is going to become cherry inlay in a grandfather clock to be built by my carpentering mate and firewood for warm family gatherings next winter, so also does our marriage dispel any fears that love, like this tree, can be easily uprooted. Though I am able to tug some small roots free from their grasp on the stump, the taproot goes even beyond my desire to sever its connection. Long may it hold.

Thank you for entwined roots, Lord, which are strongest with you at their core.

Read 1 Timothy 4:4.

Reading aloud by flashlight as the car travels back and forth on weekends, stepmother and stepson have read their way into a relationship no court can mandate and no willpower can create: They are friends. Together, chapter by chapter, they've moved across vacation miles and weekend visits. Hundreds, thousand of miles. Sometimes they have been en route to our house, where I've wrapped up surprise books for them—fodder for their bonding. They are my daughter and grandson.

Once when I told this tale, some sniffed in disapproval at the divorce and remarriage preceding this new family. I was stunned.

As a wife for the second time and the mother of children who, in the double twist of wedding bands, became stepchildren and stepgrandchildren, I can only sink to my knees in gratitude for the fulfillment of our wedding day text: "I am making all things new." Even leftover families.

What joy to "inherit" a ready-made grandson. What privilege and adventure to watch them pore over the newest book. As our children and friends—and strangers—create blended, unique, diverse families, we either can provide them wonderful tales to read and lights for the reading, or we can sit alone in the dark.

Stepfamilies—families of all sorts and shapes and sizes—may be God's way of inviting us to yet another party.

We are grateful, wise and wonderful God, for your grace found in the building of family. You know it is best not to live alone. Give us minds and words that celebrate renewal—however and wherever it is found.

Help us peer closely at these new family portraits. Yep, there you are, Lord, smack-dab in the heart of the family bosom!

Read 1 Timothy 4:4; Genesis 1:31.

It took two birds to kill a tree, but it was more than an even trade.

Although I'm a veteran at discovering more sparrows' nests than I can count, I'd never seen a nest of cardinals, those delightful redbirds with glorious morning songs. Cardinals brightened our yard all winter. One duo was truly a pair. They talked, heads cocked, as my mate and I do, and fed each other sunflowers while designing a nest in a pine tree beside the sidewalk leading to our front porch.

After convincing Abigail and Annie cats to be indoor felines, we crept past the nest. We softly thanked the birds for sharing their spring adventure with us. We promised we wouldn't harm the babies that soon would hatch beneath Mama's broody feathers. It was a promise easily made but difficult to keep.

Worms have started eating the tree, like an ice-cream cone with the redbirds as the cherry on top. These worms are the plug-ugliest I've seen, and I've turned quite a few logs in my day. In rhythmic unison, they cluster, chew, twitch-turn, bite, chew, twitch-turn, destroying our tree.

It is the tree we decorate with lights—six strands last year—to shine through the woods on dark silent nights. It is a child's drawing of a perfect triangle. It is the tree cradling Mama and Papa Cardinal.

"Spray, burn, clip, chop, spray again," advised authorities we consulted about the worms. Forget the birds and save the tree. A simple solution, but never a choice.

We're still waiting for the eggs to hatch. The babies are sure to be as bald as the tree of their birth. The worms have slithered-slunk to other yards. Or maybe they died of indigestion, or became moths smudged on windshields. Or, better yet, maybe something uglier and hungrier ate them. When the birds are gone, we'll cut down the emaciated tree.

After all, we tell ourselves, it was too big for that space, pretending we're planning instead of mourning.

Come next December, our house will be the one with the tiny outdoor Christmas tree, barely reaching the porch railing yet standing as tall as a promise to a pair of redbirds who swapped us a song for a tree.

It's our nature as your daughters, Lord, to nurture, tend, protect. Nowhere is that harder than in today's consuming, consumable world. How shortsighted we are to ignore your intricate balance of nature. We haven't yet gotten the picture that all things work together for good, from worms who become butterflies or food for birds; from weeds that hold back eroding soils; from rain forests that heal us and streams that quench us. Just as you are a broody hen for us, we promise to brood over the world you gave us. We can do it, inspired by a pair of redbirds undaunted by worms, destruction, and human threat. Give us that kind of trust.

MAY 25   **HANDS FULL OF LIFE**

Read Psalms 63:7-8; 138:7-8.

The most beautiful pictures in my photo album are a set of mammogram and ultrasound prints. Although black and white, they add color to my life, a dazzling kaleidoscope of what might have been. I'll get a set yearly, probably on my birthday, wishing many happy returns of me.

Today, the operating room gleamed—a chilly fantasy in bright, bright white. A sting, a blink, a snooze, and I was rid of two large *benign* tumors.

I am fine, not just from the diagnosis, but from what I learned this month: that God wills wholeness for all and, as our constant companion, is first to weep at our tragedies and to celebrate our joys. I also learned that I can live with unanswered questions, such as *Why illness? Why is life unfair?* As I probe questions with a trustworthy God, my response is

141

what defines and creates the peace I find—*not* facts and answers. I also learned that most lumps are benign, that discovering the others when small is life-saving, and that, although I'm sore and tired, removal is not *that* big a deal. Not removing them could be.

I've also discovered bluebirds that have always lived in my woods but I'm just now *seeing*. How long will this shock-induced clarity last? *A lifetime* is my pledge, for I've gotten the point: Life is not a dress rehearsal.

I clutch this thought to my bandaged bosom while I eat food brought by friends, lean on my mate's shoulder, and listen again to four-year-old Kali's message on our answering machine: "It's 2:30, Grandma. We know you're in surgery—just wanted to say we love you."

To love her, and all my life, is to be diligent in self-care and wise in stewardship of energy and time. It is to dance in the woods where God is as tangible as bluebirds—azure streaks against fern and trillium.

Why me, O God? It will be a joy to discover.

MAY 26   MOUNT UP LIKE EAGLES, BUT CAREFULLY

Read Isaiah 40:28-31; Psalms 61:1-4; 121; 34:4.

While recuperating from surgery, I am watching old family videos. . . . *What goes up must come down,* I was thinking, and I wanted to make sure I did so under my own steam. With a slight tilt, I could've fallen off the misty Scottish mountain.

I'd stopped at a plateau halfway up. Why go higher? To prove I could overcome fear of heights? To justify the expense of getting to my ancestral Scotland? The reason didn't matter; I couldn't do it. I was stuck. I waved the family on and sat on my poncho with my fear. We had to come to terms, for I was tired of being hostage to fear—to anything.

142

I forced my vision beyond the mountain's edge. Sea, mountains, heather, and grazing sheep lay like a scene from the Twenty-third Psalm. Could I ever hope to say, "I will fear no . . . [falling]"? I *did* fear falling.

And that's okay, sang the wind. Okay to fear? I strained to hear.

Oh yes, an icy stream answered, *for fear can be good; fear of falling off a mountain is not a silly fear. Besides, look how far you've come.*

Emboldened, I claimed the perch as *my* summit and stood to survey it, edging to my left for a better view. *Movement* is what takes us places; movement, not just climbing, for I found something wonderful by inching sideways: a woolly ewe and twin lambs nestled in coarse grass. I tiptoed back to my poncho, forgetting to fear what was becoming a familiar tilt.

The family soon swooped down and retrieved me. Over tea and scones we swapped tales of a mountain where I'd become an eagle while working on not being a chicken, secure in the knowledge that God loves both.

O God, we name our fears to you: _____ . *Your daughters are no longer willing to be their hostages. We feel you nudge us to take first steps, and your hand steadies us as we answer your call to the summits.*

MAY 27   SANDWICH GENERATION

Read Romans 15:1; Psalm 34:18.

"I can't do it," lamented a friend. Whether she meant bringing lunch to me or caring for her stroke-burdened mother was unclear to me at first. Both, it turned out. Slapped like pastrami on rye, she and many women are finding themselves sandwiched between conflicting loyalties: aging parents and their own families.

Is turnabout fair play? The quickest answer is "certainly."

Who has not wondered what a parent is owed? Who has not dreaded being asked to pay the debt, real or imagined? Who has not wrestled with guilt at hesitating when the phone rings and the summons comes? Who has not dreaded being asked to give up career and interests to become a "baby-sitter"?

So quickly assumptions are made that daughters, daughters-in-law, and granddaughters are the only ones who can do this. Guilt begets anger—and how can a good daughter be angry? How can a good daughter turn her back on turned tables as she is asked to shampoo hair, clip nails, change wet beds, fetch meals, brush teeth, cradle, and hug?

Honoring parents has come to mean something very complicated. We're challenged to believe that our love can exist with rage, sadness, and rebellion. Yet, with *honest* prayer and practical help, it can, making the task at least doable. The rest of us can pick up the slack, offering respite, running errands, listening. Our time will come. Or if it has, and we're on the other side of this pain, "been there, done that" can spur us on to lend a hand.

O dear God, what have we done? Medical intervention and our drive to thwart death have brought us a strange sight: a playpenful of aging parents. Bless them and empower us to lift them lovingly into our arms. They can be a heavy load.

MAY 28   TETANUS SHOTS

Read Song of Solomon 5:16 b; Ecclesiastes 4:9-10.

Wisely, we got matching *his and hers* tetanus shots last year before enlarging the kitchen that I'm slowly puttering around in today.

We should've gotten booster shots of humor: Marital upheaval was around the do-it-yourself corner as we tore out a wall, added a window, plastered, and wallpapered—from, as always, opposite perspectives. He needed me to plan and wait; I needed him to go with the flow and hurry.

144

For the sake of peace, we took a break to plant flowers around a tree. I arrived with a spade; he with tape, stakes, and string. All I wanted was a semblance of round! Already tired, we were headed for staple guns at high noon. Then the owls called one another up and down the river.

Their songs were no less sweet because of the distance between trees where they perched. The birds at the feeder come in different varieties, just as the best marriages do. Some are ground feeders; others prefer swaying stations. All come together, dipping their heads as if in blessing, to splash in the birdbath. It's common ground, like a stepladder when redoing a kitchen: One holds it steady while the other climbs. It is a joint triumph.

And our garden? I followed the ragged contours of roots on one side of the tree; he staked and measured on the other. It overflows with the loveliest blooms amid laughter at ourselves and each other in the blooming, for we both had the same intention: to create a place of beauty.

Would it be more lovely if I'd had my way or he, his? Or is it, instead, exquisite because the portions are perfectly joined where they meet?

I am grateful there is room for all beneath your wings, Creator, because opposites dwell in our home and world. Guide us toward appreciation and away from condemnation. Guide us to middle ground.

MAY 29   **PRAYER**

Read Nehemiah 8:10b.

The sun is warm; the air, balmy. Moving better now, I'm heading to a log overhanging the river: my prayer spot. Join me? I don't go as often as I want, and today I am tempted to give up. But I need to pray because I need company, and because Jesus prayed. So it must be important.

I like my set-apart prayers even as I am lifted by others: in traffic jams and coffee breaks, before meals and sleep.

145

Quickies get a bad rap, yet they can richly supplement longer prayer conversation. We ignore them for the same reasons we can't quite get it together in deeper times: beliefs about ourselves, God, and prayer.

We sing "Just as I am" and don't mean it! We believe God needs a spiffed-up version of us, not the real thing. We're like the gal who cleans her house before the cleaning lady comes!

We believe God's love is like that daisy I wrote about when I learned of the breast lumps: *loves me, loves me not.* We pick them off in our minds, certain that God is as unpredictable as the flower. We destroy it and wind up—bare stem in hand—with no relationship with an ever-loving God.

And prayer? Nothing complicated: It is simply sharing.

As I straddle my log, I get comfortable and become aware of sound, smell, and river. I breathe in God's love and breathe out worry. Today I focus on Nehemiah 8:10*b*: "The joy of the LORD is your strength" (NRSV). Theres no discovery that pushes me off my log. Just communion, awareness. The very act of praying changes us and is an answer in itself. We move closer to the God who's always there, a resource. Prayer: mysterious, marvelous, never the same. It reminds me who I am—a beloved, personally named child—and confirms who God is: loving Creator, Alpha and Omega.

O God, you are the parentheses within which I live and move.

MAY 30   MAKING CONNECTIONS

Read Psalms 90:1-2; 145:4; Proverbs 1:8; Joel 2:28; Acts 2:17.

Sunsets make me homesick. As this Memorial Day readies itself to turn a new page after picnics, parades, and cemetery visitations, my very marrow yearns to be sitting around a cooking fire with other women. We will be talking, laughing, perhaps singing and telling stories that connect generation to generation. Old will teach young, praising God's works to the next generation (Psalm 145:4), and the young will energize the old.

As I note scattered families today, I wonder where the connecting cooking fires are. Where can we learn from matriarchs and old ones? Where will we pick up knowledge for becoming old ones?

Not in the future, say experts who predict that baby boomers will be able to know their great-grandchildren but likely won't bother. Aging boomers are likely to be so busy fulfilling themselves in second or third careers and leisure activities that they won't have time for the young. No room around these cooking fires for stories, songs, or one another.

On the other hand, industries are springing up to teach people how to be better grandparents and subsequently better great-grandparents.

Whether we are worth knowing or have anything to pass on depends on who we decide to be: too busy and self-sufficient, or available. We must make newfangled cooking fires and create community where we can—our own living rooms, churches, committees. We have much to learn and much to share. Memorial Days can be silent and empty, or they can resound with old and young voices in chorus, like the owls calling tonight along my river.

Dear God, inspire us to draw closer, to build up fires of connection. We've been scattered so long, Lord, we've had no one to observe. Ignite in us a desire to learn from one another, O God of Sarah, Ruth, Naomi, Mary and Martha, God of ancient tribes and clans whose blood fills us. Reconnect us.

MAY 31   A STIRRING OF THE SOUL

Read Ephesians 4:22-24.

In the aftermath of today's smart-alecky storm, rose petals from an old-fashioned climber litter the ground like snow. Believing that God doesn't waste things so I shouldn't either,

147

I'm adding the petals to what we've already collected this month: joy, wonder, fear, dread, fury, humor, relief, and peace, to name a few. We're left holding a hodgepodge of feelings and experiences—petals *and* thorns, just like our month. And life. From it, we can make potpourri, "a gathering of God's plenty," and bath sachets to take as gifts and rosewater splash to wear to Mother Nature's spring fling.

BATH SACHETS

Place a few rose petals and equal amounts of dried basil, lavender, rosemary, and thyme in a four-inch fabric square. Gather and tie with a ribbon. Drop into hot bathwater.

ROSEWATER

Cover several handfuls of fresh unsprayed rose petals with distilled water in a stainless-steel pan; slowly bring to boil. Stir occasionally with wooden spoon; simmer ten minutes; strain through coffee filter; bottle; refrigerate. Use in two weeks as bath soak or body splash.

As we luxuriate in the wonder of God's re-creating power, we can hear a still, small Voice carried on the fragrance: *See how the rose bends, not breaking beneath storms that tug to uproot it or dry winds that shrink it. Have you realized that you too are a rose?*

We live our lives "as a tale that is told," the psalmist observed (Psalm 90:9 KJV). Always there is God's hand tending us. Like spices we add to petals to transform them from storm and seasonal leftovers to lasting keepsakes, it blends our days into a potpourri of enduring possibilities.

Tend us, loving Creator, and shelter us in the palm of your hand against all that would uproot and destroy us. We are flowers of your field.

June
Living by Faith

Iris R. Bellamy

JUNE 1   **VAGUENESS**

Read Genesis 1:1-2; Hebrews 11:1.

I'm having trouble focusing today. I've got so many
things to do, that I don't know what to do. Prioritize? I've
tried that, but there are so many priorities right now. Rather
than being certain, all I can do is hem and haw.

Is this the start of a bad day? Not so. Our God, who created the heavens and the earth out of nothing and who gave
life purpose, is able to bring order and purpose into my life
if I invite him in.

God can take vagueness, or lack of focus, and turn it into
purpose when our desire is to please him. God will order our
steps as we commit ourselves to his care.

We can't know how everything will work out, or whether
we'll get it all done today. But we do know that by faith, with
God's help, vagueness can become clarity, clarity can become
purpose, and purpose can become hope.

Dear God, help me to trust you today.

Read 1 Samuel 17:37.

Living the Christian faith should be a matter of overcoming each trial, each challenge that confronts us, that tries to keep us from fulfilling the purpose of God for our lives. Sometimes I question why we have to endure these trials. The response I always get, from my mentors and from God's Word, is that these situations cause us to grow. Whether great or small, these challenges are meant to strengthen us in our spiritual journey and prepare us for what lies ahead.

I don't like to think about being changed or perfected. But I have come to understand that the goal of our spiritual journey is to mature in our faith walk, to become more Christlike in character. So my response to each new challenge has been to embrace it for the benefit of my soul.

As we successfully meet our challenges, holding on to God's unchanging hand, we can glorify God, who alone has the power to perfect us. He has promised never to leave us or forsake us. That's a promise we can cling to as we press on.

Lord, help me to gratefully embrace the challenges of today.

JUNE 3   DEFIANT FAITH

Read Daniel 3:17; Jeremiah 32:27.

Defiant faith is the faith that will not waver, even when tested. Those who have this kind of faith are not easily discouraged. In spite of sickness, they are able to say, "God is able." In spite of financial hardship, they know that God is faithful. As they come up against those situations that would knock them down and take away their peace of mind, they are confident that God goes with them—even into the jaws of death. That's defiant faith.

Our God is always there. He's only a prayer away. God loves us and wants us to put our trust in him. There is no situation that is too hard for God.

Defiant faith stares adversity and hardship in the face and doesn't back down. Defiant faith perseveres and endures, even in times of trial. Don't give up, and don't give in. We serve a miracle-making God who is mighty to deliver.

Dear God, give me defiant faith.

JUNE 4   THROUGH THE STORM

Read Acts 27:25; Romans 4:20-21; Numbers 23:19.

Sometimes the struggles in our lives seem overwhelming. Our hope is slipping away. We have tried all we know to make our situation easier to bear, and still there seems no letup, no relief in sight. But take heart. God is able not only to speak words of comfort and peace to your situation, but also to bring relief.

There are times, as Paul discovered in the storm on the Mediterranean, when trouble comes because others refused to take our advice. At other times, even though we know God has promised to see us through, we may experience a moment of doubt. But remember: "God is *not* a human being, that he should lie" (Numbers 23:19 NRSV, emphasis added).

If hope seems fading, keep holding on. These trials are just a test of your faith (1 Peter 1:6-7). Stand your ground, knowing that God is with you and will sustain your life. God will keep his word.

Fill me with your hope, O God.

JUNE 5   PRAYER AND FASTING

Read Matthew 17:20; Zechariah 4:6.

There are times when my faith is at a very low ebb. Even the good I try to do seems to come up short. I feel overwhelmed and begin to fret. Sometimes I even become short-tempered and lose my sense of humor. But it's at times like these that I go to God in prayer.

Sometimes all I need is a good cry. Other times I'm just too full of myself. That's when the Lord reminds me that it's not by my own strength that things are accomplished. It is by his Spirit dwelling and moving in me that the work gets done. And sometimes the Lord wants me to rest while he sends others to help me get it all done.

Still, at times like these I am reminded that I need to keep up my discipline of fasting. When I fast, I place my reliance on God's power—not on my strength. When I rest in God, the troublesome tasks become ordinary, and the things that I think will take a long time are completed with ease. I can feel my sense of accomplishment returning as my faith and confidence in God are quickened through my fasting.

God never leaves us, even in those times when he seems farthest away. Have faith! Nothing is impossible with God.

Thank you, O God, for renewing my faith and giving me hope.

JUNE 6   INCREASING FAITH

Read Luke 17:5-6.

At times we are overwhelmed by our situation. We feel that we are all alone. But that's when God blesses us in surprising ways.

I had been praying that the Lord would increase my faith, without any idea of how he would answer. Then today, through a conversation with a woman of God, God taught me an unexpected lesson.

As we shared bits and pieces of our spiritual journey, we

listened, laughed together, and exhorted one another to continue to strive in Christ. I found that as I spoke, my words not only encouraged her but also encouraged *me* by reminding me of God's faithfulness to me. In parting, we expressed our appreciation to God for our friendship.

To increase our faith we must exercise our faith. When the disciples asked Jesus to increase their faith, he did what he always does—he bade them to call something forth. It was in witnessing about the goodness of the Lord that I was encouraged. I needed only to remember what God had already done to assure myself of God's faithfulness, and thus increase my faith. God bids us only to ask.

Has the Lord already done great things for you? Share these things with someone, and trust God to do the same today!

Lord, show me how I can exercise—and increase—my faith today.

JUNE 7   GOD'S WORD

Read Romans 10:17; Psalm 119:11.

Believers know the importance of hearing the Word of God rightly divided (2 Timothy 2:15 KJV). The Word of God can either edify or oppress, clarify or confuse; so it matters whether the messenger has encountered that word personally and been changed by it.

Think about what would happen if we woke up in a world where there were no means for hearing a word from God. Could we, would we, still follow after righteousness?

It's important not only to hear God's Word but also to study God's Word for ourselves. God's Word must be planted deep within our minds and hearts, so that we can follow Christ with integrity, with purity of heart. Bible study and Sunday school are two good ways to do this.

Still, hearing and studying should not replace doing. Christianity is more than lip service—it is a lifestyle. If we want to be effective laborers for Christ's sake, we must do more than spend one hour per week with God's Word. Let us spend time in God's Word daily, and then practice what we hear and read.

God, help me to be disciplined in hearing, studying, and acting upon your Word.

JUNE 8   FAITH THROUGH LOVE

Read Galatians 5:6; 1 Corinthians 3:4-8.

As I try to figure out how to live out my faith, Scripture shows me that faith is more than mere mental gymnastics. It is perhaps best expressed in the kind of relationships I have, with both God and my neighbors. Faith must be expressed through love. And, like love, faith is more than words—it is action.

Our relationship with God is central. If it is strong, our faith also will be strong. If it is weak, so our faith will be. Our faith is strengthened as we learn more about God through his Word. As we grow in our appreciation of how great God's love for us is, we are able to grab hold of God's unchanging hand, knowing that he always has our best interests at heart. And we will want to respond in love—not only to God but also to our neighbors.

There are times, though, when we will have to make decisions that will upset others. At those times we must remember what really matters—God comes first. God's ways are loving ways. God never leads us astray, for he sees much farther than we can. Faith expressed through love may not always be what we want it to be, but we can trust God that it is the way that has our best interests at heart. Just as love never fails, so also our faithful response to God will not fail.

Help me always, Lord, to express my faith through love.

Read James 2:14-17.

Martin Luther began the Reformation by emphasizing justification by faith alone. Viewing the institutional church of his day as merely professing faith but lacking any possession of the same, he sought to transform intellectual assent to theological truth into true repentance and reliance on the promises of God.

As James points out, however, faith without the genuiness of fruitful service is dead. A person who claims to be loyal to Christ but fails to treat his or her neighbor with love and equality offers no proof of his or her genuineness. If we mistreat or disrespect our brother or sister, who will think that Jesus Christ lives in us? Likewise, we cannot claim to be Christians and quench God's Spirit, who would cause us to grow as children of God and live out our faith.

Can we claim to love God and deny the spirit of love to operate in us? Should we have the form of godliness, denying the power? The power is in the love! Knowing Christ should make a difference in our lives—and be reflected in the way we treat one another. We should love one another sincerely.

Our faith is fruitful and true only when we accompany that faith with good works. Faith is not a head response but a heart response. Is your faith fruitful?

May I be an instrument of your love, O God, today and every day.

JUNE 10   HEART KNOWLEDGE

Read John 6:28-29; Hebrews 13:8.

Faith in Jesus Christ involves a personal relationship with him. This is more than head knowledge; it is heart knowledge. Consider your loved ones. You love them not because of what you know about them, but because of what you have experienced with them. The times you have spent together are precious. You have taken the time to really know them. So it is with Jesus Christ.

I have not always known that our Lord longs for such an intimate relationship with us. I did not understand that it was possible to know the Lord in this special way. But through prayer, fasting, Scripture reading, meditation, practicing the fruit of the spirit, and praise and worship, I sought and found this precious closeness with him. As I read about the lives of the saints, I found affirmation for what I had already experienced—that we can be ushered into the presence of the Lord. But we must seek after him diligently.

Jesus Christ is the same—yesterday, today, and forever. What he did for others, he has done for me. And what he has done for me, he is more than able to do for you.

How can we do the works of God? We are to believe in Jesus Christ—today!

I do believe in you, Lord. Help me to know you more intimately.

JUNE 11   SHIELD OF FAITH

Read Ephesians 6:10-17.

We are creatures of faith. We have faith that when we put our key into the ignition of our car, it will start. We have faith that when we sit in a chair, it will support our weight. And we have faith that when we cross a street with a green light, no one will hit us.

As Christians, we are told that we need to wear the shield of faith as part of the whole armor of God (Ephesians 6:11). The shield is one of the most important pieces of armor. It is usually both the largest and the strongest piece of equipment—protecting the whole body.

Faith in God is our shield of protection—wherever we go, and whatever we may be doing. It is our first line of defense. If our faith is strong, our bodily armament remains intact—the breastplate of righteousness, the helmet of salvation, the girdle of truth. If our faith is weak, our armor may take a beating—literally and figuratively. Without faith in God, we are defenseless.

But we have help. Jesus overcame death and the grave so that we too could overcome, could grow strong in our faith. So take hold of your shield of faith, and it will give you hope for every battle.

Clothe me with your armor, O Lord, so that I may stand firm in faith.

JUNE 12   GOD'S PRESENCE

Read Hebrews 11:5, 6; Micah 6:8.

God has always wanted human beings to have a genuine heartfelt relationship with him. Since the days of Adam, God has taken delight in communion with his people. Adam and Eve talked with God in the Garden of Eden. Enoch walked with God for three hundred years and lived in accordance to God's will, despite the popular opinion of his day (Genesis 5:22).

We should desire to have the kind of close relationship with God of which Enoch is the prototype. We are to be agreeable in spirit, fervent in prayer, and in harmony with the Word and the will of God. To do this, we must spend time with God, allowing his love to fill us. We must allow God to perfect us according to his divine blueprint—not according to our thoughts or plans.

Through our faithfulness, even nonbelievers will know that God is real, because of his presence shining in us.

Today, take care to look for signs of God's presence. Watch for his loving-kindness and tender mercies. They're all around you.

O God, I know you go with me every day. Make me even more aware of your presence today.

JUNE 13   EXPECT A BLESSING

Read James 1:5-6; Ephesians 3:20.

James offers practical advice on how to pray. Knowing that the Christian life is full of challenges and understanding that God wants to establish us and does not cause us to fail, James admonishes his readers to stand firm in their faith. If there is anything we lack—be it strength, wisdom, resources, or faith—we should ask God to help us. Because God is our source and our supply, he will not deny those who seek him. God will meet our needs.

Therefore, when we pray, we must believe that something will happen. And then we must wait. God is a liberal giver and is able to do over and above our expectation. God will meet us where we are and give us the power, the wisdom, the help, or the faith we need to carry us through any situation. There is nothing that God can't handle. Things may be impossible for us, but all things are possible with God on our side (Mark 10:27).

Make your request known to God today. Trust him, and watch him work it out for you. Expect a blessing!

Today I come to you in faith, Lord, trusting you to meet my needs.

JUNE 14   RIGHTEOUS LIVING

Read Genesis 15:6; Habakkuk 2:4.

According to the Old Testament, individuals who trusted God, who lived lives of honesty and integrity before God and their neighbors, and who were obedient to the laws of God were counted as the righteous. Theirs was a walk unlike that of the rest of the world.

For them and for us, living by faith means trusting God in every situation or challenge of life. It is like sailing a ship in a steady wind. We can travel securely, knowing that God has matters well in hand. Living by faith means knowing that God is faithful, just, and steadfast in all his ways. God will never leave us or forsake us. Living by faith is acknowledging that God is in control at all times and in every situation.

Righteous living begins with trust—trust in God's unchanging love. Keep your eyes on God; he alone will see you through.

Help me to live by faith, Lord, today and every day.

JUNE 15   THE GIFT OF FAITH

Read Philippians 3:7-11.

God gives us all a measure of faith, by which we are able to do great things for his glory. As a gift, it has already been given—it is already in our possession. We don't have to ask for it; it is already in us. Paul wrote to the Philippian church to continue in the life of faith, just as they had begun it—by trusting in Jesus Christ. He spoke of how Jesus was careful to do the will of God, living a life of servanthood. The Philippians, he wrote, were not to be self-serving, but to consider others as better than themselves (Philippians 2:3). Paul considered that seeking after God, striving to know Christ, was more important than anything else he could achieve (Philippians 3:7, 10).

To understand this gift of faith, we have to get to know the Giver of the gift. Also, our faith must be cultivated and nurtured. As Jesus walked, so should we walk—always seeking to do the will of God. We must spend time with the Lord in order to find our purpose in him. And we must submit ourselves to God and allow the Spirit of God to lead us.

In Christ, Paul knew we would find meaning and satisfaction. He knew that we could do all things through Christ (Philippians 4:13). Press on!

Thank you, God, for your gift of faith. Help me to claim it and use it for your glory.

JUNE 16   MOVING MOUNTAINS

Read Matthew 21:21-22; 2 Timothy 1:7.

Yesterday we considered how faith is a gift from God. It is important to understand that God gives us a measure of faith according to the blueprint he has designed for our lives. Each one of us, therefore, is unique. Being unique means that there is only one you. It also means that your contribution to the Body of Christ is both unique and much needed—like pieces of a puzzle.

Yet when it comes to serving God, we set up many obstacles in our lives. "Oh, I can't do that," we say when presented with an opportunity to serve. We always have an excuse. But Jesus said, "If you have faith and do not doubt" (Matthew 21:21 NRSV). The mountains in our lives *can* be moved—if we want them moved. Still, we hem and haw. We want to be blessed, but we don't want to allow God to do it. We want to be used mightily by God, but we are not willing to strive. There is nothing that we cannot accomplish for God as long as we are careful to focus on him and seek to do his will.

Some of the mountains we face are self-made—mountains of fear, doubt, and guilt. But God has not given us a spirit of fear. God has given us a spirit of power, of love, and of a sound mind (2 Timothy 1:7). Grab hold of your faith today, believing that you *can* accomplish great things because of Christ, and see that mountain move right out of your way. By faith, you *can* move the mountains in your life.

Give me the measure of faith I need, Lord, to move the mountains in my life.

Read 1 Samuel 14:6.

In today's Scripture text, we are introduced to a Jonathan few talk about. He was a hero. His faith in God gave him the confidence to go against the Philistines, even though he had only his armor-bearer with him. For Jonathan, it was enough to know that God was on Israel's side. Jonathan believed in the power of God. He knew that with God on their side, Israel would always prevail.

Jonathan's faith also made his devotion to David possible. Who but a person of deep spiritual insight would see the hand of God on David's life? Although Jonathan stood to become king over Israel after his father, Saul, he did not stand in David's way when he realized the plan of God for Israel through David. Instead of plotting against David, he loved David "as himself" (1 Samuel 18:1 NIV). It might not be easy to step aside and watch another receive what you thought God had planned to give you, but if you keep the faith and continue to be faithful to God, God will reveal his plan for your life too.

Our thoughts are not God's thoughts; his plans are not our own (Isaiah 55:9). Let us keep trusting and believing God. He knows what's best for us.

O God, I know you will never leave me or forsake me. Today I stand aside and invite you to have your way in my life. I will look toward the future with new hope.

JUNE 18   TOUGH TIMES

Read 2 Chronicles 20:12; Philippians 4:6-7.

Jehoshaphat was a cautious king. For the most part, he walked in the ways of the Lord, but especially in times of indecision he sought the Lord.

Sometimes trouble comes on us unexpectedly. It may be an undetected illness that steals our joy; it may be trouble on the job that we don't know how to handle. That's the time to go to God in prayer. I have walked with the Lord long enough to know that trials come to strengthen us and establish us in the faith. They are times that cause us to humble ourselves, to move from head knowledge of God to a vital relationship with him. The Lord desires relationship with his people. He wants us to know beyond a shadow of a doubt that if he is with us, nothing will defeat us—not sickness or conflict or death (2 Chronicles 32:7-8).

Tough times don't last. God's will for us is that we draw close to him in prayer, seeking him in all things. If we abide in him, he promises to work on our behalf. If we keep our eyes on him, he will keep us and lead us to safety.

Lord, I know that the best way to keep my eyes fixed on you is through prayer. Today I let go of my worries and trust you to lead me safely through the day.

JUNE 19   WALKING FAITH

Read Job 19:25.

Job was determined to hold on to his faith in God, despite the circumstances that had befallen him. Although he experienced great tragedy and loss, he refused to lose hope. With his physical condition at its lowest and his inner turmoil at its highest, we hear what is perhaps his greatest show of confidence in God: "I know that my Redeemer lives" (19:25 NIV).

When we are going through our storms, I wonder if we are as confident. We talk about having the patience of Job, but do we share his determination to trust and serve God? When our so-called friends try to discourage us and family members think we're crazy to endure our fiery trials; when we've examined and cross-examined our motives, do we have the courage to stand alone? In times like these, we must have "walking faith." Talking faith is nothing more than lip service. But walking faith will carry us through the tests of time. Walking faith brings humility and stability to our lives, while purifying our hearts so that we may be mightily used by God.

Job knew God. He knew that he served the true and living God. He did not trust in the idols of the pagans, whose gods never answered the worship they were given. Job knew that God cared for him—in spite of his circumstances.

Oh, for pure-hearted Christians today! For they *shall* see God (Matthew 5:8). Strengthen your determination today, and put on your "walking shoes"!

Give me the faith of Job, Lord, so that I may not only talk the faith but also walk it.

JUNE 20   A WORSHIPFUL HEART

Read Matthew 8:1-3.

Often we ask the Lord to do things for us, but we fail to live in full assurance that the Lord will do what we ask. We say we believe; we know that God is able, yet still our breakthrough does not come.

A leper came to Jesus and asked him to heal him of his leprosy. He came in confidence, knowing that Jesus could heal him. He didn't come with a story to tell or excuses to make; he came worshiping the Lord.

How often we fail to recognize that the Lord listens for our praises. He wants us to worship him in spirit and in truth (John 4:24). We underestimate the value of worship. The leper came not only with the expectation that he would be healed but also with a thankful, worshipful heart—because he knew Jesus could do it. And Jesus honored his request, "put forth his hand, and touched him . . . And immediately his leprosy was cleansed" (Matthew 8:3 KJV).

O come, let us worship and bow down,
let us kneel before the LORD, our Maker!
—Psalm 95:6 NRSV

Worship him today!

I give you praise and thanks, O God, for all you have done and have yet to do in my life.

JUNE 21   EXERCISING FAITH

Read Matthew 8:5-10.

The centurion was a man who understood order and knew how to move with authority. He also recognized that Jesus operated in the same way. The centurion sought an audience with Jesus to ask for healing for his servant. Jesus offered to come with him to heal his servant. Anybody else might have accepted the Master's offer to make the journey to where his servant was, but the centurion told Jesus that it wasn't necessary. He knew that Jesus needed only to utter the words and his servant would be healed. How great his faith was!

When you go to God in prayer, do you look for evidence before you believe that the Lord will work on your behalf? If so, then you aren't exercising faith. Until you can release your situation completely into God's capable hands—expecting him to work it out for you in his own way and time—you are only slowing down the movement of God in your life.

The centurion was not a worrier. He expected things to get done, and things got done. He recognized that Jesus had the power of God behind him and that with that kind of authority, he needed only to say the words.

Remember, we don't serve a little god but a great, big God—the God who can do all things. So, pray, expecting God to act on your behalf!

Dear God, help me to have the faith of the centurion, trusting in you completely.

164

Read Matthew 9:18, 23-26.

Jairus had worshiping faith. This meant that regardless of his situation, he gave God thanks. Even though his daughter lay at the point of death, Jairus knew that Jesus could reverse the outcome.

Sometimes we are at the very end of our rope, and our situation seems destined for failure. But there is one more thing for us to do. We can thank God for our situation and rest in his unchanging care for us.

God's care for us never ends—even in the worst of times. Even when things look hopeless, we must realize that there is always hope. Although Jairus knew his daughter was dying, he encouraged himself, knowing that all was not lost. If he could keep hope alive there might still be a chance that his daughter would live.

We, too, must keep hope alive. There will be times when we are all alone and the odds seem insurmountable. Our friends or relatives may tell us to give up. But we must never give up on God! Trials come to test our devotion to God. We've got to learn to trust God more. Remember: With God, all things are possible!

Thank you, God, for your unchanging love and care for me. Teach me to trust you more and more.

JUNE 23   TWO ARE BETTER THAN ONE

Read Matthew 9:27-33.

The Bible says that "two are better than one" because they can work together and accomplish more than one can alone (Ecclesiastes 4:9). We all have experienced those times when the support of a friend made all the difference. So it was for these two blind men. They both had awaited the coming of the Messiah, and because of their faith, Jesus was able to cast out a demon from one who was mute without so much as speaking one word (Matthew 9:32-33). Great was the return for their work of faith.

Although they could not see, their faith was unshakable. Notice that they called Jesus "Son of David." This was the Messianic title for Jesus. Matthew uses the title in the beginning of his Gospel account (1:1) to support his claim that Jesus was the promised Messiah. For these men to have that kind of faith in Jesus implied their certainty of his ability to restore their sight. Note Jesus' response: "Do you believe that I am able to do this?" (Matthew 9:28 NIV). They responded, "Yes, Lord." And according to their faith, they were healed.

We need the faith of the blind men. We also need to remind one another that our God is able to do what he promises to do. As Paul told the Corinthians, "For in him [Jesus Christ] every one of God's promises is a 'Yes.' For this reason it is through him that we say the 'Amen,' to the glory of God" (2 Corinthians 1:20 NRSV). Amen!

Thank you, O God, for Christian friends who increase my faith and remind me of your promises.

JUNE 24   CORPORATE FAITH

Read Matthew 14:34-36.

As word of Jesus' healings spread, the faith of the people escalated. By the time Jesus reached Gennesaret, the faith of the people was such that they believed they needed only to touch the hem of his garment to be made whole. If we contrast this to the time when Jesus was in Nazareth, and no one was healed because of their disbelief (Matthew 13:54-58), we see the power of corporate faith. Because of the people's faith in Gennesaret, Jesus' healing power was displayed in all its glory. And the whole region was charged with anticipation.

The people of Gennesaret were so convinced of Jesus' abilities to heal, all they needed to do was to reach out and touch him. We too can appreciate the benefits of our corporate faith every time we gather together. When we come together as a body of believers, we are all blessed. When we pray in the sanctuary, believing together in the unity of our faith, something must happen. We cannot leave in the same condition in which we came.

Just as it was in Gennesaret when Jesus passed by, so we too must bring our expectations whenever we come to the house of prayer. Once we invoke the presence of the Lord, something *will* happen!

Lord, we gather in your name expecting your holy presence to change us, and we are *changed. May we remember to bring our expectations with us each time we gather.*

JUNE 25   THE SPIRIT-FILLED LIFE

Read John 1:12; 7:37-38.

Being Spirit-filled may be understood best as doing the will of God as directed by the Holy Spirit. John Wesley called it perfection. It is a spiritual standard that we all must strive toward if we are to be conformed into the image of our Lord, Jesus Christ. When we accept Christ as Savior and are baptized in his name, we begin a spiritual journey that connects us to Christ as children of God. The Holy Spirit is that divine "stuff" of God that propels us on our spiritual journey—the "living water" that springs up inside us, empowering us to do great things in Christ.

Although we aspire to the Spirit-filled life, we start as mere "babes," seeking to discover the will of God for our lives. As we grow in the Spirit—attempting to follow the leading of the Lord—we mature in the faith through a process of testings and trials. Thus, to become Spirit-filled Christians demands that we be in right relationship with our risen Savior.

The Spirit-filled life also requires faith. Without faith, we cannot achieve the purpose of God for our lives. When we were created, God stamped his blueprint on each one of us. Each of us carries a "piece of God" inside us that waits

167

to be released. Faith unlocks the promises of God, and the indwelling presence of the Holy Spirit nurtures, guides, and sustains us. It is the power of God unto salvation. By faith, we become heirs with Christ Jesus, therefore having the power to move mountains. Speak to your mountain today!

Lord, fill me with your living water so that I may faithfully do your will.

JUNE 26   OVERCOMERS

Read John 14:12-14.

In John 14, Jesus shares with the disciples the source of his power. He makes it clear that his power comes from God, and he challenges his disciples—and us—to believe in him. If we would be made perfect in him, we must increase our faith.

Jesus explained to the disciples that their faith would be tried: They would be hated, persecuted, put out of the synagogues, and even killed (John 15:18, 20; 16:2). We too can expect tribulation. We know, however, that God will keep us in his care through every storm of life (John 16:33). It is the power of God that keeps us as we abide in Christ.

When we receive the Holy Spirit, as Jesus explained to the disciples, we know that Jesus is in the Father and that we are abiding in him and he in us (John 14:15-20). In Jesus, the power of God unto salvation is made available to us—power to be overcomers. In order to be overcomers, then, we must be tried. As Jesus was tried, we shall be tried. As Jesus suffered, we shall suffer. But as Jesus overcame, we shall overcome too. Draw close to the Power Source today!

I do believe in you, Lord Jesus. Increase my faith and make me strong enough to withstand the storms yet to come.

Read Psalm 37:3, 5; Proverbs 16:3.

It's easy to trust God in our "comfort zone," when every-thing is going well, but trusting God is not as easy when he draws us out of our comfort zone. Sometimes we find our-selves in a place we've been before where we've experienced failure. Sometimes we're in a place we never thought we'd ever find ourselves, doing things we never thought we'd do. During these times, some of us dread the change and want to shrink back. Others of us cry our eyes out. Yet God always goes before us, preparing the way.

In these times, especially, we must draw near to God, for he alone can see us through. If we will keep our focus on the Lord, who has promised never to leave us or forsake us, we'll be all right. Though we can't see what awaits us at every turn in life, we serve a God who sees everything and who cares about us greatly.

As we step out in faith, we can trust God to be with us through every situation. If we commit our work to him, he *will* establish our thoughts (Proverbs 16:3). Once we cast all our cares on him, he will work for us. Our fear, our ner-vousness, will pass away. And we'll see that it wasn't as bad or as hard or as impossible as we thought. Let God's peace go with you today. Put your trust in him. He'll never let you down.

Lord, I place all of my trust in you. May your peace go with me through all the day.

JUNE 28   DON'T STOP BELIEVING

Read Isaiah 26:4; Psalm 27:13.

Isaiah knew the Lord Jehovah from personal experience. His personal encounter with the Lord (see Isaiah 6) was such that he was privileged to see beyond his own time. He was so inspired by God that he was able to catch a glimpse of the Messiah and his coming.

So confident was Isaiah in the vision the Lord gave him that he wrote this song of praise recorded in Isaiah 26. He knew that Israel had nothing to fear as long as they kept faith with the Lord. They would lack no good thing with God as their provider. Isaiah admonished the people to trust God at all times—no matter what. Not only is God able to save and redeem his people, but "the LORD JEHOVAH is everlasting strength" (v. 4 KJV). The LORD JEHOVAH was Israel's sure defense. He would preserve his people and be their refuge. He is from everlasting to everlasting—the Eternal One.

If God has promised you something, you can be sure that he will bring it to pass. If God has given you a vision, wait for the vision to be manifested. It is closer than you think. Isaiah wrote, "Trust . . . in the LORD for ever" (26:4 KJV). God is able to do what he said he would do. Hold on, and don't stop believing!

Today I praise you, O God, for the promises that have yet to be fulfilled in my life. I will keep on believing!

JUNE 29   GOD'S SPECIAL PEOPLE

Read Psalm 125:1.

When God makes a promise, he keeps his word. If Israel knew anything about God, they knew that God was faithful. They knew that God would take good care of them. And they became secure in that promise. They knew that if the LORD JEHOVAH said it, nobody could change it; and this gave them great peace of mind over the years. Psalm 125 is a song of Israel's security.

Having the Lord on our side makes all the difference. It's not important that we have a lot to bring to him, or that we are people of status. God requires only that we remain in relationship with him; he will do the rest. God wants to make us his people. He wants to be faithful to us, so that we can be witnesses of how he has led us. God blesses us because he is pleased with his character in us. We don't bring anything to the table, really. Recall that God told Israel that they were the least and the fewest among the nations (Deuteronomy 7:7).

When we as believers show forth God's character and God's blessings, others will want what we have. The only way to receive God's special promises is to be God's special people—people who know the Lord for ourselves. "O taste and see that the LORD is good; happy are those who take refuge in him" (Psalm 34:8 NRSV).

I am richly blessed, Lord, because I know you for myself. You are my shelter and my strength, and I am grateful.

JUNE 30   STEP OUT IN FAITH

Read Matthew 14:28-31.

Peter was very impulsive. Sometimes he did and said the right things; sometimes he was wrong. Still, Peter was a man of great faith. Jesus scolded Peter for having doubted while he was walking on the sea toward Jesus. Yet who but a great person of faith would even attempt such a thing?

If we want to do great things for the Lord, we have to dare to step out on faith alone. Sometimes our own inner conviction will be the only proof we have that the Lord spoke to us and directed us to do this or that. There may be no one else around to witness the encounter. Still, we must be willing to go wherever the Lord leads us. And we don't have to be afraid, because Jesus will be right there in front of us, bidding us "Come" (Matthew 14:29).

It's time to leave the security of the crowd and walk alone with Jesus. He has destined us for great things. But we'll never see it unless we step out of our comfort zone. Yes, it's

scary, but it's also exhilarating. That's what life in Christ is—
it's a journey, an adventure.

I challenge you to step out in faith and get your feet wet!

Help me to step out in faith each day, Lord, trusting you in all things.

July
Learning to Love
Rebecca Laird

JULY 1   **KNOWING JOEY**

And a little child shall lead them.   —*Isaiah 11:6 NRSV*

We met six-year-old Joey through a church-sponsored summer puppet program. Weeks later when he was hospitalized, his family remembered the name of our church and called for a minister. Why had this full-of-mischief child stopped growing? Why was his blood count so abnormal? A transfusion given at birth had passed a terrible disease to him. Joey had AIDS.

At first when I went to visit Joey, I found myself scrutinizing him: *Does he look pale today? Has he grown in the last month?* Initially I viewed him like a health concern to be monitored—a curiosity, an oddity. Over time I realized that I had stopped looking at him as a boy with a dreaded disease. Instead, I knew him simply as Joey—a kid with a big heart and an unquenchable spirit. His disease did not define him.

Knowing Joey opened the door for me to meet others who also had AIDS. Because I knew Joey, I knew that each one was a unique person who bore God's spark of life inside, just as I do.

God, help me to see others through your eyes today. Take away my fears of those who seem different from me.

JULY 2   THESE PRECIOUS YEARS

*My heart and my flesh sing for joy
to the living God.*
                                              —*Psalm 84:2*b *NRSV*

When Joey would come to visit us, I would put extra bananas on my shopping list, for he routinely emptied the fruit bowl. I rolled up the hall carpet because he discovered that the hardwood hall was really a great long-jump pit. He sprinted from the dining room, planted his feet on the floor furnace grate, and hurled himself toward the front entrance as our eager dog, Brewer, slid to a stop beside him. Every year Joey called me the week after Christmas with a reminder to bake him a chocolate birthday cake.

One Saturday Joey stayed overnight. At breakfast the next morning he prayed, "Lord, thank you for these precious years. Thank you for this food. And please help Brewer to behave better. Amen." We laughed, then almost began to cry. A smile, a banana, a new pair of boxer shorts, a good romp with the dog, or release from the hospital after yet another stay were the good stuff of life for Joey. Precarious health couldn't dampen his zest for life. He was a human being, fully alive, who knew how to savor the simple joys—the best stuff of life.

God, make me aware of the simple joys of my life today.

JULY 3   CALLED TO CARE

Rejoice in hope, be patient in suffering, persevere in prayer. Contribute to the needs of the saints; extend hospitality to strangers.   —*Romans 12:12-13 NRSV*

Soon after we met Joey, a group from our church began to meet weekly to pray for the increasing number of people we knew who had HIV/AIDS. We read Scripture and discussed our fears of disease and the difficulties of seeing others in pain. We talked of our own mortality.

As we struggled to focus our energies, some in the group kept saying, "Can't you see? It's Joey and the children whom we are to care for." Others of us thought we were to offer care to everyone God led across our paths, regardless of age or how they became ill. But we saw that we all were called to care, though in differing ways. We claimed the wisdom we'd learned from Mother Teresa of Calcutta: "I am one, I am only one, I cannot do everything, but I can do something." Individually, our efforts seemed limited, but when joined together, the impact was tangible. A couple of our members became chaplains on the AIDS ward of a local hospital; others volunteered with existing caregiving organizations. As needed, I organized volunteers to deliver meals and visited those who were housebound. And I prayed. Sometimes my efforts felt so small. But God's word to me was simply to be faithful in the little things. If there was more for me to do, I'd discover it in God's good time.

God, help me to be faithful to what you have already asked me to do.

JULY 4   "SOMEBODY THERE LOVES ME"

Teach us to count our days
that we may gain a wise heart.
—Psalm 90:12 NRSV

I was on my way to visit Daniel, a friend who was sick, when I passed the animal shelter and stopped in to take a look. In the puppy room, potential owners vied for three jostling puppies. A fourth puppy, the runt, wholeheartedly leaped up and down in the back of the cage, trying to see and be seen. Soon, the three were claimed, and he took his place at the front of the cage, bewildered by his newfound soli-

175

tude. I meant only to pet him. But then he looked at me with his eager eyes—and I claimed him!

With this toy-sized puppy cradled in the crook of my arm, I continued on to Daniel's house. Daniel, a strikingly handsome man, was now skeletal, and often seemed faraway when I visited him. Today, however, his face lit up with pleasure when he saw the black and brown face peek from under my jacket. The dog gingerly padded across the bed, then plopped down beside him, snuggling close.

As he petted the puppy, Daniel said, "Little things, like this little guy's soft fur, hold me here in this world." He went on: "I am living between two worlds. Sometimes I can see a greenish glow that seems to be the border of the next world. I can even smell it." He sensed that God was preparing a welcome. "I look forward to going now," he said, scratching the contented pup. "Somebody there loves me."

Thank you, God, for loving me and claiming me as your own.

JULY 5   A TUG ON MY HEART

You shall go to all to whom I send you,
and you shall speak whatever I command you,
Do not be afraid. . . .
—Jeremiah 1:7b-8a NRSV

After work one evening, I flipped on the news. The camera panned rows of tiny abandoned babies in a hospital nursery. Some lay in plastic incubators; others had tubes protruding from tiny, heaving chests. The newscaster described the search for foster parents with medical backgrounds to open their homes to these little ones, most born with drug addictions or the HIV/AIDS virus.

I felt a tug on my heart. But getting involved with kids who needed special care didn't make sense. *I don't have any medical training,* I thought. *But why can't I get those babies out*

176

of my mind? I'd been moved by seeing the plight of others before, and the impulse to help had gone away. But all week long, the image of those babies kept returning to my mind and stirred my heart. God was calling me to action. God was waiting for me to say "yes." As I admitted my willingness to obey, I began to trust that God would show me my next step.

I say "yes," Lord, to your plans for me. Show me the next step you would have me take.

JULY 6   "I'LL BE YOUR PARTNER"

Two are better than one, because they have a good reward for their toil. For if they fall, one will lift up the other; but woe to one who is alone and falls and does not have another to help.   —Ecclesiastes 4:9-10 NRSV

The Saturday after the newscast seeking foster parents for medically fragile kids began to tug at my heart, I spied Lorie across the room at our prayer group. As a nurse, she would be a perfect candidate for the program. I rushed over to talk to her about it. Before I finished, her eyes shone with tears. "I'd like to become a foster mom," she said, "but I'm afraid to do it alone."

"I'll be your partner," I rashly promised.

Before we could count the full cost of our commitment, we were attending training sessions, propelled by the belief that somewhere out there was a child who needed us. Lorie had the medical skills. I had a helping hand to lend. We did not know exactly what or whom the future held. We simply did what we knew to do; we prayed, readied her apartment, and she filled out the thick sheaf of forms. Then we waited. Only God could mastermind the next step.

Thank you for those with whom I work and serve. Strengthen those who offer me the support I need from day to day.

JULY 7   LOVE TAKES HARD WORK

Let us love, not in word or speech, but in truth and action.
                                    —1 John 3:18 NRSV

Within short weeks of committing myself to support my
friend as she became a foster parent, Lorie received word
that a baby awaited her. Together we drove to the hospital
and brought home a tiny boy, just a few weeks old, whose
drug-addicted mom had abandoned him at birth. On Thurs-
days, while Lorie went to a support group for single parents,
I watched Cornelio. The residual effects of the drug addic-
tion his birth mother had passed on to him led him to con-
vulse stiffly when he was afraid or tired. He was difficult to
comfort. Humming softly as I held him, I paced the long
hardwood hall in my Victorian cottage. He wailed. I bit my
lip and prayed and paced until he finally calmed and slept.

As I watched for the headlights of Lorie's car to shine
through my living room window, I wished that I had more
patience. I knew that she carried the overwhelming burden
of care. I was simply her weekly helpmeet. Still, on those
nights when the baby cried, I wondered if we had bitten off
more than we could chew.

Loving this child was the right thing to do, but it was
harder than I had imagined. Real love takes hard work.

*Dear God, help me to be willing to do the hard work of
loving others today.*

JULY 8   "YOU'RE MINE"

I have called you by name, you are mine.
                                    —Isaiah 43:1 NRSV

Six months after Lorie took her first foster son home, a second call came from the city's social workers. Would Lorie also
take in Patrick, a nine-month-old with AIDS? I was wary. How

178

could she say yes to another child? But as her support person, I agreed to go with her to meet Patrick. He lay sleeping in his room in the pediatric intensive care unit while two large teddy bears, an intravenous pole, and a myriad of monitors stood sentry. He was a beautiful child with curly black hair, flawless cocoa-colored skin—and, as he awoke, I saw sad, brown eyes. His mother had died of AIDS, and a relative had kept him until he was admitted into the hospital for failure-to-thrive.

My doubts about helping Lorie take in a second child evaporated as that little boy warily watched me. A divine call to care for a child with AIDS had propelled Lorie and me to travel this path. And here waited a tiny boy who, by the best medical guesses, would need love and a home for a few months, perhaps a year, until he died.

Lorie came into the room, bent down, and said, "I love you, Patrick. You're mine." She was ready to risk taking him home, knowing that heartbreak awaited her.

"We've got to take him, Lorie," I said. She nodded but never took her eyes off him. We vowed he'd live and die knowing that he was wanted and loved.

Thank you, God, for calling each of us by name and caring for us as your own.

JULY 9   GIVEN BY GOD

For this child I prayed; and the LORD has granted me the petition that I made to him. Therefore I have lent him to the LORD; as long as he lives, he is given to the LORD.
—1 Samuel 1:27-28 NRSV

When Patrick turned one, Lorie brought him to our church to be baptized. I stood beside her and read the words of Hannah, who had prayed so long for her son, Samuel:

> My heart exults in the Lord;
> my strength is exalted in my God.
> —1 Samuel 2:1 NRSV

179

On that happy day, Lorie presented this child to God and affirmed that for the length of his life, Patrick would be a member of God's household. We publicly acknowledged that God had added a member to our family of faith. Patrick became my godson—a son given by God for me to love for the length of his life. God had deemed me, and others in the household of faith, important stewards of this child. Because of our faith, we belonged to each other for better or for worse.

Who has God entrusted to your care? For whom have you prayed for so long? Today, recall that this one you love is God's child, lent to you to love and care for the duration.

I commit my loved ones to you today, God. Thank you for making us a family.

JULY 10   A SMILE AND A KISS

Blessed are the pure in heart, for they will see God.
                                        —Matthew 5:8 NRSV

Patrick loved Elmo, *Sesame Street's* red monster who rarely says the word *I*. Instead, as many toddlers do, Elmo cheerfully says, "Elmo did it." Patrick couldn't claim to have done many things according to the standard child development charts. He rarely ate solid foods; a nutritional supplement kept him going. He liked to come to the table and mischievously pretend to eat while dropping pieces on the floor—checking regularly to see what reaction he could muster from his tablemates.

Patrick learned to crawl and then to walk. But as time went on, he needed a scooting board and a wheelchair. He spent hours hunched over a wooden train set that he scooted and circled around the track. He learned to best his brother, Cornelio, at games and claim his share of the toys and attention.

At each good-bye, Patrick would take a break from his play and say, *"Beso,"* the Spanish word for kiss. He'd throw kisses and smile. And when this often-serious child smiled, his eyes became backlit and his already beautiful countenance turned angelic. Many adults worked endless hours and traveled many miles for one of his smiles. Love radiated from him.

God chooses to dwell in the lowly. God exalts the pure in heart.

Create in me a clean heart, O God, and put a new and right spirit within me (Psalm 51:10 NRSV).

JULY 11   AN EXTENDED FAMILY

God sets the lonely in families.   —*Psalm 68:6 NIV*

It was a couple of years later. I walked up the long flight of steps to my friend Lorie's flat. Once inside the door, one of her four cats flew by, one of her two toddler boys aimed his trike toward my knees, and the other hollered a hello over the din of *Sesame Street*. Lorie waved as she talked to a social worker on the phone. An alp-sized heap of laundry towered by the back door. I washed dishes, did laundry, and made macaroni and cheese. Each week an army of caring souls enlisted to help. Lorie's travel agent became a surrogate aunt. Friends, colleagues, church family, and neighbors who learned about this special family pitched in. Someone bought groceries and another took the cats to the vet. Others watched the children while Lorie took a break.

Lorie's boys loved the many comings and goings. They began asking at breakfast time, "Who's coming today, Mama?" Two little boys, both born to loneliness, now had an amazing extended family. No longer was it Lorie and me offering love to two little boys. God's love had built a fullfledged extended family where none had been before.

Lord, widen the borders of my family to include someone who is lonely, today.

181

Teach me your way, O LORD,
that I may walk in your truth;
give me an undivided heart to revere your name.
—Psalm 86:11 NRSV

In mid-July, celebration plans would begin for a big birthday bash for Patrick. A roomful of balloons was ordered, and an apartment full of people of all ages was invited. Hors d'oeuvres for the adults, pretzels and munchies for the kids, and a big cake for all lined the kitchen table. Before the piles of presents were opened, we stopped the noise and chaos and offered a blessing for Patrick. For a few brief, meaning-filled moments, we offered words of gratitude for the wonderful gift of another year of life, and we prayed for health and strength to live fully the months ahead.

One year at Patrick's birthday celebration I read from Psalm 86 (v. 16 NRSV):

> Turn to me and be gracious to me;
> give your strength to your servant;
> save the child of your serving girl.

The words of the Bible became ours. Lorie needed God's strength, and Patrick needed God's miracle to live for another year. We claimed the promises of God and set off to live the coming year one day at a time.

O God, give me an undivided heart, so that I may honor all that you are doing in my life.

JULY 13   A NEW LIFESTYLE

Lead a life worthy of the calling to which you have been called.   *—Ephesians 4:1 NRSV*

Patrick outlived all medical expectations. Rather than living for a few months, as doctors first predicted, each July brought another birthday. As Patrick grew so did my own family, with the birth of two daughters. They too were grafted into Patrick's extended family. When my friend Lorie and I had made our initial commitment to help each other care for a child with AIDS, we envisioned caring for one child for a limited life span. Instead, her once-quiet home now buzzed with the noise and needs of her two sons, as did mine from my two lively daughters. What we thought was a short-term ministry led us into a new lifestyle full of children. Isn't that often God's way? We step forth thinking that we'll care for this one need and then go back to our "normal" lives. Before we know it, reaching out in new ways has become a lifestyle.

Give me the energy and strength for this day, God, to live a lifestyle of caring toward others.

JULY 14   LIVING WITH RISKS

The apostles said to the Lord, "Increase our faith!"
—Luke 17:5 NRSV

One day while visiting my mother-in-law, I told a story about Patrick's recent birthday party.

"What about your girls?" she asked, looking at my daughters. "What if they are exposed to the AIDS virus while you are helping Patrick? Isn't their safety your top concern?"

Her words were laden with honest fear. To answer her, I described the precautions we took: the latex gloves donned for changing Patrick's diapers or caring for cuts; the special biohazard bins for disposing of items that might have come in contact with body fluids. His intravenous treatments were administered through a tube that had been surgically placed in his stomach.

Yet my mother-in-law held firm, "But they play together. They touch the same toys. Precautions don't take away all the risk."

The fact remained: Yes, there were some risks—extremely slight ones for my daughters, large ones for Patrick. A common cold germ passed from us could be lethal for him. Yes, loving Patrick held some risks. But isn't love always risky? I wanted my girls to know and remember a boy named Patrick. He wasn't a hothouse plant, nor was he a leper to be shunned. He was a fun kid who loved parks and toys and playmates. I wanted my kids to grow up knowing that faith without risks is no faith at all.

God, give me the courage to love and the faith to believe that you are with me.

JULY 15   ASKING FOR HELP

If in my name you ask me for anything, I will do it.
—John 14:14 NRSV

The energy in Lorie's home both enlivened and exhausted me. And still she needed more help. I started feeling guilty when too many days passed between visits. I despaired at my own lack of availability. I also knew that a cross-country move might be ahead for my family. What would Lorie do? What about my commitment to her? Only then did I pray. And God reminded me, "You have not because you ask not."

Not long after that I preached at a church in our city where I described Lorie and her foster sons. After the service a woman handed me a business card to pass on to Lorie. Within days, Theda, a nurse with a commitment to medically fragile babies, became like the boys' second mother. When Patrick was hospitalized, as he was many times, Theda was on call, day or night, to care for Cornelio. Theda, so well suited for the task, arrived just at the right moment. It was what some would call a "Godincidence"—a coincidence that shows us God's invisible fingerprints are everywhere.

I come before you in faith today, God, to ask for what I need.

As a mother comforts her child,
so I will comfort you.
—Isaiah 66:13 NRSV

My godson, Patrick, spent much of his third winter in the hospital. One night the phone rang in the wee hours. Lorie was terrified that Patrick would die that night. The infection he was battling had resisted all treatments. Lorie was asking his loved ones to gather around his bed.

But I couldn't go. I was torn in two. My own infant daughter had a cold and needed me. I certainly couldn't take her into the intensive care unit. So my husband, Michael, went to the hospital in my stead.

For hours Patrick teetered on the edge of life and death. All who were there that night agreed that Lorie's fierce love, her urgent calls, "Fight, Patrick. Hold on, baby. Mama's here," were what willed him back to life that night.

When I first met Patrick, he was an abandoned child who didn't seem to have the will even to whimper. Now he fought hard for his life. He knew that someone loved him, and so he gave his all and struggled back into life.

Perhaps God is revealed to us in the ways we can most readily understand and at the point of our most basic need. When we suffer, God comes to us as what we need—a loving mother who gives us the will to hold on.

Let me know, O God, that you will meet me at the point of my most basic need today.

JULY 17   GIVING AND RECEIVING LOVE

Thanks be to God for his indescribable gift!
—2 Corinthians 9:15 NRSV

One Christmas morning, I opened piles of presents, many of them sent for my daughter's first Christmas. The tag on one special present for me read, "To Mommy—Love, Rachel." The writing and wrapping were unmistakably my husband's. I was glad that Michael had expressed what Rachel was unable to say. The morning was peaceful and picture-perfect. But my friend Lorie kept coming to mind. I had two families, I felt, my own and Lorie's. I'd committed myself to help her, since she was the sole parent to her two foster sons. That afternoon I drove to the hospital where the corridors were empty and the staff cheerless. I peeked into the room and saw Lorie bent over Patrick's bed, entertaining him with his wooden trains, just as she always did, hour after hour, while he was hospitalized.

When she looked up, relief spread across her face. My heart soared at Patrick's unrestrained joy when he opened the new truck book I had brought. Then I handed another package from my bag to Lorie. The card read, "This is from your boys to their mother—Merry Christmas." Her eyes overflowed with tears. This mom who gave everything she had to give, day after day, also needed to receive. She had shouldered the impossible job of loving a special child, knowing that she would lose him all too soon. I sat down and gazed at this child, born to suffering, whose love was pure and deep. That Christmas, God's love again broke through, this time in a city hospital.

Thank you, God, for giving me so many good gifts as reminders of your lasting love for me.

JULY 18   FACING THE FUTURE—WITH LOVE

Father, if you are willing, remove this cup from me; yet, not my will but yours be done.   *—Luke 22:42 NRSV*

Patrick's brush with death forced me to admit that his illness would soon take him from us. Somehow we had to continue to pray for a miracle while simultaneously accepting the medical realities that the HIV was weakening his defenses.

186

Early one blustery day, I met Lorie and Theda, Patrick's "second" mom, at a local coffee shop to talk about the impossible subject that loomed before us: How should Patrick's last days be lived?

Lorie had thought a lot about the subject. She wanted him to die at home, if possible. He hated the hospital and longed to be home with his toys, playing on his favorite spot on the couch.

With tears, and with fears that we were hindering the miracle we so fervently wanted, we set forth a plan to let him be surrounded by many friends and loved ones every day of his life.

Lorie closed her eyes. "Sometimes, I can imagine Patrick running free through the fields of heaven," she said.

More than anything she wanted him to have that freedom here and now. But she had to trust that, one day, all would be well again for Patrick. We all knew what we wanted. But again we placed the future of this young boy in God's hands.

God, help me to pray, "Not my will but yours be done today."

JULY 19   REMAINING IN TOUCH

I am with you always, to the end of the age.
                        —Matthew 28:20b NRSV

Lorie and I were spending a glorious afternoon in Golden Gate Park. As our kids fed the ducks, I mustered my courage and told her that my husband and I were considering a move to the East. Her face showed sadness, yet the dread I had felt did not return. I'd promised to be there for her while she was the foster parent to her two boys. Four years had now passed. She had adopted Cornelio, and Patrick had miraculously lived beyond our initial hopes. It appeared that my family's path was moving us elsewhere.

"I understand," she said. "But I don't know what I'll do without you."

I promised that wherever I lived, whatever the circum-

187

stance, we'd remain in touch. "When Patrick's time to leave us arrives," I told her, "I'll be there." Though separated by distance, we'd have to trust God to keep us close.

God, when friends are far away, help me to rely on your abiding presence with me.

JULY 20   MAKING HARD CHOICES

*Trust in the LORD with all your heart,
and do not rely on your own insight.
In all your ways acknowledge him,
and he will make straight your paths.*
                                    —Proverbs 3:5-6 NRSV

Patrick's health was up and down during the fourth year of his life. Local doctors suggested that he participate in the tests of a new drug that had promising preliminary results. His mom had to decide—should she take the risk of possible unknown side effects, based on the doctors' educated guesses that this drug would prolong his life? If he were given the drug, he would need to fly cross-country periodically to be monitored by the government researchers. What would she do with Cornelio while she traveled? What if the drug made him worse?

Lorie knew she held Patrick's life in her hands. She talked to other doctors, to parents of other children with HIV/AIDS, and she sought godly counsel. She did research. And she prayed to discern God's best for Patrick. Using the tools she'd been given, she chose to go ahead with the treatment.

God, teach me to discern your ways. Help me to listen to you as I face what seem to be impossible decisions.

JULY 21   NO SEPARATION

It is right for me to think this way about all of you, because you hold me in your heart.   *—Philippians 1:7 NRSV*

188

After our family had moved to the East, we planned an out-of-town weekend trip and discovered that our friend Lorie and her two sons would be in the same city at the same time. They were traveling east so that medical researchers could monitor the effects of the new AIDS drug Patrick was taking. Our itineraries would overlap only by hours, so we met in the airport. My husband and I pushed our kids in strollers down the long corridors on the way to their gate. *Would the boys remember us after a year's separation?* we wondered.

We spotted them just as Cornelio spotted us. He put his head down and exuberantly charged toward us. He threw himself into my husband's arms, burying his face in his neck, and wouldn't let go. As my husband carried the long, lanky four-year-old back to his mother, I said, "We weren't sure if the boys would remember us." Lorie replied, "We talk about you all the time. I don't think he realizes he hasn't seen you for a while."

Neither distance nor time need sever the heartfelt connections between God's family members.

God, today I bring before you those that I hold in my heart, both near and far, and ask you to keep us connected across the miles.

JULY 22   LOVE BROKE THROUGH

Love one another with mutual affection.
           —*Romans 12:10 NRSV*

The next summer, our family headed from our home in the East to visit our extended family and friends in the West. Patrick was back in the hospital, so one of the first things we did was to drive up the hill to the hospital with the beautiful view of San Francisco Bay. Our first child had been born in this same place. This time, though, we did not enter the hospital with joy. I knew this would be the last time I would see Patrick.

189

Patrick had failed noticeably. His voice was barely a whisper, and his smile was dulled by pain. My husband and daughters played in Patrick's room while his mom went with me downstairs for coffee. We caught up on each other's life, and I learned the latest details of Patrick's condition. The afternoon passed quickly.

As each of us in turn bade farewell, I bent down to say good-bye to Patrick, not knowing how much he would understand through his fatigue and pain. I looked in his soulful brown eyes and said, "I love you, Patrick. You're a champion." Just as with every other parting, Patrick played his part in the ritual. His eyes lit up from the inside. Then he smiled and rasped, *"Beso,"* and threw me a kiss. Even in his suffering, love broke through.

God, show me who needs to be loved today. Help me to know how to love as you have loved me.

JULY 23   DIVINELY CARED FOR

Where can I go from your spirit?
Or where can I flee from your presence?
If I ascend to heaven, you are there;
if I make my bed in Sheol, you are there.
　　　　　　　　　　　　—Psalm 139:7-8 NRSV

We were staying with relatives on the West Coast when the phone rang. Lorie was calling about Patrick. After a few days' respite at home, Patrick had been hospitalized again. As she stared grief in the face, Lorie wondered if God cared. God felt so absent. Then, she told me, Patrick had been placed in the very same room with the very same attending nurse he had had when, more than five years earlier, she had first met him and had been asked to become his foster mom. In all these years that had never happened before.

Several similar events seemed to show that Patrick's life

190

was coming full circle. No one could have scripted these events. They were what some call "Godincidence." In Lorie's great pain and confusion, God found a way to remind her that she and Patrick had been divinely cared for every step of the journey.

God, give me eyes to see your fingerprints in my life today. Help me to trust that you always care, even when I can't feel you.

JULY 24   COMING TO THE END

My grace is sufficient for you, for power is made perfect in weakness. ·   *—2 Corinthians 12:9 NRSV*

After our summer vacation, we returned to our home in the East. Not long after, my work took me out of town again. During a break, I retreated to a secluded patio, lost in my thoughts. Out of the blue, a voice—not audible, but clear—said four words: "Call Lorie—Patrick's birthday." *Oh, yes,* I remembered, *tomorrow is his sixth birthday!*

I went inside and dialed Lorie. When she answered, her voice betrayed tears. Watching Patrick lying motionless day after day, unable to communicate, was too much. For more than five years she had cared for this little one with AIDS as both mother and twenty-four-hour-a-day nurse. Never before had she said that she couldn't cope. This day she had said, "This is a nightmare. I've looked inside for strength. Always before I've found it. But now there isn't any more." She didn't want to see him die, Lorie told me, but she had no more strength to watch him suffer.

I paraphrased from Scripture what I trust to be true: "God promised not to give you more than you can handle."

God, thank you for keeping your promise to give only that which you give me strength enough to handle.

He will wipe every tear from their eyes. There will be no more death or mourning or crying or pain, for the old order of things has passed away.   *—Revelation 21:4 NIV*

The next day I returned to my hotel room. A pink note was taped to my door. I knew without reading the message what it would tell me—my godson, Patrick, was gone.

I dialed Lorie's phone number. That afternoon, she told me, on his sixth birthday, Patrick had begun to slip away. Lorie played some special music in preparation for his passing: *"Calling all angels. Walk me through this life."* Soon Patrick stopped breathing. His expression was without pain for the first time in weeks. He had traveled on in peace.

Since it was Patrick's birthday, friends arrived soon after, expecting cake and ice cream. Helium balloons were delivered and an unplanned party took place—a party celebrating Patrick's spirit, which finally was running free through the fields of heaven. He no longer needed his wheelchair, his IV pole, or his many medications.

When Lorie finished talking, I cradled the phone, left my hotel room, and went outside. To the brightest shining star in the heavens, I threw a good-bye kiss. Patrick's life had come full circle. This boy, born to suffering and sadness, had died peacefully on his sixth birthday knowing he was deeply loved.

Thank you, God, for surrounding me with love, even in times of sadness and confusion.

JULY 26   LOVED AND HEALED

Blessed are the merciful, for they will receive mercy.
                                   —Matthew 5:7 NRSV

At Patrick's funeral, I gave the eulogy. I tried to capture the radiance of his six years of life. But words were hardly necessary. His struggle to live with AIDS, his smiles, and his ease at expressing joy had touched all those he met. Over two hundred people, all of whom knew this child well, gathered to celebrate his life. As the service neared its close, Patrick's mom stood and struggled to speak.

"All of my life," Lorie said, "I've felt unworthy of love. The other day, I was in the shower, crying, missing Patrick so much, feeling unloved. Then I felt his presence and heard him say, 'Mama, I have loved you, really loved you. You can never say that you are unloved ever again. You can't fall back on that excuse. I love you.'"

People often had told Lorie she was heroic for taking this child into her home, but she felt that she was the lucky one. Patrick had offered his love freely. And in loving and being loved, both had found healing.

Love heals, God. Free me to love and be loved each day of my life.

JULY 27   NO SECOND-GUESSING

No one has greater love than this, to lay down one's life for one's friends.   —John 15:13 NRSV

The evening after Patrick's funeral, friends gathered at his home, just as we had in previous years for his birthday parties. Kids dodged around the adults' legs, and pretzels ended up scattered across the floor. The apartment seemed larger. The intravenous drip pole and wheelchair were gone. Patrick's favorite place on the couch was empty. His trains were put away. We missed him.

In the hours after Patrick's burial, Lorie greeted guests and I wiped up spills. Soon my family would catch a plane for home. But then Lorie's son and my daughter ended up in the bathroom at the same time. There, separated by tired kids and a training potty, Lorie looked at me, her eyes clear. "You know," she said, "I never would have done this without you."

In that moment our eyes locked and nothing more needed to be said. Without my support, she wouldn't have chosen to become a foster mom to medically fragile kids. Without her, I never would have had the courage to commit myself to an unwanted child. Even on the day we buried the joy named Patrick, there was no second-guessing. We had pleaded for God to heal Patrick and leave him with us. God didn't. Yet in our deep sadness, we would not trade the days of suffering or the hours of sheer joy for easier years. We'd learned that *easy* isn't a synonym for *better*. Loving and caring, even in dire times, is best.

Do you have a job for me to do today, God? Show me, and give me the courage it takes to really love.

JULY 28   LOVE HAS MORE IN MIND

I pray that you may have the power to comprehend, with all the saints, what is the breadth and length and height and depth, and to know the love of Christ that surpasses knowledge, so that you may be filled with all the fullness of God.
                                        —Ephesians 3:18-19 NRSV

When Lorie and I had, with great idealism, opened our lives to Patrick, we thought we had something to offer a child in need. But after Patrick died, as I reflected on the past six years, I began to see that God's plan had more than Patrick's welfare in mind. God had been thinking of us too. Lorie's need to be loved was as great as Patrick's need for a loving mother. His smile and his perseverance through pain helped her to grab on to the present moment, rather than wait for some hoped-for future. My need to widen my definition of family, to broaden the group of people to whom I belong, was real too.

Loving Patrick wasn't just about helping a boy with AIDS. Love always has more in mind. The main benefit of giving is its effect on the giver. Because we followed that early

194

impulse to love a child in need, God imperceptibly stretched many hearts—including mine—to include the weak, the sick, the humble. I needed to love as much as Patrick needed someone to love and care for him.

God, today I give you my life anew. Use the hours of this day in ways that bring healing and hope to the world.

JULY 29   WE NEED EACH OTHER

Therefore confess your sins to one another, and pray for one another, so that you may be healed.   —*James 5:16 NRSV*

A physician was speaking about healing: "Patients with a high degree of connectedness fare better than those with little social support." Her words brought Patrick to mind. He had a committed mom, a sibling to love and fight with, and dozens of surrogate aunts, uncles, cousins, and church friends. Many medical workers cared about his well-being.

As a child born with full-blown AIDS, Patrick wasn't expected to live for six years. But the doctors based their views on the lack of appropriate drug treatments. They hadn't factored in the variable of the healing community. Isolation, fear, and a lack of hope are risk factors for health. Vital relationships, trust, and hope help keep us well. The Bible has been telling us this for centuries: We really do need each other.

I rejoice today in the people all around me, God. Give me a healing word to offer to another today.

JULY 30   A MYSTERY BOX

Now I know only in part; then I will know fully, even as I have been fully known. And now faith, hope, and love abide, these three; and the greatest of these is love.
                      —*1 Corinthians 13:12-13 NRSV*

I met a missionary once who told me she had a mystery box for unanswerable questions. Into this box she put her questions: Why did my husband die in the war? Why was I kept as a prisoner of war for so long? Why did I survive when others did not? Sometimes she wanted to take those questions back out of the mystery box and shout them at God. But she had lived long enough to know faith demanded a choice of her: Would she believe even when life's circumstances seemed to question God's power and compassion?

When Patrick died, I had to get a mystery box of my own. Why wasn't he healed? We certainly prayed and believed. Why hadn't he lived long enough to benefit from some new treatments that might have prolonged his life? Why would God allow a child to live his entire life combating a terrible disease? Why would God allow a deadly disease to pass from mother to child?

My list of questions is long. I want answers. But there are none that satisfy. So I choose to believe and trust that one day I will understand.

God, when I am baffled by life and my prayers seem to go unanswered, give me faith to believe that you are God and that is enough.

JULY 31 THE ALL-IMPORTANT QUESTION

Jesus said to her, "... Those who believe in me, even though they die, will live, and everyone who lives and believes in me will never die. Do you believe this?" —*John 11:25-26 NRSV*

Henri Nouwen, my husband's former seminary professor, came to dinner. He had left academics to work among the disabled and the suffering. Over our meal, we shared stories of those we had loved and lost to disease in the past decade.

In coming to grips with his losses, Nouwen had turned to the Bible. "In the Bible," he said, "people ask Jesus about all sorts of tragedies and calamities. Martha says to Jesus after

196

her brother dies, 'Lord, if you had been here, my brother would not have died.' She seems to be wondering why Jesus hadn't hurried to help." Nouwen went on to say that when people asked questions of Jesus, often they were asking from below—that is, from a perspective that means to bang on the door of heaven for answers. But Jesus' answers came to them, and come to us, from above—that is, from a panoramic perspective that allows for a different view of suffering and confusion.

Jesus didn't defend his time of arrival in Bethany. He made a declaration: "Those who believe in me, even though they die, will live, and everyone who lives and believes in me will never die. Do you believe this?" (John 11:25-26 NRSV).

While we bang on heaven's doors for answers, what we receive is an all-important question in reply: *Will you believe?*

God, help my unbelief. Today, I declare anew that I will follow your way.

August
Of Scars and Stars

Becky Durost Fish

AUGUST 1   **THE GOD WHO IS THERE**

Be strong and courageous. Do not be afraid or terrified because of them, for the LORD your God goes with you; he will never leave you nor forsake you. —Deuteronomy 31:6 NIV

*A*lthough our calendars say December is the last month of the year, August feels more like the end of the year to me. That's when many people go on vacation and make plans for the new school year. Most churches plan their Sunday school programs for September through August. Because I live in an area of the country with many retirees, August is when I notice more and more RVs being taken out of storage in preparation for a trip south for the winter.

I've found that August is a good time to reflect on where I've been, assess where I am now, and plan for the future. That process can be painful. Sometimes God gently reveals a scar from some past hurt that I haven't recognized before. I may discover a change I need to make in my life. At times, God's promises for the future seem too good to be true, and I find I'm reluctant to step out in faith. I can understand why Sarah was so unimpressed when she learned that God planned on her descendants outnumbering the stars!

Acknowledging pain from our past, confronting the difficulties of change, facing our fears about the future—all take strength and courage. But whether our concern is with the past, present, or future, we can be sure we are not alone. God makes that journey with us, and we will never be abandoned.

AUGUST 2   OF REUNIONS AND QUESTIONS

Anyone who comes to him [God] must believe that he exists and that he rewards those who earnestly seek him.
—Hebrews 11:6 NIV

There's nothing like spending time at a family reunion to remind me of where I've been.

Now that my family is scattered from Germany to Maine, Iowa, and Oregon, getting us all together at the same time can be a bit of a challenge. But this year we managed the impossible for the first time in five years.

Inevitably, much of the conversation involved reminiscing about growing up. My brother will never let me forget the tofu cutlets I inflicted on the family (I still like them!). My mother shivers at the memory of the spider eggs she discovered hatching in my bedroom while I was at school. (I wanted to know what those gray eggs were—and I'd carefully placed them in a jelly jar. Of course, the lid had holes in it so air could get in. . . . You can fill in the rest of the scene yourself.)

As I listened to the stories my family enjoyed telling about me for the benefit of my husband, I began to notice some themes. My family remembered me as constantly asking questions and trying new (my brother would say *weird*) things.

Though my family largely tolerated my questions over the years, other people sometimes found them disturbing. Rather than help me work through pain, they'd give pat answers intended to end conversations:

Why can't my friends' marriage be restored when they're both trying to save it? "There must be sin."

200

Why have these people been healed while my loved one is dying? "The ways of God are mysterious."

What do I do with my anger toward God? "You shouldn't be angry at God."

God, however, knows my pain and confusion. God never tires of my questions, never tells me to stop wrestling or to keep quiet. As I am honest with God in the darkest situations, eventually I see a glimmer of light. In that faint light stands Christ crucified—the ultimate proof of God's love for me—and his hands reach out for mine.

I probably will ask tough questions until the day I die, and many of them will go unanswered in this life. But no matter how painful or complicated my world becomes, nail-scarred hands will still grasp mine, reminding me of God's unfailing love.

AUGUST 3   OF PAIN AND PRESENCE

Our hope for you is firm, because we know that just as you share in our sufferings, so also you share in our comfort.
                              —2 Corinthians 1:7 NIV

When I was growing up, my dad used to take me along with him when he'd visit some of the older members of our church who were either confined to their homes or living in nursing homes. By watching him, I learned how to ask questions that would trigger fascinating stories about their lives, and I became comfortable holding the hands of people I barely knew.

When I started living on my own, I continued this tradition, often becoming involved in the nursing home ministry of whatever church I attended. One Sunday afternoon, our church was conducting a service at a local nursing home. I asked an aide about a woman who was sitting off by herself, and the aide explained that the woman was blind, couldn't talk, and was extremely hard of hearing. They doubted that she could hear the service, but they had brought her out because the family wanted her to have the opportunity.

Not knowing how I could help but being uncomfortable

with the thought of this woman being left by herself, I pulled up a stool beside her, reached over, and held her hand in both of mine. I gently stroked the back of her hand and looked up at her face. Sightless eyes stared blankly at the opposite wall. Suddenly, her hand squeezed mine. Tears filled her eyes and slipped down her gaunt cheeks. A smile crossed her face. By simply holding her hand, I was able to communicate that she was not alone, that she was loved.

Reasons other than physical impairment cause people not to hear. Pain can freeze souls, causing words of concern and comfort to ricochet off the hard surface. At times like these, we can offer others the gift of a hug, a warm squeeze of the hand, or the simple presence of someone who cares and will prayerfully walk with them through the hardships they endure.

AUGUST 4   OVERWHELMED?

We do not want you to be uninformed, brothers, about the hardships we suffered. . . . We were under great pressure, far beyond our ability to endure, so that we despaired even of life. Indeed, in our hearts we felt the sentence of death.
                                    —2 Corinthians 1:8-9 NIV

Overwhelmed. Despairing. Having difficulty facing another day. Have you ever felt like that?

The Bible is full of examples of people struggling with overwhelming pressures. From the psalmists to Elijah, from Jesus in the Garden of Gethsemane to Paul in today's passage—it's clear that life can be overwhelming.

When five friends and relatives died within three months, I was overwhelmed. I have friends with chronically ill children; other friends have three children under the age of five. All feel overwhelmed. A company downsizes—hundreds of families feel overwhelmed.

Obviously, when we are despairing, depressed, and having difficulty functioning, we should have a doctor examine us to make sure no physical problems are contributing to our emotional state. Counselors can help us sort out our options when life gets too complicated; they are essential if we become seriously depressed or suicidal. And our relationships with God and with other friends are essential during tough times.

But today, we need to remember that we live in a fallen world, that bad things do happen, that we share in Christ's sufferings. The resurrection will come, but that doesn't make the suffering hurt any less. Jesus himself felt abandoned. He cried from the cross, "My God, my God, why have you forsaken me?" (Matthew 27:46 NRSV). When we feel that cry echoing in our own hearts, we can have confidence that he is with us and understands our pain.

AUGUST 5   SCARS

But this happened that we might not rely on ourselves but on God, who raises the dead. He has delivered us from such a deadly peril, and he will deliver us.
                                          —*2 Corinthians 1:9-10 NIV*

I have some small scars under my lower lip. Few people notice them. I hardly notice them myself. Most of the scars resulted from a fall on ice, but one little scar is a reminder of the day I decided that I wasn't a little girl anymore.

I was about three years old, and my mother was busy in another part of the house. I decided I was going to be a big girl and help her by doing the dishes. So I dragged my little stool next to the kitchen sink and climbed up. Stretching forward on tiptoe to reach the faucet handles, I lost my balance. My feet flew out behind me and my lip landed on the edge of the cast-iron sink. That was the first of many lessons in learning to live within my limitations.

For generations, our society has valued self-reliance and independence. We solve our own problems and make our own way in this world. But God wants us to rely on him. When things are going well and our only problems are manageable, it's easy to say we're trusting God, but usually we're trusting our own abilities to handle things. It's when we are over-whelmed, when we no longer can manage the situations that confront us, when we are in deadly peril, that we discover what trusting God is all about. Although we may not see how he is going to do it, God promises that he will deliver us.

AUGUST 6   THE MYSTERY OF PRAYER

On him we have set our hope that he will continue to deliver us, as you help us by your prayers.
—2 Corinthians 1:10-11 NIV

For the third night in a row, I woke at 2:00 A.M. My mind was seething with vague but disturbing images of two friends. I was filled with apprehension and a conviction that they were in great danger. My friends were missionaries in an area of the world where many people hate American citizens almost as much as they hate Christians, so I knew they could be in danger. But I had no way of knowing whether my dreams reflected my underlying concern for them or a truly dangerous situation that they were facing.

As I had done the two previous nights, I sat in bed and prayed for my friends. "God," I said, "I don't know if your two children are in danger, but you do. If they are at risk, protect them and bring them to safety."

After that night, the dreams stopped and I almost forgot about them. Then I received a letter from my friends. During those nights I had been praying for them, they had been in grave danger. The husband had almost died. Then God had delivered them.

There are many things about prayer that are a mystery. We may not know how, but we do know that God works through the prayers of his children. Our faith is not simply a matter of our individual relationship with God. God works through the Christian community. Let's be faithful, then, both in praying for others and in asking for their prayers for us. Our lives may depend on it.

Are not five sparrows sold for two pennies? Yet not one of them is forgotten by God. Indeed, the very hairs of your head are all numbered. Don't be afraid; you are worth more than many sparrows. —*Luke 12:6-7 NIV*

Finances had been tight in our family for a while. Dad worked for the post office, and Mom took care of us four kids—including the two-year-old twins. There'd been surgery and major medical bills. We ate a lot of hot dogs, macaroni and cheese, and baked beans.

One Monday evening before supper, Dad made an unusual announcement. "Friday is payday, but we don't have enough money for the milk and eggs we'll need until then. We're going to pray that God will provide us with the food we need."

So we did. Monday and Tuesday passed. There were no answers. Then, just when we were finishing our last gallon of milk, a knock sounded at the door. A man from our church stood there, his arms full of grocery bags. "I don't know what came over me," he said sheepishly, "but when I stopped by the store, they were having a sale on milk and eggs, and I bought more than we could ever use before it goes bad. My wife suggested I bring the extra over here because she figured with the size of your family, you could always use milk and eggs."

Some people like to think that God is so big, he doesn't involve himself in the details of our lives. Jesus told us otherwise. Whatever you are facing—an event of great happiness, a time of sorrow, or an ordinary summer day—remember that the God who gave his Son for you is with you each step of the way. His love never fails.

AUGUST 8 OF BREAD AND CANDY

Your attitude should be the same as that of Christ Jesus:

Who, being in very nature God,
. . . made himself nothing,
taking the very nature of a servant.
—*Philippians 2:5-7 NIV*

Some of my favorite memories from childhood center on visits to my grandparents' farm in Maine, where they had lived since before my mom was born. There were lots of great places to hide and fun things to do on the farm.

Early each week, my grandmother filled her kitchen with the yeasty aromas of baking bread. When we were little, she'd give my older sister and me enough dough to make a loaf in a toy bread pan. Then one year she decided Vickie was old enough to make her own bread. Vickie spent hours mixing dough, kneading, shaping loaves, and baking.

I was bored—and a little jealous. So my grandmother let me make layer candy. All I had to do was measure and layer graham cracker crumbs, melted butter, chocolate chips, chopped walnuts, coconut, and sweetened condensed milk. It was easy, and did it taste good!

From my little-girl perspective, I had the better deal. With very little effort, I'd made candy that looked good and tasted fantastic. All Vickie's hard work had resulted in only four loaves of boring bread.

Time has certainly changed my views. Given the choice today, I'd take a homemade loaf of bread over layer candy every time. It's much more satisfying and better for me.

Maybe I'll find the same thing true when I reach heaven. It seems God has given me some things to do that are like making layer candy. Taking flowers to new neighbors or calling a sick friend, for instance, don't involve much of my time, look great, and are appreciated. Then there are other things that are more like bread baking—time consuming yet taken for granted: caring for my mother-in-law, for instance, or doing the laundry. They're a lot like the things a servant would do. Maybe that's why from God's perspective, they hold so much value.

In everything he [Amaziah] followed the example of his father Joash.   —2 Kings 14:3 NIV

I got my love of baseball from my grandfather Durost. Some of my earliest memories are of him leaning his crossed arms along the top of the refrigerator (he was over six feet tall), his chin resting on his wrists, listening intently to radio broadcasts of games at Fenway Park, home of the Red Sox. In spite of their failure to win a World Series since 1918, the Red Sox have been a constant source of entertainment for me.

Unfortunately, not everything that's handed down from generation to generation is positive. Even the best families have attitudes, behaviors, and sayings that can be destructive. When my grandfather died, my father and his seven brothers and sisters, along with their families, got together for a meal. As my aunts and uncles talked with my dad, they made a disturbing discovery. My grandfather had the habit of telling each one of them what they were doing wrong and what their siblings were doing right. He would praise his children behind their backs, but not to their faces.

This behavior had caused great pain for decades. In spite of their best efforts to treat their own children differently from the way their father had treated them, some family members found it very difficult to express approval directly to their children.

Every day we are passing on a heritage to our families and to generations yet to come. What behaviors and attitudes should we get rid of? What new traditions should we start?

AUGUST 10   FAMILY DIFFERENCES

Be completely humble and gentle; be patient, bearing with one another in love. Make every effort to keep the unity of the Spirit through the bond of peace.   —Ephesians 4:2-3 NIV

Although my family shares many traits, I sometimes think we have more differences than should be allowed. Thirteen years stretch between the oldest and youngest in the family. My older sister and younger brother are tall, but my younger sister and I both stand under 5'3". Two of us see the world in shades of gray while the other two see almost everything in black and white. Our professions include music, publishing, the military, and medical technology. We do not attend the same church or even belong to the same denomination; we belong to different political parties; and our addresses spread from Germany to Oregon. If the choice had been left to us, I doubt we would have chosen one another as friends.

But through no choice of ours, we all were born into the same family. And as we grew up together, we were forced to get along with one another. We learned to appreciate our differences. Today we truly love one another, and usually we manage to get along. If I hadn't been born into my family, I would have missed out on knowing three special individuals, not to mention their spouses and children.

It isn't an accident that God refers to the church as his family, or that today's verses instructing us to bear with one another precede a description of our different gifts. Usually, it's more comfortable to spend time with people who are like us, but God has other plans. He enriches our lives through brothers and sisters who are quite different from us, yet who are loved by the same Father and share the same name.

AUGUST 11   FINDING REST

And God blessed the seventh day and made it holy, because on it he rested from all the work of creating that he had done.
— Genesis 2:3 NIV

Most of my friends laugh at the idea of resting. Otherwise they'd cry. By the time they've taken care of kids, put in their hours at work, made a stab at fixing dinner and cleaning the house, and gone to church and community activities, they have just enough time to tumble into bed for too little sleep before the circus begins all over again.

I can sympathize. Although my husband and I don't have children, we've spent the past two and a half years being primary caregivers for his mother, maintaining her home and ours, and running a home business. We knew enough to cut back on our church responsibilities when we became responsible for Bruce's mom, but because her condition was deteriorating so slowly, we didn't notice how much added stress we continued to absorb.

This past year, her deterioration accelerated. Even though we were receiving support from home health care and other caregivers, our days off disappeared. There were extra meals to prepare, schedules to create, new medications to dispense, and changed behaviors to compensate for.

Then we went on vacation, leaving her in an excellent respite care facility. At first, we simply felt exhausted. Gradually, we relaxed. We noticed that we weren't as easily upset, that we were able to enjoy life again. Getting time away gave us perspective on our situation, and we realized that we needed to make changes. We're now in the process of putting Bruce's mom in a long-term-care facility where we can visit her, have her over for dinner, and continue to be part of her life, without having *constant* responsibility for her well-being.

There is work God wants us to do, but he designed our bodies to need rest on a regular basis. I was trying to carry my responsibilities seven days a week, and it was destroying me. If situations in your life prevent you from having one day a week when you can relax, what steps can you take to bring your life in balance again?

AUGUST 12   CALM AMID CHAOS

Be still, and know that I am God.   —*Psalm 46:10 NIV*

The first story I heard about Susannah Wesley (mother of Charles and John), captivated me. She lived in a small house with lots of children. Life was not always well ordered, and even when a day was going well, the household could hardly be described as tranquil. Susannah wanted time alone with God, but she couldn't get away from her family responsibilities. So periodically she would flip her apron over her head to create a quiet space where she could pray. I loved that image. It was so practical. It reminded me of friends who had young children and would lock themselves in the bathroom to get two minutes of solitude—even though the kids would stand outside the door, knocking and crying.

So often we imagine that when the Bible speaks of being quiet, it means we have to go off on a retreat, totally removing ourselves from the real world. Though retreats have their place, Psalm 46 suggests more involvement with real life. It talks about mountains falling into the sea, earthquakes, cities under attack, nations in uproar. It is in that context that we are told, "Be still, and know that I am God" (v. 10 NIV).

When the earthquakes of change throw our lives into upheaval, when chaos floods our souls, we are tempted to let ourselves be carried off. It is precisely at those times that God calls us to be still. Instead of reacting to people and events, we're encouraged to focus on who God is. When we are certain of his presence in our lives and are assured that he is our refuge, strength, and help, we can respond with peace—no matter what life brings.

AUGUST 13 WHAT REALLY MATTERS?

Therefore I tell you, do not worry about your life, what you will eat or drink; or about your body, what you will wear. Is not life more important than food, and the body more important than clothes? —*Matthew 6:25 NIV*

When we decided to put my mother-in-law in a long-term-care facility, a number of other challenges appeared. Her house needed to be sold. Friends and businesses needed to be notified. Decisions abounded: Which pharmacy should provide her medications? Which possessions should we keep and which should we sell? What was the best way to pay for her care? All this along with the normal responsibilities of work and life.

I was drowning in details, and when I'm drowning in details, I find it tough to do menu planning—much less get any perspective on life. But as my husband and I discussed the issues that were bombarding us, we recognized an important truth. Most of these decisions were not critical. No matter which pharmacy service we chose, Bruce's mother would receive excellent care. If we sold the wrong table, we could always get another one. And if we had to go through most of our financial resources to provide her the care she needed, at least our relationship would be intact.

Recognizing that our well-being and my mother-in-law's well-being were the important issues didn't remove all the stress. But it did help me keep things in perspective. I was able to focus my energies on the important things and relax about the other choices I faced. I even planned some meals.

Maybe you're facing some decisions today that seem overwhelming. Looking at them in light of what's important—what you really want to last—may help your perspective.

AUGUST 14   WORRYING OUR LIVES AWAY

Therefore do not worry about tomorrow, for tomorrow will worry about itself. Each day has enough trouble of its own.
—Matthew 6:34 NIV

Shortly after my maternal grandmother was diagnosed with breast cancer, I discovered a lump in my breast. I was eighteen years old. At first I didn't want to tell anyone because I was afraid of what might be discovered. I knew that having a maternal grandmother with breast cancer increased my chances of developing it myself. Was this lump the beginning of the end of my life?

For three months that lump was my secret. But every time I took a shower or brushed my hand against my breast, I felt that lump. Was I about to die? What would it be like to have a mastectomy? Would anyone marry a woman with only one breast?

Fifteen years later, another friend had a similar experience. She put off having her lump checked for a year because she was afraid that it might be cancerous. She envisioned her husband a widower and her children motherless. She even imagined what her funeral would be like.

The thought of cancer terrifies most of us, and that's perfectly understandable. But when we let worries about what might happen prevent us from dealing with the realities of today, we put ourselves at risk.

My friend and I were lucky. Neither of us had cancer. But if we had, our delays in seeking treatment might have cost us our lives. Is there a trouble in your life that you've avoided confronting because you're afraid of what might happen? Why not deal with that problem today?

AUGUST 15   DELAYED HARVEST

A man reaps what he sows. The one who sows to please his sinful nature, from that nature will reap destruction; the one who sows to please the Spirit, from the Spirit will reap eternal life. Let us not become weary in doing good, for at the proper time we will reap a harvest if we do not give up.
—Galatians 6:7-9 NIV

Last year, one of my friends planted some seed potatoes in an ideal spot in her garden. She watered and fertilized them. Looking out her window one day, she could see a faint tinge of green in the potato patch. She rushed to the garden to examine her little potato plants more closely. Her face fell. What she'd thought were potato plants proved to be weeds. No matter what she did, those potatoes refused to sprout. The rest of the garden was a huge success, but she missed tasting the indescribable sweetness of new potatoes.

212

This spring, her husband plowed the garden. My friend planted vegetables. When the first blush of green covered the soil, she ran down to see what had sprouted, fully expecting to find weeds. The green wasn't weeds. Nor was it the vegetables she had planted. Potato plants covered her garden. Apparently, when her husband plowed, the old seed potatoes had been cut up and scattered throughout the garden and somehow had gained a new lease on life. Now in August, it looks like a healthy crop of potatoes is in the works.

So often as we follow the Spirit's leading, we can't detect any results—and our society has taught us to expect immediate returns on our investments. But doing good, like gardening, takes patience. If we don't give up, we will reap a harvest, and the reward will more than repay our efforts.

AUGUST 16   OF WEEDS AND BEANS

No discipline seems pleasant at the time, but painful. Later on, however, it produces a harvest of righteousness and peace for those who have been trained by it. —*Hebrews 12:11 NIV*

My parents have always had a vegetable garden, and each of us four kids has had a turn at being chief weeder and bean picker. Whenever I think of my childhood summers, I remember weeding unending rows of bush beans while the sun seemed to burn right through my clothes. There was nothing romantic about weeding. I'd hunch over the bean plants, search with my fingers for the base of any weed, pull it out, and toss it in a bucket. Then I'd move on to the next few plants. By the time I was done, my back and thighs ached, my shoulders burned, and strings of hair were plastered down on my cheeks with sweat.

Picking beans wasn't much fun, either. The aesthetics of hearing beans snap away from their stems has always escaped me. I'll admit that a bowlful of green beans fresh from the garden looks beautiful and tastes even better, but it's easier to talk about the beauty of beans when you haven't had to pick them.

Though today there are no beans in my garden, I did learn one thing from those hot summer days: If you don't weed, you won't have many beans; and if you don't pick the beans, you won't have any to eat.

God does his own weeding and harvesting in our lives, but he lets us choose whether we will participate. The cost is backbreaking discipline and great struggle, but without such challenges, we will never experience the harvest of righteousness and peace we so long for.

AUGUST 17   WILDFIRE

Who can stand when he appears? For he will be like a refiner's fire.   —Malachi 3:2 NIV

The night sky glowed red. Five miles away, a wildfire surged forward, blown by strong southeast winds. It rolled rapidly over everything in its path, blazing a direct line toward town—toward our home.

My husband and I drove to a nearby spot where we were out of the way of firefighters but had a clearer view of what was happening. A raging mass of flames covered the horizon. Flashes reached out above the fire's horizon like solar flares every time a tall ponderosa or straggly juniper ignited. Although common sense told me that bulldozers and air tankers would bring the fire under control long before it reached town, I was cold with fear.

The next morning, we woke to find our cars covered with bits of burned pine needles and ash. Although it was a cloudless day, smoke hid the sun. The good news was that the fire had been brought under control. That knowledge didn't console the nineteen families who had no home to return to.

Just as the East Coast has its hurricane season and the Midwest its tornado season, the West has fire season. Recent fires have been more intense and destructive for many reasons: drought, pine beetle infestations, and more homes being built in wooded areas. But one of the most significant reasons is that for decades forest fires were totally suppressed. That action increased the fuel loads in the forests to unnatural levels. Instead of simply cleaning out unhealthy growth, fires now burn hot enough to sterilize the soil.

It's human nature to want to suppress wildfires. When seen in person, they are terrifying. It's also natural to want to avoid the hard things in life. But just as wildfires were designed to create a healthier forest, so also God uses the difficult experiences in our lives to purify us, to make us more like his Son. Will we let him bring good from the difficulties in our lives, or will we let the impurities in our lives build up until they destroy us?

AUGUST 18   RESURRECTION

Be glad, O people of Zion,
rejoice in the LORD your God,
for he has given you
the autumn rains in righteousness.
He sends you abundant showers,
both autumn and spring rains, as before. . . .
I will repay you for the years the locusts have eaten."
—Joel 2:23, 25 NIV

It's easy to trace a wildfire's path. Charred trees. Blackened chimneys standing guard over hollow foundations and twisted metal. What's not so easy to identify is any good that can come from a fire. Over time, however, the good appears. Some trees release their seeds only when exposed to the heat of a forest fire. Branches and trunks that fall into rivers provide the perfect habitat for some species of fish and slow the speed of the water, thereby decreasing erosion. Gradually, the forest recovers and is healthier for the stress it experienced.

I was thinking about that the time a friend described some

horrible experiences he had gone through. "I would never want to repeat those years in my life," he said, "but because of what I've gained both in my relationship with God and my understanding of myself, I wouldn't trade those years for anything."

He was quick to admit that such thoughts had never occurred to him when he was going through those personal fires. "I would have given anything to change my circumstances," he said. But he had no control over what other people were doing. All he could do was trust that God was with him and that eventually God would bring good from a situation that was clearly evil.

The situation changed. My friend looked at the blackened fragments of his life. There seemed to be no hope that anything positive could come from what had happened. And then God stepped in, and the process of redemption began.

Redemption leads us to heaven, but it involves so much more. What people intend for evil, God uses for good. You may be experiencing the fires of life right now. There may be nothing but a charred wilderness in front of you. Don't give up. God will redeem your life.

AUGUST 19   THE UNNOTICED DEVOTION

Devote yourselves to prayer, being watchful and thankful.
—Colossians 4:2 NIV

One of my college professors was a very practical woman, using her time efficiently and getting more tasks accomplished than seemed humanly possible. Her husband was a priest at a small church in New York City that ministered to poor families. They lived in a troubled neighborhood, and their home had been broken into twice. Stress was a daily part of their lives.

While I was visiting their home one evening, my professor's husband mentioned a convent on Long Island run by their denomination. Not aware that this denomination had convents, I asked him what the nuns did.

"They pray for the churches, priests, and families in our area, as well as for the church around the world," he explained.

"Do they do anything else?" I asked.

"No," my professor said crisply. "And it's always been a mystery to me why our church provides a living for people who don't do anything other than pray."

"Well, I know for me," her husband inserted gently, "there are times when the knowledge that someone is praying for me is all that gets me through the day."

I've thought about that conversation many times over the years. Obviously, the vast majority of us cannot devote ourselves exclusively to prayer, but that doesn't mean it's unimportant. Through prayer, we not only get to know God better, but we also play a part in God's mysterious and powerful ways, for God uses our prayers in the lives of others. Is there someone you need to pray for today?

AUGUST 20   FREE FALL

There is no one like the God of Jeshurun,
who rides on the heavens to help you
and on the clouds in his majesty.
The eternal God is your refuge,
and underneath are the everlasting arms.
—Deuteronomy 33:26-27 NIV

Trapeze artists amaze me. Hurtling through the air, trusting that someone or something else will be at the right place at the right time to catch them—these things are not my idea of a good time. I've wondered what it must feel like to spin through the air, stretch out my arms, and wait for the reassuring grip of hands and arms that will pull me to safety.

Then someone suggested that I might know exactly how it felt. Having never mastered the basic skill of doing a somersault above a trampoline, I was somewhat incredulous. I could relate to falling. Successfully defying the law of gravity was not part of my life experience.

In his book *Yearning,* M. Craig Barnes compares much of our faith experience to being a trapeze artist. We are spinning through life, there is no net underneath us, and we are hoping that God's strong arms will catch us before we are destroyed. Time and again, God proves himself. Yet that moment just before we feel his arms can be terrifying. We can't see God, and we don't know what he's doing.

I don't want to be suspended in air. I don't like unpredictable outcomes. But during those times when I'm surrounded by uncertainty, there is one thing I know: Whether I can see him or not, God is with me. His everlasting arms will not fail.

AUGUST 21　　　　　UNABLE TO SAY GOOD-BYE

Even though I walk
through the valley of the shadow of death,
I will fear no evil,
for you are with me.
—Psalm 23:4 NIV

My mother-in-law is dying. She's been in the hospital for four days. We visit her every day, hold her hands, stroke her face, talk to her—but whereas before she would at least squeeze our hands, now there is no response.

I sit in a chair by her bed and notice how the morning sun pouring in through the window touches her face, bringing into sharp relief the S-shaped curves of the wrinkles that flow over her cheek and down toward her ear. The artist in her would have loved those lines, would have used them as the foundation for a beautiful abstract painting. But it's been years since she's been able to hold a paintbrush, years since her mind has been able to conceptualize in that way.

For ten years, our family has watched Kay's mind slip

away. We've learned to appreciate the description another person gave of her own mother's dementia: "She was unable to say hello, and we were unable to say good-bye."

Now the time has come for Kay to leave, but still we wait. We're like a family seeing someone off at a small airport. Kay has gone through security, but her flight's been delayed. Although we still can see her through the translucent barrier, her thoughts are closed to us.

So we wait. And in the waiting we trust that her heavenly Father is walking with her where we cannot go, that his loving arms are providing the reassurance she needs as she makes that last step toward her final home where she will at last be whole.

AUGUST 22   WHEN WE CAN'T FOLLOW

I lift up my eyes to the hills—
where does my help come from?
My help comes from the LORD,
the Maker of heaven and earth. . . .
he will watch over your life;
the LORD will watch over your coming and going
both now and forevermore.
—Psalm 121:1-2, 7-8 NIV

It's Kay's eighth day in the hospital. The dementia that has taken her mind from us is now taking her body as well. Her brain can't coordinate her immune system, and pneumonia fills both her lungs. Antibiotics have failed to stem the inexorable progress of disease. She's getting medication and oxygen for comfort, but her breathing is very shallow. Though we've been told that she is functioning just above brain-stem level, it's agonizing to listen to the periodic outbursts of nonsense syllables that, during the last few months, have signaled anxiety or distress.

Holding her hand, I look out the windows toward the east and see the shadows of clouds racing across the distant line of purple buttes. My mind travels back fifteen years to my grandmother's funeral in Maine. After the committal service, my father, who with the loss of his mother had been made an orphan, looked across the cemetery toward Mars Hill and whispered, "I will lift up mine eyes unto the hills, from whence cometh my help[?]" (Psalm 121:1 KJV).

Now it is my husband who is about to be orphaned, and I carry his pain as my own. But my love cannot keep Bruce from feeling alone. And much as I grieve with him, how can I—with my parents, brother, and sisters all living—possibly comprehend the feelings of an only child about to lose his last parent?

There are places our loved ones travel where we cannot follow, journeys they must make on their own. When those times come, we can rest in the certainty that both our help and theirs come from the God who made the universe. We are never alone.

AUGUST 23   LIVING WITH HOPE

We would not have you ignorant . . . concerning those who are asleep, that you may not grieve as others do who have no hope.
—1 Thessalonians 4:13 RSV

After spending ten days in the hospital, Kay was released to the nursing home. That afternoon she rested comfortably in bed, and as evening approached, she simply stopped breathing.

Though Bruce and I have been grieving for over ten years as we have watched Kay gradually decline, we still are saddened by her death. Kay could be charming, and she was a gifted artist and musician. She enjoyed being with people and had a meaningful relationship with God.

Yet Kay's life also was defined by serious problems. She faced difficulties that outside of heaven she was unable to overcome. Her life was shadowed by an untreated anxiety disorder that darkened her friendships and created unnecessary conflict. Some of Kay's struggles were the result of her own poor choices; some were brought on by a combination of mental illness and increasing dementia that she could not control. During much of her life, she chose not to make good decisions, but by the end of her life she could not have made good choices if she had wanted to.

Kay's extreme confusion, anxiety, and anger are not the final statements on her life, however. Bruce and I can take comfort in the knowledge that through death she has been fully healed. In heaven, she is able to love God, her husband, and her friends in ways she was unable to do during life.

Because of our faith, we can look forward to the day when we will be reunited with Kay, when our tears will be wiped away, and when we will enjoy the relationship with Kay that God intended all along. This hope does not diminish our grief, but it does fill the future with meaning.

AUGUST 24   STORING TREASURE

Do not store up for yourselves treasures on earth, where moth and rust destroy, and where thieves break in and steal. But store up for yourselves treasures in heaven, where moth and rust do not destroy, and where thieves do not break in and steal. For where your treasure is, there your heart will be also.   —*Matthew 6:19-21 NIV*

Since Kay's death, Bruce and I have spent many evenings going through her things, deciding what to keep, what to give to others, what to throw away. As we've gone through this process, I've been struck by the things that were important to Kay but aren't so important to us. Kay had a wonderful collection of lifelike porcelain birds that she treasured. Although we appreciate the fine workmanship that went into creating these pieces, Bruce and I will give them to someone who likes porcelain figures more than we ever will.

This isn't the first time I've sorted through someone's belongings. Each time it makes me evaluate my life. So often what I treasure isn't as valuable to other people. Does this mean I shouldn't keep things that give me joy? Of course not. But it does mean I need to keep my possessions in perspective.

Ultimately, the things that last are the intangibles that build the kingdom of God: showing Christ's love to a person in pain, nurturing children who cross our paths, being an agent of redemption in a fallen world.

As I consider where I want my life to be headed, I need to ask myself, *Am I storing up treasure that will last?*

AUGUST 25   A NEW CHAPTER

"For I know the plans I have for you," declares the LORD, "plans to prosper you and not to harm you, plans to give you hope and a future."   —Jeremiah 29:11 NIV

In central Oregon, August is the hottest month of the year. We'll often have a couple of weeks with temperatures in excess of one hundred degrees. But usually toward the end of the month, a few days sneak in that are only in the seventies. Red begins to show on the leaves of the vine maple. Change is in the air.

As Bruce and I finish taking care of the details of Kay's death—notifying friends, selling her home, paying bills—I feel a similar change blowing through our lives. Much of our energy the past few years has been focused on helping Kay make the transition from life in this world to life in heaven. Now that responsibility has ended. We're beginning to think of the future in terms of our goals and dreams.

All of us can point to moments in our lives where such major transitions took place—moments such as marriage, a career change, children leaving home, or the loss of a spouse. Though they usually mark the end of a chapter in our lives and often are accompanied by pain, these transitions do not mean the end of life itself.

Developing new patterns in life, new relationships, new ways of doing things is challenging and can be a little scary.

222

But God's plans for our lives are full of opportunity and hope. The blank page of a new chapter lies open before us. Will we keep rereading the old chapter, or are we ready to embrace our future?

AUGUST 26   SURVIVING THE GOOD TIMES

[The Lord] took [Abram] outside and said, "Look up at the heavens and count the stars—if indeed you can count them." Then he said to him, "So shall your offspring be."
                                    —Genesis 15:5 NIV

Growing up in the densely populated Northeast, I never realized how many stars could be seen by the naked eye. Then I moved to the high-altitude desert of central Oregon. For the first time in my life, I *saw* the Milky Way. Watching for meteor showers in August—and actually seeing them—has become something of a tradition.

Now when I read about God's promise to Abram that his offspring would be as numerous as the stars, I can better picture what an incredible image that must have presented to that desert nomad who peered into the inky black, Middle Eastern sky.

Life had not been easy for Abram. He had left the city of his birth and the people he knew. He had survived a famine. His nephew Lot had left him on bad terms, and then Abram had rushed to rescue Lot when the younger man was taken captive during a war. Abram and his wife were not young, and they had no children. In the context of these struggles, God promised Abram the impossible: His offspring would outnumber the canopy of stars shining over him.

Believing God's promise took more than simply accepting that God could perform miracles. It meant that after years of discouragement and difficulty, Abram had to hope. He had to accept the promise of something good for what it was—a gift with no strings attached, no accompanying problems.

Sometimes it is more difficult to believe that things will get better than it is to tough out the hard times. We get used to expecting life to go from bad to worse, and when something appears to be going right, we wonder what the catch is, what will inevitably go wrong. When God brings stars of promise into our lives, do we have the courage to simply embrace them as his gift?

AUGUST 27 DETERMINING THE FUTURE

A generous man will himself be blessed,
for he shares his food with the poor.
—Proverbs 22:9 NIV

My grandfather is ninety-five years old. Although you'd never know it from talking with him, an eye disease prevents him from reading or seeing the birds he so easily identifies by their call. Both of his knees have been replaced, so he can no longer kneel down by the plants in his garden. The circle of people who knew him when he was a boy is shrinking. "I've reached the age where you go to more funerals than weddings," he once said to me.

In spite of these limitations, my grandfather has more zest for life than many twenty-year-olds I know. A farmer all his life, he doesn't let minor things like being legally blind and lame stop him from gardening. He will concede that it's better to have one of his sons-in-law rototill in the spring, but then the garden becomes his territory. He'll carve a row with a hoe, and then because he can't bend down to the soil, he'll sprinkle seeds down the hoe handle and press them in with the hoe blade. Sometimes he can't tell that a row has been planted, so he'll plant it again—Grandpa's salad rows, we call them.

When fall comes, he always has more food than he and my grandmother could ever eat, so he takes potatoes, carrots, turnips, and beets by the bushel to church for people who could use some food. Grandpa may depend on others for transportation, but he's never retired from his love of being able to help people in need.

224

Grandpa didn't learn to focus on life's possibilities when he turned ninety. It's a habit he developed in childhood, practiced as a young father during the depression, and developed into a fine art through mill closures and the loss of friends and family. If I'm going to be able to enjoy life in my senior years as my grandfather does now, I'd better start nurturing those same habits today.

AUGUST 28   REAL FANS

Therefore, since we are surrounded by such a great cloud of witnesses, let us throw off everything that hinders and the sin that so easily entangles, and let us run with perseverance the race marked out for us.   —Hebrews 12:1 NIV

One of my favorite things to do on a summer evening is go to a baseball game. Bend has been the home of minor league and professional baseball teams for years, and we can walk to the baseball park from our home. There's something about watching the sun set behind the Cascade Mountains, smelling hot dogs and french fries, and listening to the crack of a wooden bat making contact with a baseball that is eminently satisfying.

Two thousand years ago, baseball hadn't been invented, but the writer of Hebrews used a similar image—competitive games in an amphitheater—to describe the life of faith. There's one big difference between the crowds at a baseball game or at an ancient amphitheater and the crowds that surround us as we live out our lives. Most people watching athletic events have not been professional athletes themselves. They may understand quite a bit about the game they are watching, but they've never actually been in the same position as the players they are cheering on.

The witnesses referred to in Hebrews 12, however, are the people of faith—some well known, others anonymous—who are listed in the previous chapter. They know what it's like to make difficult choices, face seemingly impossible tasks, and obey God when the consequences appear to be grim. They've been where we are, and with all of heaven, they are rooting for us to keep going. When we're tempted to give up, it's good to remember that heaven is on our side. That's a home-field advantage that can't be beat.

AUGUST 29   FAITH THAT WORKS

If anyone considers himself religious and yet does not keep a tight rein on his tongue, he deceives himself and his religion is worthless. Religion that God our Father accepts as pure and faultless is this: to look after orphans and widows in their distress and to keep oneself from being polluted by the world.
                                                    —*James 1:26-27 NIV*

My grandfather was one of twelve children, eight of whom were girls. Four of those girls are still living, and three generations of nieces and nephews have referred to the family farm where they live as "the ant hill."

One of my great-aunts died in her twenties, but the others have lived long, industrious lives. Three were missionaries, two were homemakers, two helped run the farm, and one operated a number of nursing homes. They spent decades as independent, self-reliant women.

As the aunts got older, however, physical limitations set in. One by one, they fell prey to various illnesses: stroke, recurring malaria, crippling arthritis, disabling back pain, and dementia. Whenever a sister became ill, the other sisters gathered together to provide the nursing care that was needed. They set aside their independent ways and strong opinions so they could more effectively help the sister who was facing adversity.

I often think of my great-aunts when I hear bickering at church business meetings or when I notice people arguing endlessly about fine points of doctrine but never getting around to doing God's work. Correct teaching is important, but if it never results in godly action, it has failed. Christian brothers and sisters are in need. Can we set aside our arguments long enough to make sure that those who need our help receive it?

AUGUST 30 THE POWER OF SILENCE

Carry each other's burdens, and in this way you will fulfill the law of Christ. —*Galatians 6:2 NIV*

I've always loved words and loved to talk, so it's no surprise that my older sister was ecstatic every time I got laryngitis when we were growing up. The doctor would order me not to even whisper for at least seventy-two hours, and as soon as we left his office, the teasing would begin.

Vickie would try everything in her power to get me to talk. She'd embarrass me, tease me about boys I didn't like, pretend she couldn't understand my hand signals—all, of course, while my parents were out of earshot. To be fair, I must admit that I wasn't defenseless. Over the course of our childhood, I did plenty of things to exasperate Vickie.

Frustrating as it was for me not to be able to talk, the experience gave me my first lessons in listening. I noticed that I was picking up on nuances of conversation that I'd missed before; and when I wasn't able to rush in with answers, my friends were more likely to tell me how they really felt about situations.

Did a few cases of laryngitis transform me from an inveterate talker to the world's greatest listener? No. I still need to remind myself to talk less and listen more. But I am learning that an important part of bearing my friends' cares is to let them unburden their hearts. I'm more helpful when I simply listen than when I rush in with answers that may not even address the real problem.

All of us need to be heard. Is there someone in your life who needs your listening ears today?

I always pray with joy because of your partnership in the gospel from the first day until now, being confident of this, that he who began a good work in you will carry it on to completion until the day of Christ Jesus.
                                        —Philippians 1:4-6 NIV

It was 6:00 A.M.—not my favorite time of day—but that late August morning it didn't matter. I was bicycling through the early morning quiet to my friend Sue's house. The sounds we made as we carried her kayak down to the river carried through the humid air. It wasn't hot yet, but we knew the day would be a typical warm and muggy day in northern Connecticut.

The kayak slipped easily into the water from the grassy bank, and we dipped our oars through the river's smooth surface. Mist hung around us, obscuring the opposite bank, but we barely noticed. For thirteen years, ever since we had first caught the bus to kindergarten together, we had been best friends.

Now our relationship was about to change. Later that day, I was leaving for college. Sue would be staying at home, building a career in insurance. Our futures were as indefinite as the vague outlines of the shore we were leaving. And we realized that as close as our friendship had been, inevitably it would change. We didn't say much to each other that morning. We didn't need to.

I still have the Bible Sue gave me in which she inscribed the verses from today's reading. They comforted us then and continue to give me confidence today. No matter what scars we may carry from our past, or what challenges of faith lie in our future, God will be with us. He continues to work in our lives, and he won't give up until our journey is complete.

September
God at Work
Debra K. Klingsporn

SEPTEMBER 1   BACK TO SCHOOL

September 1: the first of the month. Something about turning the calendar page from August to September brings a halt to summer's carefree spirit—and like an automatic alarm—back-to-school mentality kicks in.

Never mind that I'm over forty and haven't been to school in years. September marks a radical change. It's time to get *serious*—about the clutter control I put off until fall; about the piles of books and projects I've amassed on my desk; about the most sobering of all realizations: pulling on jeans I haven't worn since last spring and—ugh—ten unwanted pounds have returned.

The hot, humid days of August don't change in perfect timing with the flip of a calendar page, but something within me does. September is synonymous with get busy. It's the month to "get back on program." Exercise more, eat healthier, be more intentional about prayer and reflection, be more serious about what really matters. The back-to-school mentality is contagious.

But do we have to be more serious? Is it really up to us?

Paul says that the One "who began a good work in you will

bring it to completion" (Philippians 1:6 RSV). The source of what really matters isn't found in our efforts. God the Creator is at work within us. What an awesome thought. What a humbling truth. What an incredible gift. Say the words out loud; say them slowly: *God the Creator is at work within me.* Something far more grace-filled than a "back-to-school mentality" is determining who we are becoming.

God is at work within us. The time we spend in prayer, reflection, and study is merely a way to cooperate in the process; the results are due to God's action in our lives, not to our efforts at self-improvement.

SEPTEMBER 2　　　　　　　　　　CHANGING SEASONS

"Can you believe it's already September?"

So the question goes. In the grocery checkout line, at the beginning of a meeting, in hallways at the office. Can it really be September . . . already?

Where I live, September brings warm days and cool nights, trees with splashes of yellow beginning to overtake the green, mums and pumpkins sitting on front porch steps. But if I close my eyes, blinding myself to the telltale signs of autumn, I wouldn't know it's no longer summer. The sun is warm on my face. The grass is lush and green—and begs for bare feet. Dragonflies flirt with the flowers and bask in the September sun.

Autumn comes quickly here in Minnesota—subtly, but quickly. By the end of August, we're already opening our closets and reaching for jackets. A simple change in weather patterns brings a radical change in wardrobe. One day we're wearing shorts and T-shirts. The next morning we're scrambling to find sweaters, jeans, and jackets.

We reluctantly surrender summer. Change is not something we readily embrace. In fact, change often is something we actively resist. Yet growth doesn't happen without change. Through the changing seasons, nature renews itself, and growth silently, slowly transforms the world around us.

Change always precedes growth—for humans as well as for trees. We open ourselves to new beginnings only by opening ourselves to change.

SEPTEMBER 3   THE WORD OF GRACE

My first-grade daughter is learning to read. She's been writing letters of the alphabet since preschool, but the letters had no meaning for her. Now she's beginning to learn how words are formed from the lines and arcs that shape the letters, and in so doing, she's discovering the wonder of leaving behind a message even after she's walked away.

She taped one of her first love notes, written in the proud lettering of a six-year-old's misshapened handwriting, to the top of my computer where I couldn't miss it—and it probably won't be removed until she goes away to college (if then).

God wanted to leave us a love note we wouldn't miss. He tried the miraculous to keep us mindful of his love, but we didn't get it. He tried rainbows and angels, burning bushes and parting waters, but we didn't get it. We saw the signs but missed the message. God is nothing if not persistent.

In the great wonder of words left behind long after the messenger is gone, God gave us a love note that doesn't go away. He gave us the Incarnation: the life, death, and resurrection of Jesus Christ.

God wanted to get our attention. And it worked. Not only Christ's followers took note, but history itself was redirected. Now we come into each day as a six-year-old learning to read. We can see the lines and arcs that form the Word of God, but we miss the meaning. Or we can listen for the message, the word of grace that daily transforms, renews, sustains:

> Because you are precious in my sight,
> and honored, and I love you, . . .
> Do not fear, for I am with you.
> —Isaiah 43:4-5 NRSV

231

I have the best of intentions. Each day I set out to seek a few moments of quiet, a time apart for prayer, reading my Bible, seeking God's presence. Yet my journal reveals otherwise. Gaps of days and even weeks between entries provide evidence of time gone by without a moment captured to be still, to come into the Presence.

Busy movement determines my day. As I move from one load of laundry, to a phone call, to a repairman, to yet another distraction, my day dissipates into a seamless pattern of activity. When I do finally sit down in the quiet of a sun-room warmed with oak and wicker and the golden sunlight of September, I am easily distracted as thoughts of the many things I have to do dance through my mind.

I'm not alone. Teresa of Avila, a contemplative and mystic sixteenth-century nun, whose writings are considered among the classics of spirituality, wrote:

> Over a period of several years, I was more occupied in wishing my hour of prayer were over, and in listening for the clock to strike, than in thinking of things that were good. . . . When I was enjoying worldly pleasures, I felt sorrow when I remembered what I owed to God; when I was with God, I grew restless because of worldly affections. (As quoted in Avery Brooke, *Finding God in the World* [San Francisco: Harper & Row, 1989], pp. 55–56.)

And Teresa was a saint! In her honesty, I find both comfort and hope. She shows me, first, that even the saints weren't always saintly, and second, that our piety isn't as important as our perseverance.

Even Jesus struggled to find time apart. What we offer to God is not a slice of our schedule, but our whole self: our day, our duties, our busyness—our heart and soul. On the days we fail to find time apart, when quiet moments are elusive despite our best intentions, we still live, work, and have our being in the grace of the One who began a good work in us.

A Saturday morning. The day lies before me. What will I do with this first Saturday of the month? Errands? Shopping? Chores?

In Minnesota, September is the month when winter preparations begin: putting up storm windows, cleaning out gutters, raking leaves, getting the furnace checked out.

Against the backdrop of chores and responsibilities that have to be taken care of before the snow flies is the panorama of a captivating season—the most alluring season of Minnesota. The colors are vibrant, the smells are woodsy, the textures of each day are rich with autumn's fullness. September beckons: drives in the country, walks in the woods, or one last picnic in the park before winter turns outings into occasions for down jackets and long underwear.

Duties, tasks, and responsibilities so easily take priority. Lists of things we need to do fill our minds if not our days. We can attend to the immediate and miss the most important.

On the road to Emmaus, the disciples were attending to responsibilities, taking care of what needed to be done. The risen Christ came alongside them, walked with them, listened to their concerns—and they were so preoccupied that they didn't recognize him. They were concerned with the immediate and almost missed the important: Christ in their midst.

No matter what our responsibilities dictate, we miss the most important if we fail to recognize the kingdom of God present within the sights, sounds, and smells of this day—the gift of life in this moment.

Perhaps today Jesus is calling us away from duties and tasks, responsibilities and preparations. Perhaps the errands and gutters and storm windows can wait. Listen to the sounds of the season and embrace that which calls you—the drive, the walk, the picnic in the park. Fill your heart and soul with the gift of this moment, and in so doing, come back to the preparations and responsibilities with a grateful heart.

SEPTEMBER 6   FACING UNCERTAINTIES

On Sundays I look at sections of the newspaper that I never glance at any other day of the week, including the employment listings. In every Sunday paper I see the words "bright, responsible, creative self-starters." As I read them, I wonder about the individuals looking through those listings who've lost their jobs or who can't find one. Whether we face unemployment, illness, financial struggles, or some other difficult circumstance, change and loss can be challenging at best—overwhelming at worst.

When Paul wrote to the Philippians, he had every reason to be fearful, discouraged, and overwhelmed. He was in prison—again—wondering, *Will I ever see my friends at Philippi again, or will this be the day of my execution?* Yet he wrote, "I know that through your prayers and the help of the Spirit of Jesus Christ this will turn out for my deliverance" (Philippians 1:19 NRSV).

How do we trust in deliverance when nothing seems certain? How do we trust in God's timing when a mortgage has to be paid and family responsibilities loom? How could Paul be so confident that "this will turn out for my deliverance"?

Paul's assurance relies on two underpinnings of faith. He writes, "I thank my God every time I remember you" (1:3). Our memories of God's care and keeping in the past can carry us through difficult times in the present. He didn't bring us this far to let us down now. The God of grace didn't abandon the Israelites in the wilderness. God won't abandon us in our wilderness.

The second source of Paul's confidence is found in the first phrase of verse 19: "through your prayers and the help of the Spirit of Jesus Christ."

When tensions are high and futures uncertain, when each day is stressful, exhausting, or overwhelming, let us remember that God has brought us to this place, and that Christ will see us through. From the wrenching experience of losing a job to the exhilarating promise of new opportunities, we are sustained by the Spirit of Jesus Christ in the present as we hold on to the remembrance of God's faithfulness in the past.

SEPTEMBER 7   A DAY OF REST?

Labor Day: special outings, cookouts, family gatherings. When I was a little girl, Labor Day meant fried chicken, potato salad, baked beans, Jell-O, and brownies. Not until I was in my thirties with two children of my own, did I realize how much *work* holidays are.

I don't peel potatoes, chop celery, or boil eggs. My potato salad comes in those little plastic containers from a deli. I've never fried chicken (why work so hard to do something the Colonel does so well?). Yet even with concessions to readily available conveniences, family outings don't just happen. Someone puts time and effort into making holidays memorable—and we know who that someone is. As they say in the South, womenfolk. You and me.

For women, holidays are rarely a "day of rest." Even when preparations are being made for a day of play, preparations are still work. For many of us, Labor Day can be a day of "overtime," instead of a day of rest.

Yet Jesus says, "Come to me, all you that are weary and are carrying heavy burdens, and I will give you rest. . . . For my yoke is easy, and my burden is light" (Matthew 11:28-30 NRSV). Is this verse only for those doing "serious" work of the Lord, such as those who labor in food pantries or hospices? Or is there something in that verse for me? For us? For a day like today?

I find a clue for my day in the words *easy* and *light*. When my efforts are born of love, my spirit is easy and light. I look forward to the day's activities—even the necessary work of preparations. But when my spirit is heavy—when my feet are reluctant and feelings of resentment and fatigue are working overtime—the words of Jesus call me to step back, listen to my feelings, and question my efforts. If the day's plans aren't something I look forward to, perhaps I need to rearrange the plans, not my feelings. When we open our hearts to God's leading, plans and preparations may go out the window as we allow an adventure to begin.

SEPTEMBER 8   TREASURE HUNTS

We're a family of treasure hunters. We began the practice in the days of strollers and holding hands and toddlers' steps, but my daughter's love for this family ritual is at least a third-generation tradition. Even before they could walk, we'd pick up rocks and leaves and twigs and feathers and bits of bark. No matter what part of the country we're in, we find treasures: acorns and sumac, cotton bolls and shells, rocks and birds' nests. We no longer rely on pockets; plastic bags now accompany our treasure hunts.

Once we pulled over to the side of a dusty, hot Texas farm road to pick a cotton boll in full bloom. Another time we paid an outrageous sum to ship autumn leaves overnight to "Granny B" so she could share the wonder of our September treasures: crimson of maples, gold of birch, burnished rust of oaks. My daughters took great care arranging the leaves in a Federal Express envelope, and from Minnesota to Texas, autumn leaves flew.

A single red maple leaf is taped to my computer table with a post-it note saying, "You needed this today. I love you." That solitary leaf joins a growing collection that appears on my desk throughout the year as the seasons change. From dandelions in May to maple leaves in September, the treasures change. But the message is the same: *I love you. I saw beauty in the world and thought of you. I wanted to share this with you.*

As summer's warmth is overtaken by autumn's chill, the season's changing splendor is a treasure, a message to each of us when we pause to look. Not subtly, not gently, but with a riot of color God says, "I love you. I created this world for you. Winter will come. Cold and darkness will enfold you. But I am as faithful as the seasons. I am with you."

SEPTEMBER 9   REDEMPTION 101

"MOM! I messed up! I'm going to have to start all over again," came the cry of despair from the other room.

"Bring it here," I said. "Let's look at it together and see what you can do with it."

I looked at the drawing, an earnest effort at a first-grade homework assignment—one being taken *very* seriously.

"Well, you're right. You did mess up," I replied, "but you don't have to start over. You can change your idea a little and just draw around the goof. Work what you think is the 'goof' into your picture. Did you know Grandma K makes a goof on purpose in every quilt she makes?"

"She does? Why? Are you telling me this just to make me feel better?" she asked, skeptical that a grown-up would intentionally mess up.

"No. It's a quilter's tradition. Every quilt is made with an imperfection, sometimes known only to the quilter. It's a way of acknowledging that we're all imperfect and that God uses us in spite of our imperfections—just like quilters use each scrap of fabric in spite of its imperfections. In fact, most famous artists make big goofs in their paintings and just paint over the mistakes."

"Cool!" came the incredulous response. And with that, she was off to complete her homework.

Redemption 101, I thought. Her teacher gave her an assignment. God gave her a teachable moment. No matter what goofs we bring to God, he simply works them into the fabric of our lives. Nothing is beyond God's power to redeem. What a simple concept. What an incredible gift.

SEPTEMBER 10   EARLY-MORNING WHISPERS

I love getting up before daylight breaks and having my first cup of coffee in the gentle light of early-morning darkness. September mornings in Minnesota are always cool, if not downright chilly. The morning air and awakening sky inevitably lure me outside, and I find myself sitting on the front porch—the warmth of my coffee in direct contrast to the frost in the air. I watch a sleeping neighborhood slowly come to life. The lights in the house next door are always on before ours—a one-year-old baby is an early wake-up call. Darkness is broken as lights come on in first one house and then another. A new day is beginning.

"Timeless time . . . when being hangs suspended, unadorned by will or intention," wrote Thomas Merton of this moment, "the virgin point between darkness and light, between non-being and being . . . when creation in its innocence asks permission to be once again as it did on the first morning that ever was" (Patricia Hampl, *Virgin Time* [New York: Ballantine Books, 1992], p. 206).

I wonder what God's thoughts are in that space between morning and night, when the day is new and headlines have yet to be written. What does the Holy One whisper to those who speak his name in the early morning quiet?

In the timeless time between darkness and light come the words:

> Listen to me in silence. . . .
> For the windows of heaven are opened,
>   and the foundations of the earth tremble. . . .
> I have called you by name, you are mine. . . .
> Do not fear, for I am with you,
>   do not be afraid, for I am your God;
> I will strengthen you, I will help you,
>   I will uphold you.
>   —Isaiah 41:1; 24:18; 43:1; 41:10 NRSV

Holy moments come when we least expect them. Before the morning light breaks through the night and you hold the first cup of coffee in your hands, welcome the inbreaking of the holy. Listen to the gift of a new day.

I thought my days of homework were over—a high school diploma, a college degree, the rigors of my husband's Ph.D. I didn't realize I was only on leave. Then my daughters came of age—school age—and homework assignments reentered my life.

I hated homework the first go-round. Now it's worse. Now I watch my daughters struggle with subtraction, multiplication, and fractions, and I have to answer questions with cognitive thinking skills long since dormant.

Addition, subtraction, multiplication, division—basic math skills they have to practice, review, practice, review. Over and over. Again and again. These skills they will use the rest of their lives are not mastered in days, weeks, or months—they take time. I have forgotten how slowly the learning is accomplished.

I find myself wondering, *Is this the way God watches us struggle to learn life's basic lessons?* We begin with counting fingers and toes; we progress to more complicated versions of adding to, taking away. We grow through times of blessings multiplied and sorrows divided. We experience the fractionalization of multiple roles, demanding lives, and fragmented spirits. Again and again we revisit the same problems, the same issues, the same principles—only to relearn them in a new way. Over and over again we come back to the Master Teacher with our pencil and paper in hand—the eraser marks showing where we've tried unsuccessfully to solve the problem on our own. With the simplicity of a child we ask, "Lord, will you help me with this problem?"

Each time my daughters sit down with their addition or multiplication, they handle the problems with a little more proficiency. Every time we confront issues with which we wrestle, we see things differently. Theologian Frederick Buechner has said that faith is more of a process than a possession. Spiritual growth is not a process of learning and moving on; it's a process of learning and revisiting.

September brings an end to TV network reruns. 'Tis the season of premieres, pilots, and new episodes. As a writer, I often think about villains, the bad guys. I grew up watching Saturday morning cartoons and the early "good-guy, bad-guy" programming: *Sky King, The Lone Ranger, Lassie.* What story holds our attention without bad guys? "Barney" skips the bad guys, and his show loses most audiences over age five.

Think of the biblical story from the "good-guy, bad-guy" perspective. What if we reversed the plot development and suddenly all the foils became good guys? What if Eve had looked at the Tree of Knowledge, shrugged, thought, *Nah, I don't think so,* and walked away? What if Joseph's brothers had pampered and coddled their baby brother? Or what if Pharaoh had simply said, "Oh. You want to move across the continent? Well, why didn't you say so?"

The villain is usually the person we love to hate. But the truth is, within our souls are both heroine and villainess. No matter how we long to be women of God—righteous, gracious, fair, compassionate—we still lose our temper, disappoint and hurt those we love, or fail to be all we aspire to be.

If the biblical foils suddenly rewrote their parts, the biblical story wouldn't be *our* story. The biblical story is our story precisely because it records the comedy and tragedy of what it is to be human in relationship with God. But the plot takes a dramatic twist. Into the inner tension between hero and villain comes the unexpected development—the element of grace. No matter what the plot line of our lives looks like, the biblical story, God's story, is one of creation, redemption, and forgiveness. The grace of God continually rewrites the script of our lives.

SEPTEMBER 13   APPLES AND EVE

Apples are part of Minnesota just as tamales are part of Texas. Macintosh. Cortlands. Haralsons. Orchards dot the countryside, and September is the month to "pick your own." From apple pie to apple butter, apples are a symbol of early fall.

Biblically, apples have gotten a bum rap. Adam and Eve took an ill-fated bite of one tempting apple—and it was downhill from there. Had Eve given in to the temptation of a hot fudge sundae, *that* I could understand. But an apple?

Actually, there's no biblical evidence that the proverbial bite was made in an apple. The earliest texts simply say "fruit." What if the bum rap all these years was unfounded? An editorial whim of some scribe or biblical translator hundreds of years ago?

Well, if the apple got a bum rap, perhaps Eve did too. I grew up with the Sunday school version of the Temptation and the Fall—and Eve's unmitigated culpability. Granted, maybe she used poor judgment, but before that fateful decision, Eve was created in God's image—as we all are. What about Eve the woman instead of Eve the temptress?

In defense of Eve, consider a few of her strengths. She was a woman of action. She was willing to take a risk. The fact is, Eve wanted knowledge—and we're no different. We hate uncertainty. We think if we know enough, we can change it, fix it, control it, or improve it. But when it comes to faith and our understanding of God, knowledge isn't everything. Sandra Carey says, "Never mistake knowledge for wisdom. One helps you make a living; the other helps you make a life" (*She Said, She Said: Strong Words from Strong-minded Women*, ed. Gloria Adler [New York: Avon, 1995], p. 154). All Eve needed to do in the Garden was trust; she thought she needed to know. Eve made a mistake, one that we too make when we confuse knowledge with holiness. We can learn from her mistake.

SEPTEMBER 14   CRABBY, GROUCHY, GRUMBLY DAYS

Some Mondays are worse than others.

This morning my daughter couldn't find clean clothes to wear. All the laundry was still buried in laundry baskets. Homework, ignored in the excitement of Friday afternoon and forgotten over the weekend, was pulled out of back-packs, untouched, at 8:00 this morning. The class gerbil who spent the weekend with us went back to school with her cage in serious need of cleaning. (At least it was still alive—no small feat in our household!)

We oversleep, run out of gas, bounce a check, lose our keys. The aggravations may differ, but the result is the same: We feel grumpy and irritable for no good reason.

Some days Paul's encouragement to live life "in a manner worthy of the gospel of Christ" by doing "all things without [grumbling]" (Philippians 1:27; 2:14 NRSV) is less than encouraging. After a day like today, I find myself thinking, *Easy for him to say. He wasn't a mom!*

Nonetheless, I still wonder, *What does that mean for me?* How do I live my life in a manner worthy of the gospel of Christ? Does it mean I'm not to be crabby, grumpy, aggra-vated, or angry? If that's true, I'm in trouble.

Yet Paul himself wrote harsh words in many of the Epis-tles. He had his moments of aggravation and irritability with others in the Christian community. Paul was not superhu-man—and neither are we.

Living each day—even the crabby days—in a manner wor-thy of the gospel of Christ means living the "good news," ever mindful that we are loved, forgiven, redeemed. In the midst of aggravations and grumpy moods, we can turn our thoughts to "whatever is true, whatever is honorable, what-ever is just, whatever is pure, whatever is pleasing, whatever is commendable" (Philippians 4:8 NRSV). Bad days come and go. The good news is ever-present.

SEPTEMBER 15   BUS-STOP INTIMACY

Let your tenderness encircle everyone you meet.
—*Macrina Wiederkehr**

We have a friendship born of bus-stop intimacy. Weekday mornings we meet at the corner to see our kids off to school.

The school bus route has brought our lives to an intersection. Each morning we have a five-minute conversation, and I hear the latest in a year of tumultuous events: her mother's death, her father-in-law's terminal illness, her husband's estrangement from his family.

"This is Gethsemane," writer Vicki Covington says. "If you are past thirty-five, you're surely grieving something. If nothing else, you're simply grieving for the passing of time—for the swiftness with which your children are growing and changing . . . for the helplessness of knowing that tragedy can occur instantly, with no warning" (from a sermon by Vicki Covington, preached on Maundy Thursday 1996, at Vestavia Hills Baptist Church in Birmingham, Alabama).

Where is the word of grace for those who suffer and grieve? Where is the good news when sadness hovers? What can I offer to one whose load is so heavy?

At the intersections of our lives, when we realize God has chosen us to walk through Gethsemane with another, we need not lessen their pain—we need to *listen* to their pain. When Jesus asked the disciples to wait with him at Gethsemane, he didn't want them to change the events to come; he simply needed their presence.

We proclaim the good news of Christ when we do the listening and leave the healing to God.

---

*(Macrina Wiederkehr, *Seasons of Your Heart: Prayers and Reflections*, revised and expanded (Harper/San Francisco, 1991), p. 79.

SEPTEMBER 16   WHAT WE DON'T KNOW

"Mommy, I don't want to go to school today."

The special blanket was clutched tightly. Tears began a slow rise in her eyes. Her usual bravado was visibly absent.

"Well, love, going to school is not optional. You have to go, but is something going on at school that's troubling you?" I asked.

"Mommy, I miss my blanket and we don't get to have pajama days and I want to go back to kindergarten," came

243

her words tumbling out without a breath or pause as the tears began their descent.

She curled up in my lap like a kitten, hugging her blanket, longing for things to be the way they used to be—when she was in kindergarten. Just days ago, she excitedly played "school" in our family room for hours with her new school supplies. Reality differed from expectations, and reality had closed in.

As I wrapped my arms around her, I embraced her fears as well as her body, knowing we never outgrow those feelings. Our circumstances change, but our feelings don't. Unmet expectations, unnamed insecurities, and unspoken disappointments send us running to the nearest source of comfort and reassurance.

Holding my first grader, I couldn't tell her of all the excruciatingly wonderful discoveries she has yet to experience. She can't hear what she doesn't know. We are no different. We have trouble hearing what we don't know.

John Claypool says, "Despair is always presumptuous. We are housed in a universe full of mystery. We know some things, but we don't know everything. [God] is rarely obvious or predictable in how he works, but again and again, he takes the worst of times and does the best of things with them. If for no other reason, we have hope because of what we *do not* know" (a composite quote from "Good Luck, Bad Luck—Who Is to Say?" a sermon preached Sept. 10, 1989, and *Tracks of a Fellow Struggler* [Waco: Word Books, Key Word edition, 1974], p. 33).

SEPTEMBER 17   THE DIVINE PARADOX

Around 3:00 each afternoon I start getting restless. I find concentrating difficult as I watch the minutes on the clock creep slowly, more slowly than any other part of the day. The sixty minutes before a yellow school bus rumbles down our street bringing two little girls with blonde ponytails and stuffed backpacks home are the longest of the day.

"Mom, I'm hungry!"

"Mom, can I go over to Beba's house today?"

"Mom, we had a substitute today!"

"Mom, can I ride my bike over to Brian's?"

The questions and exclamations come tumbling out as back-packs are thrown aside and the quest for after-school snacks begins. Glimpses of their day come in rapid-fire clips as we engage in the staccato conversation of mothers and daughters.

The quiet of my day is shattered—and I welcome the chaotic moments of their return. I pour out my life for these two little people, and in so doing my heart is filled with the fullness they bring to my world. Their enthusiasm fills the house with energy. Their exuberance fills my day with joy. Their tears fill my heart with compassion.

"For those who want to save their life will lose it, and those who lose their life will . . . save it" (Luke 9:24 NRSV). As Christians, we live a paradox. In losing our life, we find it. In giving ourselves away, we gain everything. In letting go, we take hold. The Resurrection itself is the divine paradox—in saying "yes" to death, Christ said "yes" to life. "To sacrifice something is to make it holy by giving it away for love," writes Frederick Buechner (*Wishful Thinking* [San Francisco: Harper & Row, 1973], p. 29).

SEPTEMBER 18   LISTENING FOR THE
                               IMPERATIVES

As I read through the Gospels, I find it interesting that when Jesus is talking with an individual his words are almost always imperatives. "Follow me" (Matthew 4:19 NRSV); "Your sins are forgiven" (Matthew 9:2 NRSV); "Stand up, take your bed and go to your home" (Matthew 9:6 NRSV); "Daughter, your faith has made you well; go in peace" (Mark 5:34 NRSV); "Let the little children come to me" (Mark 10:14 NRSV), "Let anyone with ears to hear listen!" (Mark 4:23 NRSV).

Time and time again, if Jesus was not asking a question or telling a parable, he was speaking in imperatives—and, no

245

doubt, he had someone's attention. The person to whom he was speaking was *listening.*

Perhaps we underestimate the importance of listening—in our relationship with God, in our relationships with others, in our relationship with self.

"We are swept into the web of belief that action is always preferable to inaction, that doing is always preferable to being," writes theologian Phyllis Zagano. "[Yet] without prayerful inaction, we can never be sure when action is best; without prayerful being, we can never be sure when doing is called for" (*Woman to Woman: An Anthology of Women's Spiritualities* [Collegeville, Minn.: The Liturgical Press, 1993], p. 1).

Before we can hear the gentle imperative for our day, we first must enter into the stillness, into the cloister of prayerful "being" before determining what "doing" is truly the priority.

SEPTEMBER 19   CHESTNUT CRAB APPLES

Every September our annual outing to the apple orchard is a seasonal rite of passage as significant as birthday parties, valentines, pumpkins, and garlands.

We time our trip to coincide with the availability of our family favorite, chestnut crab apples, a hybrid relatively unknown outside the upper Midwest. Barely bigger than golf balls, chestnut crab apples are the orchard's best—in disguise. They aren't picture-perfect or shiny red. These diminutive apples actually are quite ugly: small, scabby, and usually discolored with brown spots.

But beneath an unappealing exterior is a treat for those who don't let appearance define preferences. The ugly little chestnut crab is as sweet as apples get right off the tree—an unexpected delight for those willing to let go of the polished apple's appeal.

During our annual quest this year, as I helped my daughter climb apple trees to look for the best picking, I found myself musing on my spiritual affinity with chestnut crab apples. I'd like to be a polished apple: shiny exterior, perfect shape, pleasing appearance. More often, I'm a chestnut crab: imperfect, less than I'd like to be, quite capable of being crabby. And when I inevitably compare myself to other polished apples, I often come up short in my evaluations. But the problem isn't in my imperfections. The problem is in my comparisons.

Comparisons between apples—or people—seldom serve a useful purpose. "We are all ugly, but we are all dear to God who has faith in us. Would [God] otherwise have taken the risk of calling into eternity—not for a passing moment—each one of us?" *(Meditations on a Theme* by Anthony of Sourozh, quoted in *A Guide to Prayer for All God's People,* eds. Rueben P. Job and Norman Shawchuck [Nashville: Upper Room Books, 1990], p. 109). We are created in God's image, and God pronounced his creation good. We can trust in the goodness of that creation. We can trust in the goodness of who we're created to be.

SEPTEMBER 20　　OF PRAYER AND HURRICANES

Eighteen years ago we unknowingly set our wedding date right smack in the middle of hurricane season on the Texas Gulf Coast. The possibility of a hurricane arriving as an uninvited guest never occurred to us. We were blissfully ignorant—until a friend of the family, a professional caterer on the Gulf Coast, asked my mother, "Why did they choose *that* date? I hope we don't have a hurricane that weekend!"

Her question opened Pandora's box of worries. Of all the things that could go wrong, I hadn't considered a hurricane—until then. I fretted. I prayed. I worried. I casually asked several florists, "Have you ever done a wedding when a hurricane hit?" Their answers did nothing to allay my fears. In fact, the horror stories were everything I feared—and worse—because on the Gulf Coast, hurricanes are not an "if" but a "when."

247

That September was no different. The weekend before our wedding, a hurricane blew in, bringing high winds and heavy rains—just the kind of weather every bride dreads. Yet the weekend of our wedding was one of South Texas's best: clear, sunny, and breezy.

Only years later did I question, *What about the weddings the weekend before ours? Were my prayers for perfect weather answered and theirs ignored? If prayer made no difference, why pray?*

Prayer did make a difference that weekend, although the difference wasn't in the headlines announced by local weather forecasters; the difference was within me. What matters is not *what* we pray, but *that* we pray.

We come to God not to control the forces of nature, but to calm the raging storms within. We lay the fears and worries of our lives before him and then pray beyond the particulars, allowing the peace of the Spirit to calm the flood of worries, fears, and concerns. "Do not worry about anything," Paul wrote to the Philippians, "but in everything by prayer and supplication with thanksgiving let your requests be made known to God. And the peace of God, which surpasses all understanding, will guard your hearts and your minds in Christ Jesus" (4:6-7 NRSV).

SEPTEMBER 21   A SPIRITUAL COMPANION

With both my daughters in school, I realize from a new perspective the significant influence that gifted teachers have on a child. My daughters are tutored, taught, challenged, questioned, and befriended each day as they tackle their assignments. They are open and eager—but their teacher is the one who guides them through the learning process, who "brings it to completion." Their teacher opens windows in their minds, turns on lights that dissipate confusion, and leads them down new pathways in problem solving.

At a time in my life when confusion reigned, direction was lacking, and the many books lining my bookshelf provided more torment than comfort, I read these lines by Avery Brooke: "My own prayers, which had made so many choices clear for me, were no longer of help, but I persisted. Day after day, I spoke to the God I could no longer hear. But the darkness remained impenetrable" (*Finding God in the World* [San Francisco: Harper & Row, 1989], p. 25).

Brooke's words easily could have come from my own journal. Her writing was a light in my darkness. As I read farther, she introduced me to a possibility I'd never considered, a rich tradition in Christian spirituality now being "rediscovered": the tradition of spiritual direction. According to Brooke, spiritual direction is helping someone build a relationship with God through prayer—not only through our spoken prayers, with their times of silence, but also through the "prayerful perceptions of life around us." I found myself longing for this kind of spiritual guidance, and I began to inquire about the tradition of spiritual direction.

Whether we call it spiritual direction, discipling, or mentoring, sometimes we need a teacher, a companion—someone to tutor, teach, challenge, question, and befriend us spiritually, much in the way that my daughters' teachers guide them educationally.

A spiritual companion is someone through whom God can open windows in our soul, offer wisdom to dissipate confusion, and lead us in new pathways of prayer. Listen to the longings of your heart, for often it is through the longings within that God leads us out of the impenetrable darkness.

SEPTEMBER 22   LOVING THOSE WHO SUFFER

I'm a mother. I pack school lunches, plan holiday activities, and drive through mud puddles in the middle of the road because I hear a playful plea from the backseat: "Mommy, can we go through it?" In fullness and joy, I feel profound gratitude for the blessedness of my life.

Yet as the years accumulate, pain becomes an all-too-constant companion. Friends divorce. Cancer is diagnosed. A child dies. People I love walk through the valley of the shadow of death.

Pain and joy daily intertwine in my life. I take a meal to a family whose child is undergoing aggressive chemotherapy; I plan a birthday party for my own. When I pray for those who suffer, my prayers seem inconsequential, inadequate, and I struggle with feelings of helplessness.

Life is full of terrifying tumbles: illness, broken relationships, aging, financial failure. Fear, loneliness, and grief are inescapable. I look at shattered lives around me and remember John Masefield's line: "The life too wrecked for man to mend" (*The Everlasting Mercy,* rev. ed. [New York: Macmillan, 1915], p. 25). Yet it is in the wreckage and the brokenness that we experience what Roberta Bondi calls the most fundamental Christian reality: "Not the suffering of the cross but the life it brings" (*Memories of God* [Nashville: Abingdon, 1995], p. 170).

In the midst of things "too wrecked . . . to mend" stands the God of resurrection, the God who restores wholeness to that which is broken. When our prayers seem to make little difference, we enter into the covenant with the God who says "yes" to every human "no."

When your heart feels heavy, you can be confident that God's love is bigger than any human need, confident that the most fundamental Christian reality is not the suffering of the Cross but the life it brings.

SEPTEMBER 23   WISH LISTS

September was the month my grandmother would start asking for Christmas lists. She was as consistent as the seasons. When the quest for wish lists began each year, we couldn't get away with generic categories such as "books," "socks," or "sweaters." She wanted specifics: sizes, colors, titles. She wanted to know *in detail* what we wanted.

She planned early; she shopped early; she didn't leave anyone out. Despite a limited income, she made sure she had something to put under the tree for everyone in our family.

Even if she could have, my grandmother wouldn't have given us everything we wanted. Every parent knows that a child who receives everything he or she asks for is a child who is demanding, self-absorbed—insufferable. But she wanted to know our wants and wishes simply because she cared. By asking for the detailed lists, she stayed in touch with our tastes, our preferences, our longings.

Throughout the Epistles we find verses telling us to let God know our wants, our needs, our longings. "Pray without ceasing" (1 Thessalonians 5:17 NRSV); "Let your requests be made known to God" (Philippians 4:6 NRSV); "Pray in the Spirit at all times in every prayer and supplication" (Ephesians 6:18 NRSV).

The definition of *supplication* is "a humble request." God wants to know our humble requests, not because everything we ask for will be forthcoming, but because God cares. Prayer is no more than a conversation with the God who can hear, know, understand, care, and respond to our humble requests—and no less.

SEPTEMBER 24   ASKING FOR FORGIVENESS

More often than I care to admit, I speak first and think later. Today I lost my temper and said some things I wish I could take back. But words can't be unspoken, and anger can't be erased. My first response is to say, "I'm sorry." I want everything to be okay: I want to make it all better.

But saying "I'm sorry" doesn't necessarily make it all better. Instead, it puts the burden on the other person; an apology gets me off the hook by putting the ball in the other person's court.

We tend to equate saying "I'm sorry" with asking for forgiveness, but they're not the same. In fact, the difference between the two is significant. Saying "I'm sorry" acknowledges regret but not responsibility. Asking for forgiveness goes much farther. It says, "I know I failed you. I know I wronged you in this situation."

251

"I'm sorry" keeps the focus on me; "Will you forgive me?" puts the focus on the other person. Asking for forgiveness seeks a restoration of the relationship in a way that an apology never does.

In *Wishful Thinking,* Frederick Buechner writes,

> When somebody you've wronged forgives you, you're spared the dull and self-diminishing throb of a guilty conscience. When you forgive somebody who has wronged you, you're spared the dismal corrosion of bitterness and wounded pride. For both parties, forgiveness means the freedom again to be at peace inside their own skins and to be glad in each other's presence. (San Francisco: Harper & Row, 1973, p. 29)

Nowhere in the New Testament does the phrase "I'm sorry" appear, yet forgiveness is as biblical as the Crucifixion. That probably tells us something.

SEPTEMBER 25   QUESTIONING THE QUESTIONS

We tend to think that the important spiritual goal is to find the answers to our questions of faith. But sometimes the opposite is true. Sometimes the challenge is to ask the right questions.

Thomas Long tells a story of a geology professor who wrote an unclear instruction for a final exam. Expecting the students to answer with the names of minerals and rock formations, the professor wrote: "Name three things which are found on the earth which are not found on the moon." One student, quick to realize a dumb "question" when he saw one, responded, "Roller skates, Bruce Springsteen, and the Republican Party."

"The most difficult part of any examination is asking the right questions," concluded Long (from "Jesus' Final Exam," a sermon by Thomas G. Long, preached in November 1986 at the Duke University Chapel and published in *The Princeton Seminary Bulletin*).

When Jesus was asked a question, the Gospels show that

he frequently replied with a question. Nearly every encounter recorded in the Old Testament involving direct interaction between a human and God centers around questions asked of the Holy. We can echo Long's observation: The most difficult part of deepening our spiritual life is asking the right questions.

When the answers we seek are met with silence, when what we ask of God is met with a resounding "no"—or nothing at all—perhaps we need to question the questions themselves. God has a way of turning our perspective inside out. Sometimes the questions that go unanswered are a door opening before us, inviting us to walk a path of deepening spiritual growth.

SEPTEMBER 26   LETTING GO OF FEAR

I love words. Always have. I began journaling in the days of diaries with gold-toned locks and little girl secrets. I noodled and doodled my way through college, writing stray thoughts in the margins of spiral notebooks and snippets of phrases on napkins.

I've made a living by writing, first as a reporter and later as an advertising copywriter and publicist. I began freelance writing to keep from going stir-crazy when my youngest daughter was born, weighing just over three and a half pounds, and the pediatrician put us under "house arrest."

Yet even though writing is my vocation, I never thought of myself as a "writer." Writing was a skill, not an identity. To call myself a "writer" seemed to presume a certain level of talent that was beyond my efforts. Flannery O'Connor was a *writer*. Frederick Buechner is a *writer*. Madeleine L'Engle is a *writer*. I wrote for a living, but I wasn't a *writer*.

Only after I'd written three books and a friend matter-of-factly said, "Debra, you *are* a writer," did I begin to question my reluctance to call myself a writer. My reluctance had nothing to do with humility and everything to do with fear: fear of not being "good enough," of falling flat on my face, of trying to put my heart and soul into words and staring instead at a blank piece of paper. Our fears only serve to hamstring our dreams and hobble our deepest longings.

Throughout history God calls his people to take risks, to follow their dreams, to live life as a sanctified adventure. The One who leads us into the unknown has a lot of experience with fear stopping us short. Over and over in the Bible we find the phrase "Do not be afraid," "Fear not," or "Have no fear." Letting go of our fear is believing that when God says, "Fear not for I am with you," he means it.

SEPTEMBER 27   LOVE LETTERS

After systematically studying one of the Epistles for the first time in a number of years, I was struck by the irony that we call these writings "books" of the Bible. Paul's words to the Christians at Philippi are clearly a letter. In fact, of the twenty-seven books in the New Testament, only five are narratives—the rest are letters written by a specific individual to a specific people at a specific point in time.

Letters. Whether reading a passage from Romans or Philippians or any other New Testament epistle, we are overhearing a living conversation—at times deeply personal and intimate; at times more formal and purposeful; but always intended to address the concerns, conflicts, and challenges that the early Christians faced.

I seriously doubt that Paul gave much thought to the potential longevity of his words as he sat in prison writing to a small group of people in Philippi. Yet his words have transcended time. Preserved through the centuries, passed down through generations of Christians, these living conversations inspired by God's leading are living conversations for us nearly two thousand years later.

Artist and author Sark says, "Letters are chances for the soul to speak. A mood captured in the fibers of the paper, a world in an envelope which will not exist until it is opened. Love letters make love stay visible" (*Inspiration Sandwich:*

Stories to Inspire Our Creative Freedom [Berkeley: Celestial Arts, 1992], p. 19).

The functional purpose of a letter is the same today as it was when Paul wrote to a small band of countercultural Jews and Gentiles. It is written to bridge the geographical distance between two parties. I think God has another purpose for letters—one as true for us as for Paul. Letters make love stay visible.

SEPTEMBER 28   WHERE OUR THOUGHTS LEAD US

I was sitting in a Weight Watchers meeting—yet again—letting my mind wander, when the leader asked for three volunteers for a demonstration. That request got my attention. A demonstration at a Weight Watchers meeting is not the norm.

The leader asked the volunteers to sit in the three chairs placed at the front of the room. She handed them each a string with a light weight tied to one end. "Hold the string out away from your body," she told them, "by extending your arms. Now close your eyes, hold your arms still, and visualize the string moving forward and backward with a gentle swinging movement."

The rest of us watched in disbelief as the strings began swaying with no apparent movement by the three volunteers. "Now visualize the string coming to a complete stop," the leader instructed them. "Now visualize the string swinging from side to side." Again, the movement of the strings followed the visualization of the volunteers, first coming to a complete stop and then swaying from side to side. All the while the volunteers sat perfectly still with their eyes closed.

The demonstration was uncanny—and powerfully convincing! All of us left that Weight Watchers meeting pondering the incredible effect our mind has on our behavior. Our actions follow where our thoughts lead.

No wonder Paul wrote to his friends, "Finally, beloved, whatever is true, whatever is honorable, whatever is just, whatever is pure, whatever is pleasing, whatever is commendable, if there is any excellence and if there is anything worthy of praise, think about these things" (Philippians 4:8 NRSV). As we think, so shall we do.

SEPTEMBER 29   GOD DOES THE GROWING

A Minneapolis farmers' market in September is alive not only with the bounty of autumn's harvest, but also with a cornucopia of human diversity. The air is filled with a hubbub of many voices, music styles, and languages. Patterns of red, green, and yellow fruit and vegetables arranged carefully in baskets or spread on tables create a colorful patchwork effect.

As I walk through crowded, narrow aisles lined with vendors of Hmong, Korean, Hispanic, African-American, and European descent, I marvel at the skill, expertise, and effort that have gone into bringing the fruit and vegetables through the growing process: the careful cultivating, planting, weeding, watering, and fertilizing that have to take place before the patchwork patterns can appear for me to choose from. Bringing crops to harvest takes skill, time, effort, and patience.

Farmers do the work, but the growth comes from God.

"I come from a long line of farmers, and I served in rural churches full of farmers for a decade," writes David Fisher, "yet I have never heard a farmer take credit for growing crops. Farmers are very aware that they plant, fertilize, cultivate, and harvest but that germination and growth to maturity lie completely outside their ability" (*The Twenty-first Century Pastor* [Grand Rapids: Zondervan, 1996], p. 186).

A farmer does the work, but God does the growing. So it is with spiritual growth. We can plant ourselves in a vibrant community of faith, fertilize our hearts and minds with worship, prayer, and study, and do the work to which God has called us, but we can't make ourselves grow, heal, or mature. The growth is up to God.

Today my daughters are going on a field trip. Their excitement is contagious. They awoke before they had to, got dressed before I asked them to, and headed to the bus stop before they needed to. They are anticipating a day in which routine is thrown out the window and the schedule is turned upside down. A field trip rearranges the day's patterns, shuffles the schedule, and awakens imaginations. Their day is an adventure waiting to happen, tingling with possibility.

With the image of my daughters' giggling faces framed by the yellow and black metal of the school bus window, I wave good-bye as the bus pulls away and walk back to the house, thinking about their excitement and anticipation. *What about grown-ups?* I wonder. *Have we "outgrown" the purpose of field trips?*

When time separates us from the regimen of the classroom, we easily forget the monotony of school days—the long classroom hours, the unending assignments, the effort of trying to pay attention when what lies beyond the windows is much more inviting. Even though we have more freedom than schoolchildren to determine our own schedule, most of us seldom take advantage of that freedom. Routine and responsibility usually determine what we do with each day.

When you think about it, God was always sending his people on field trips—directing them to new places, turning their routine upside down, leading them into the unexpected. Jesus also kept the disciples on the move—walking with them to new places, surprising them with the unexpected, inviting them to think new thoughts. When we stay within the confines of the predictable and familiar, God's voice is easily muted.

When was the last time you took *yourself* on a field trip? Think about the possibilities: a slow, unhurried morning at an art museum, a guided tour, a visit to a historic site, a bird-watching expedition with binoculars in hand, a browse through a favorite antique shop.

"This is the day that the LORD has made; let us rejoice and be glad in it" (Psalm 118:24 NRSV). Think about the possibilities!

October
God's Presence in My Life

Maxine Dowd Jensen

OCTOBER 1   **A HUG OR A TEAR**

Read Isaiah 11:1-2.

There was a time, when I was a little girl, that I knew something was going wrong. I heard the words *strike, scab, union,* and I knew they made Mother and her friends unhappy.

When Daddy lost his job, we left the beautiful house in our small Missouri town and took a train to Chicago, where we lived for a while in one room. Mother began making friends with other new Chicagoans, and soon we found an apartment with six rooms. On Sundays, while Daddy and I walked across the park to church, Mother stayed home to cook. She earned money by serving Sunday dinner to our neighbor Mildred and the two Guatemalan brothers who roomed with us. On Sundays we ate in the big dining room instead of the kitchen.

Mildred loved to read, and she never went to the library without taking me along. The brothers were waiters at a restaurant near our home. They owned a big stringed instrument and at least once a week played and sang duets for us in Spanish. I loved those evenings.

During those times, I'd often put my hands on Mother's knee or crawl up in her lap and say, "God will take care of us, Mother." Often a tear would fall on my cheek, and she would give me a hug and a big kiss. When those days were over, she told me she could never have lived through them if it had not been for me and my childlike faith.

None of us can see into another's heart, but a hug or a tear can comfort and say a lot.

OCTOBER 2   A QUARTER ON A CARD

*Read James 1:17*a.

As long as I can remember, I sang Bible verses to the off-key tunes I hummed around the house. My voice wasn't much. Mother used to say, "You're just like your aunt Becky. She couldn't carry a tune in a bushel basket, either."

But one day a friend of Mother's said, "I think Maxine could sell some of those verses she's singing. Will you let me try?"

I'll never forget the day the envelope came with my name on it. Enclosed was a quarter on a card. I jumped for joy. I don't remember the verse, but its title was "Mother." I hugged Mother and her friend and told them I *knew* I was going to be a writer.

Thanks to the encouragement of Mother's friend, I began to write down my verses and send them off to the *Daily News*, which published children's verses every weekday on the comics page. The column was called "Topsy Turvy Times." On Saturdays, the paper had a whole page of stories and articles written by children. "Topsy Turvy Times" sent large certificates for published items, but the "Wide-Awake Club," which appeared on Saturdays, awarded books. Before I was in high school, I'd received quite a collection of both, a few of which I still have!

Today there are many more opportunities for children to develop their talents. Perhaps all they need is interest and encouragement. What child in your life needs a caring and concerned adult?

Read John 15:9-16a.

There are only two years of my life I would never want to repeat: my eleventh and twelfth. I was smart, but I was small, I wore my hair in a Dutch bob, I wore horn-rimmed glasses, and I had only one friend—a girl who was just as smart and small as I but who lacked detrimental features.

For some reason, I thought the celebration of my thirteenth birthday would change me into a swan. My mirror told me it had not.

The first of October drew near, the day of our annual church picnic. I didn't want to go. My mother made me, looking out the bay window to be sure I got on the bus.

Later in the day, I sat alone on a hillock, my chin in my hand. My only friend was Greek, so she wasn't there. As I looked up, I saw my Sunday school teacher approaching me. As we talked a little, I told her how unhappy I was. "Let's go to a quiet place," she suggested. "I think God is talking to you."

In the old washroom, kneeling on the broken concrete floor, she prayed; and then I prayed, asking Jesus into my life. It must have been a miracle that followed. I could feel a load lifted from my heart. I rose a new person—a happy one.

The word of what happened spread, and during the rest of the day people hugged me and commented on the choice I had made. At testimony time around the evening bonfire, a sharp elbow dug into my side. As I rose, my tears blurred the flames. I don't remember what I said, but I knew I'd never regret my choice. My image in the mirror was the same, but I no longer cared. God loved me.

It wasn't until several months later, as I read what was to become one of my favorite Bible books, that I learned I had not chosen Jesus. He had selected me and called me to bring forth fruit. But, what kind of fruit? It didn't take long to find out. He'd tuned my vocal cords at the same time he tuned my heartstrings. No longer could Mother tell me I was like Aunt Becky.

God has supplied all of us with something he intends for us to use for him. Have you found it yet? You can be certain he wants to reveal it to you.

OCTOBER 4   SING FOR JOY

Read Isaiah 65:11-14.

Shortly after the picnic, the pastor asked me to sing in the junior choir because he knew I could read music. Mother had let me take piano lessons because she knew I loved music. However, I liked to sing more than play the piano.

In my first year of high school, the music teacher tested all of the students' voices. When she got to mine she said, "You have the widest range of anyone I've ever tested!" She insisted that I join the Glee Club and then recommended me for the Opera Club. I was in heaven.

Since the Lord had given me my voice, I felt I should use it more often for him. I didn't have to worry. The pastor asked me to join the adult choir when I was fifteen, and I started singing solos.

In all my years of singing, I've had some wonderful and exciting experiences. Just singing hymns in church inspires me. But one Sunday, when I couldn't sing because I had a scratchy throat, reading the words of one hymn showed me something I had never seen all the times I'd sung it. In the second stanza of "Praise to the Lord, the Almighty," the music breaks the sentence in two. But what a wonderful truth when you read it straight through: "Hast thou not seen how thy desires e'er have been granted in what he ordaineth?"

Sing for joy. And if you can't sing, read the words!

OCTOBER 5   FACING CHANGE

Read Philippians 4:10-13.

A junior college graduate in January of the year I turned eighteen, I was asked to work full-time at the bakery where

I'd been employed weekends and summers since I was sixteen.

I'd envisioned enrolling at Northwestern University as a journalism major in the fall. However, life was to change.

In March my father was brought home from work never to return. My mother had been aware of my father's physical deterioration. She also knew that her mother-in-law had died after a slow loss of equilibrium sometime before she and my father married. I only hoped my friends didn't think my teetotaler father was a drunk.

A week later I learned my job had ended. The bakery was folding. I looked at the want ads that night.

Early the next morning I started out to apply at a bakery a mile away. From there, I went downtown to Woolworths. "We don't have an opening at the Loop store," the interviewer said, "but we'll put you on our waiting list." At the telephone company headquarters in the Loop, I took a test. Though my test results supposedly were among the highest, I was told, "All of our service representatives are at least twenty-three."

Subdued and slightly depressed, I plodded home.

The bakery had called. "If you want to go in at four in the afternoon and work 'til midnight, you're hired," Mother said. I went, thanking God for the speed he'd taken to answer my prayer. Though I was "book smart," I didn't know much about life—what it takes to support three adults, to anticipate emergencies, to try to save for a dream. In this ignorance, I never thought to be angry or to blame anyone, especially God. I took life one day at a time, believing God would supply all our needs.

If you find yourself in a somewhat similar situation, trust the Lord. He knows the road and will help you do your best.

OCTOBER 6   A CHRISTIAN SHOULD BE HONEST

Read James 4:1-3.

The new bakery swarmed with jolly customers. The sticky buns and triangular Chinese sweet rolls were scrumptious.

After 6:00 P.M. I was alone until midnight, when the bakers came in. Mr. or Mrs. Penker, the owners, picked up the cash a little earlier. Often they shoved some goodies into my hand to take home. The salary was not too bad—enough to pay the rent and feed us if we pinched pennies.

However, my off days were Monday and Tuesday. This meant I could not attend church on Sunday or Wednesday nights—or go out on Saturday nights.

As May approached, the heat and lack of contact with young people my age made me restless. When a deacon at church, who knew I'd subbed as a part-time soda jerk, asked me to come to work at his business, I did. I later found out it wasn't his business but a concession owned by the head of the department store. Anyway, I was fired because I didn't make sandwiches fast enough. (I'd never even made a sandwich for myself!) I was livid.

"I'll never work for a Christian again," I told my mother. "You can expect a non-Christian to lie, but not a Christian."

"Calm down," Mother said as she put my head on her shoulder and patted me on my neck. "All Christians aren't perfect." Then she repeated what I had said to her as a child, "God will take care."

OCTOBER 7   CHASE YOUR DREAM

Read 2 Chronicles 16:9a.

At age fifteen or sixteen, my mother left her rocky farm home across the river from Hermann, Missouri, to go to Sedalia. She wanted to help pay off the farm mortgage for my grandparents. She obtained a job working for a rich family, cooking, baking, and serving. She became a very proficient cook.

My favorite dish of hers was a combination of meat, potatoes, navy beans, and onions. Mother, however, would raise her eyes in amazement every time I'd cut up green onions and smear horseradish through it. It's a good thing I liked that dish. We had a lot of it during our early days in Chicago.

It was in Sedalia that Mother met my father. Daddy was terrific in math and wanted to design and build bridges. But his father wanted a doctor in the family. Daddy worked his way through the University of Missouri and two years of medical school before finally rebelling against his father. By that time, a blacksmith's job on the railroad was his only option.

Dad always told me, "Even if you want to dig ditches, I'll never stand in your way." What hurt he must have felt as he saw that I wasn't able to pursue my dream of studying journalism and becoming a writer because of his three and a half years of deterioration. I wonder if he's smiling in heaven as he knows I'm succeeding?

Are you encouraging your sister, brother, husband, or child in his or her desire for a special lifework? It's true they may not possess all the qualities needed. If so, is there a way they can?

Have *you* given up a dream? It's not too late to take it out, dust if off, and try again.

OCTOBER 8   HARD DECISIONS

Read Joel 3:14a.

It was Memorial Day weekend, my first Sunday night back at church. Unknown to us single girls, two seminary students who attended our church had established a "matrimonial agency." Apparently, they'd shown our pictures around and told eligible students of our talents. They suggested we all meet the next morning and go to the Brookfield Zoo.

I sighed in relief when I discovered none of the boys standing across the street from my home had "picked" me. For some reason, I wasn't interested in suitors at the time. As it turned out, my date was waiting at the zoo. I couldn't help wondering why he hung around me instead of my best friend.

Perhaps God chose Art to give my life a little spice during

265

that first year I was the breadwinner for our family. Art had a terrific ability to witness for Christ. He'd chat with waiters as we ate at a restaurant or with strangers as we visited museums. He had a special knack for turning conversations toward Christ. I'm sure each stranger parted from us wondering, "How did we get on that subject?" yet thinking about salvation.

Early in our relationship I told Art that I would never marry a minister—though I didn't tell him why. I didn't tell him about my father's illness—neither Mother nor I knew then that there would be nothing a doctor could do to stop the deterioration process—or about the need for me to provide for my family. I knew that a minister didn't make enough money to support four adults—not to mention potential children.

The day after meeting Art, I dressed to go job hunting. The telephone rang as my hand touched the doorknob on the front door.

"Miss Dowd, we have an opening. If you are still interested, can you report to the downtown Woolworths at 1:00 P.M.?"

Of course I could!

Before Christmas was near, I think I loved Art. Yet I couldn't marry him. So I began refusing his calls. I believe I startled both Art and my mother, but I gave no reason.

Perhaps you have had to make a hard decision in your own life. It's never easy, and sometimes, as in my case, God leaves it to you.

OCTOBER 9   WORK FOR A DREAM

Read Ecclesiastes 5:1-4.

Within six months of starting at Woolworths, I was put in charge of the paint counter where I was responsible for the cash drawer. But I hadn't forgotten my goal of becoming a writer, especially after reading that "a dream cometh through the multitude of business" (Ecclesiastes 5:3 KJV).

About two weeks before my promotion, I had signed up for an 11:30 A.M. typing and shorthand class at my former high school. (I hated the shorthand.) After my promotion, my lunch hour came at 11:00 A.M. Because I always had to wait for the cash box to be picked up, I would run to the "L," grab a candy bar from the concessionist, and at the other end, run three long blocks. I was always late. The teacher kindly held the typing speed test for me. At least I learned how to place my fingers on the typewriter.

About a month later, during my regular mile-and-a-half walk home after work, I began to cry. Of course, I couldn't "fix" my face a block from home so that mother wouldn't know.

My sweet mother. She gathered me in her arms and told me, "Quit the classes. We'll get along."

I did.

Inspired by Ecclesiastes 5:3, I began to write after Mother and Daddy were in bed. I hand printed my first manuscript and sent it away. *Moody Monthly* bought it and set it on the opposite page from a piece called "The Girl That I Marry." Mine was called something like "The Man That I Want"! I began to save for a typewriter, though I wasn't able to buy one until three years after my father's death. My savings instead helped me pay for Daddy's funeral and for two operations my mother had within those years. Then Dad Crit, founder of our church, discovered a place where I could buy a typewriter for $25, exactly the amount I had stashed away.

I had had just enough practice in my typing class to learn the fundamentals of typing. I began to write every night.

Do you want something so much that you are willing to work, save, and wait? Maybe you'd like to take voice lessons or pursue a career or new skill that will help you serve Christ in some way. Nothing is impossible when God is on your side.

OCTOBER 10   MAKING YOUR JOB INTERESTING

Read Ephesians 4:32.

A job is always more fun if you can learn helpful or interesting things about it. God gave me interesting times at the paint counter. I read all the paint tips that appeared in the newspapers. I even had customers return to thank me for suggesting they buy the cheap brush and soak its wooden handle overnight in a glass of water so the bristles wouldn't cling to the only chair they wished to paint.

I also caught some shoplifters! One, when searched as he left the store, was carrying something from nearly every counter in our big downtown store, and I was the only clerk who had noticed.

My next job was in an insurance office. I always liked medicine, and I learned a lot of interesting medical facts from the accidents that factory workers would report. I still remember the man who worked a night shift alone. His sleeve got caught in a machine, and it tore his arm loose at his shoulder. He'd carried it two blocks to the factory's nursing station. Unfortunately, he lost the use of that arm. However, he always wore a smile and had a nice word for me. Others with less severe injuries were not as pleasant.

My job at the telephone company was always interesting. One customer never paid her bill on time but was so creative with her excuses that I liked to call her about it. One day she said, "Oh, Miss Dowd, I was on my way to pay when I dropped my money in the snow. Will you wait 'til the snow melts for me to bring it in?"

If you have a job you don't like and for some reason feel you can't quit, why not see how you can get a laugh out of it or try to find an interesting story. Our God has a sense of humor, or else he couldn't put up with some of us!

OCTOBER 11   UNKINDNESS

Read Ephesians 4:30-32.

A new head man was transferred to our main office at the telephone company. We loved our immediate supervisor for her personality, her fairness, and her knowledge—as well as for her interesting names for things. We laughed inside and enjoyed hearing that she'd taken her nieces and nephews to Ziegfield when she meant the Brookfield Zoo. She often asked an employee to get something from the "Bobbin" drawer. We all knew she meant the bottom one. There were other novelty names she used.

The new head man wore white pants, winter or summer, so I always thought of him as "white pants." I probably never would have done that if he hadn't acted so superior and always let Miss Burns know each time she spilled one of her creative sayings. None of us "girls" liked him.

I've been guilty at other times as well of branding someone in my mind with a name that I think fits, a habit I suspect I got from my mother. I never say the name except within my own mind, but still it's not a nice thing to do. I'm trying to stop. Often our labels are related to something an individual can't change, such as the color of his or her skin; and I pray about this fault whenever it surfaces.

Each of us has bad habits that we do not always see but that God can reveal to us. If or when you realize something you are doing is not Christlike, I invite you to join me in asking God to help you erase this habit.

OCTOBER 12   PRAY FOR PATIENCE?

Read Romans 5:1-5.

I was eighteen when I began my years as the breadwinner for our family. That was when I prayed for patience. I didn't know my Bible very well, so I didn't know what I was letting myself in for. During those first years of my father's illness, he still could do some things for himself. So Mother decided to help me. She got a job caring for a boy with erysipelas while his parents were at work. The parents did not warn my mother of the danger. A neighbor next door told her to be careful, but it was too late. My mother caught strep infection. For five weeks the doctor tried to heal her, but she was allergic to sulfa. Glasses were not plastic then, so Daddy could not safely help her to gargle, because he tended to drop things. Church women were wonderful to come in and care for her while I was at work at a book company—another prayed-for job.

At night, I tried to wake up and see that she gargled every half hour. During the day, I often found my head bowed in the shadow of the bookcase in front of me. I worried about losing my job.

One Wednesday, the night of our weekly prayer meeting, a friend was at our home when the doctor came. He told her he didn't know what to do. "Mrs. Dowd is now too ill to even stand the ride to the hospital," he said. That night, I understand, nearly everyone in our little church prayed for her. The next day the doctor brought some serum and injected Mother with it regularly until Saturday. Finally her temperature came down to normal for the first time in five weeks. But Mother was too weak to do much, and Daddy was growing more feeble.

The founder of our church discovered a hospital for my dad and a group that would take care of the charges. I wasn't fired from my job. And Mother began to regain strength.

At the end of that period, I found Romans 5:3, and I told God I'd never pray for patience again. I never have. You see, I didn't know his word said that "tribulation worketh patience" (KJV)! I also praised him, with tears running down my cheeks, for continuing to supply all our needs.

I'm no different from you. Are you having one of the worst set of conundrums of your life right now? I wouldn't suggest praying for patience, but I know that God will answer your prayers when you trust in him. As an old hymn says, "Take it to the Lord in prayer."

OCTOBER 13   HEALTH OR HAPPINESS?

Read Philippians 4:15-19.

Sometimes our work can make us lose our verve and our interest. Perhaps 50 percent of the working population do not like their jobs and wish they could find something else.

I've always thought there is no sense in ruining your stomach, living in fear of being fired, or enduring some of the things to which employers subject their employees. Usually, it comes back to money. Money is a necessary evil, but the lack of a lot of money should not be allowed to ruin your life.

At one of my first jobs, I regularly ate lunch with some of my fellow workers. Every lunch hour Hildur complained. One day, naive me asked, "If you're so unhappy, why don't you look for a change?" The result was a tongue-lashing directed at me. Thank goodness I don't remember what she said.

An older man at one place I worked coughed repeatedly— a harsh, from-the-belly cough. I asked him if he couldn't find a town or state where he'd be able to breathe better. He replied, "I couldn't get the money I get here."

Some people fear leaving locations that are familiar, working with new people, learning a new process; others choose money rather than bodily health. Many hope for a promotion.

When I left one job, a fellow employee said, "I wish I had your guts. I'm beginning to hate my job."

Every time I wanted or needed a change, I prayed about it. Then I weighed the pros and cons. Once I accepted a job that was quite a distance from my home, but there was good transportation to it. So it had an added advantage of giving me some extra reading time.

When you dislike your work or place of employment, consider what this feeling may be doing to undermine your health or your happiness. Don't sacrifice these two Hs for money; it may not satisfy. Make a list of the pros and cons as you pray for guidance. Philippians 4:19 doesn't refer only to money. It says "all your need[s]" (KJV). Believe it!

OCTOBER 14   DON'T GIVE UP A DREAM

Read Psalm 45:1-2.

The quarter I received on a card for a poem called

"Mother" began my dream of becoming a writer—a dream that God allowed.

An older Arkansas woman I knew always loved flowers. She wanted to take pictures of them that others would enjoy. She bought a cheap camera and signed up for a photography class. When the teacher saw her camera, he scoffed; but she didn't let that put her off. She picked up tips in the class and tried them out. The last I heard of her, she had succeeded in publishing three books of her pictures.

My dream of becoming a writer began with my childish verses and stories published on the kids' pages in the Chicago *Daily News*. However, my burning desire to attend Northwestern University didn't come to fruition until after my father's death. The first night in journalism class, we were asked to describe a member of our family. Each of us sat in front of a typewriter. I hadn't been able to buy one of my own yet (this was before I got my first typewriter for $25), and all I had learned in my typing class was how to place my fingers on the typewriter. So I attempted to hunt and peck.

At our next class, the professor said, "Only one of you thought before you wrote. It shows."

I knew I had looked around before beginning, and I had seen just about everyone begin typing immediately.

He went on. "The writer didn't tell us her mother had long hair; instead, she shows her pushing a hairpin into the knot at the nape of her neck."

My heart skipped a beat. He was talking about my piece! *I have it,* I thought. *I can write adult pieces too.*

This professor gave us another tip that I'm passing on to you: "Don't give up because of a rejection slip. The editor might have had an argument at breakfast or spilled a cup of coffee on a manuscript. Keep trying."

Isn't that the way God encourages us to live? We falter sometimes, but God wants us to keep on the right road and keep trying. Therefore, I recommend that you "polish up" whatever is your dream!

272

Read Luke 24:1-8.

One year I was asked to be part of Chicago's ongoing Easter Sunrise Service Committee for the 6:00 A.M. services held in Chicago's Soldier Field each Easter. How wonderful that always was. Three women and twelve or more men were on the committee.

Perhaps my biggest thrill during those years was the Easter when Billy Graham, who was not very well known then, was our speaker.

At the dinner Saturday night before Easter, Billy Graham said, "The weather forecast for tomorrow all across our nation is excellent. If this doesn't happen here, it will be God's will."

When we woke up in our hotels the next morning, we saw that rain and wind covered our city. We plodded over to the field and found our decorations in shambles. We three women stood in one of the entryways to the seats, and a sparse audience crouched in the rain. Some of the men tried to hold an umbrella over Mr. Graham and tried to protect him with a blanket. I don't think he even knew it was raining. I can't remember the theme, but his message poured out with all the energy he possessed.

When rain falls on my attempts to succeed for Christ, I sometimes remember that rainy Easter and Billy Graham's enthusiastic message. How do we react when the rain beats down and the storms whirl about us? Let's thank God for the blessings we have had in the past and ask him to strengthen us for future blasts.

OCTOBER 16   KEEP TRYING

Read 1 Peter 4:7-11.

Every time I saved enough money for another journalism class, I went.

One night as I rode the "L" home, I wondered what the teacher would think when he read the names of my favorite book characters: Jo of *Little Women,* Scarlett of *Gone with the Wind,* and Sidney of *A Tale of Two Cities.* All were rather oddballs for their period. I guess I was still unsure of myself.

A little later, I attended what I think was the first Christian Writers Conference in Chicago. I couldn't afford the full two and a half days, but a Saturday half-day was allowed. I entered a manuscript and went.

My manuscript was read. As the critiquing started, I began to sink down in my seat, glad I knew no one. The criticism mentioned every flaw.

At home I read the critique, put it in my lowest dresser drawer, and said to myself, *I had ability when I was younger, but I guess I no longer have it.*

Two years later, while cleaning out my drawers, I found the piece and turned the comment page over. On the back I read, "But this writer can really write. You can feel the tension as Rhoda creeps through the city. . . ."

I looked up at the ceiling, as I often do when talking to God, and shouted, "Two wasted years!"

Have you had a similar experience of being turned back in your attempts to succeed? Press on. God is with you.

OCTOBER 17   JUST SHY

Read Proverbs 18:24.

If you asked any of my friends what my outstanding characteristic is, they'd probably tell you I talk too much! And I do! One friend says, "Max, you have a story for everything."

My mother never wanted me to travel alone. When I found out why—"Because," she said, "you talk to everyone"—I told her that that was the pot calling the kettle black!

When I was on vacation and would go for walks with my mother, I could see that I got the trait naturally. Once she asked some woman how her son's broken arm was coming along, and when I asked, "Who was that?" she replied, "I met her at the butcher's."

I've discovered, however, that this personality trait can be a good one. I still have some friends I've had since my late teens. I've helped them to increase their ability to be friendly rather than shy, all because I've been willing to say the first word. One of these friends I "match-made." Now a minister's wife, she speaks to groups at times and sings in the choir—another ability that, because of a mean word she heard as a child, she thought she could never do.

A few friends saw my joy in Jesus and wanted what I had. I'm so glad I played a part in helping them to know my Lord.

Have you shied away from someone because he or she looked unapproachable? This person may be hoping you will show yourself friendly. Don't feel rebuffed if your first effort receives a cold shoulder. Try again!

OCTOBER 18   GRACIOUS ACCEPTANCE

Read Matthew 10:40-42.

My mother had a third operation for suspected cancer. She improved every day following the surgery. On the day the doctor released her from the hospital, he said, "No cancer; so, if her heart holds out, you'll have your lovely mother back again."

Christmas was a day to remember. At about 11:00 A.M., our pastor and his wife visited us. He gave mother a gift of $300, collected from the church members—a large sum from our little church. He'd suggested that they help a member who was such a faithful and hardworking woman of the Lord.

At the time he'd brought the idea to the church members, I was livid. "I can take care of my mother," I almost shouted. "We don't want charity."

It was then that he taught me about "gracious acceptance," something I've never forgotten. Gifts given because of love deserve gracious acceptance, not refusal, he told me.

I've made a practice of this with friends since then, accepting their gifts with thankfulness; and I have appreciated the graciousness they've shown in accepting my loving gifts.

Do you reject things people wish to do for you? Do you, in pride, turn away their gifts? Please don't. Joy is in the giving and the receiving.

OCTOBER 19   ANGELS

Read Exodus 23:20-22.

I believe in angels. I've heard the voice of mine.

After I'd been working a while, I was able to start voice lessons. I had to travel to the other side of Chicago to a neighborhood that was unfamiliar. One October night, the next student didn't appear, and my teacher extended my time. When I left it was dusk, but the streetlights had not yet been turned on. Because it was later than usual, I decided to ride the speedy "L" instead of the every-stop streetcar, even though I'd have to walk a few blocks to get on. I didn't want my mother to worry about me.

I passed three-story apartment buildings in the first block, and then I came to private homes, whose fronts faced the streets I was crossing and whose garages faced the streets on which I walked.

As I stepped up on a curb, I heard a voice. "Be careful," it said. Then I heard footsteps—they increased in speed as I crossed an alley. "Turn around," the voice said. I did.

A man, arms outstretched, was less than five feet behind me. I opened my mouth to scream. Nothing came out, yet he fled down the alley. I ran the rest of the way to the elevated station and poured out my story to an elderly lady on the platform.

"God was with you," she said. She was so right.

In my voice lesson that night, I'd hit high F above high C in my vocalizing. Even so, I could never claim my voice was my savior. It was God's angel.

You may not have had an experience like mine, but it is still true: God is always near.

Read Isaiah 66:13.

The day after Mother's wonderful Christmas when she received the $300, I heard the voice again.

As I looked at the Christmas lights on the Merchandise Mart while the "L" crossed the Chicago River, I heard these words: "This is the night."

"Help me, Lord," I prayed.

Walking into our apartment, I saw Martha, a friend, standing against the bedroom window, her eyes swollen and red from tears.

My mother faced the wall and pleaded with someone in what sounded like a foreign language. She knew none. Her tone was argumentative—strangely so.

Three times I asked, "Mother, what do you want?" before she answered.

Martha said she'd had a heart attack—at exactly the time I had heard the voice. The doctor had been there and had left a prescription and his telephone number. Martha went to get the medicine.

I propped Mother up on the pillows, as she asked me to, and her countenance changed, as did her voice. She looked calm and content. Then she said, "You've done so much for me. Some day I'll pay it all back."

She smiled a big smile when I said, "What do you mean? You paid it all in advance," and we hugged and kissed.

Those were our last words. The nurse, who had been in our church youth group, had once said, "If you ever need me, I'll come." She folded me in her arms while Mother's breathing slowed.

I'll have to wait until I get to heaven to be sure, but I believe Mother was begging God to let her stay until I got home.

Perhaps in your youth you experienced some queer happenings and were afraid to voice them. Now I do not hesitate because I feel they are from God, who constantly watches and comforts those of us who trust him.

OCTOBER 21   GOD'S WAYS ARE THE RIGHT WAYS

Read Judges 6:36-40.

I knelt down that first New Year's Eve after my mother's death. That was the night I always chose my Bible verse for the following year. As I prayed, I told God, "For the first time in my life I am responsible for only myself. I'm willing to go anywhere or do anything you lead me to do." The only option I didn't give him was marriage. In fact, I never even thought of marriage. I'd had dates, but as soon as a guy started to get serious, I always fled.

When I got to my desk on the first workday of the new year, I noticed a note attached to my calendar. It said:

I.O.U.

If you're not married by one year from today, I'll take you to any event of your choice and to any restaurant you choose.

Virginia Kelly

"You did this to get a laugh out of me," I said as Virginia approached.

"It will come true," she replied.

I laughed again. "At my age? All the best men are married, and I wouldn't want any of the rest."

"You just wait," she answered.

Several weeks later, another friend approached our break table and said, "Max, I don't know how old you are, and you may think a forty-five-year-old man is too old for you, but Cliff is a fine Christian who's active in his church. His wife was killed in an auto accident a little over a year ago. Would it be okay with you if I try to fix you up?"

"I may be older than you think," I replied.

As I said this, my friends circling the table said, "What have you got to lose? Take a chance. Go ahead."

My friend began to talk to Cliff, but still there was no

278

meeting. In the meantime, I continued to seek God's leading. "But no marriage, God," I prayed.

It wasn't until the Memorial Day weekend that Cliff and I met. We were obviously attracted to each other, but I kept telling God I didn't know how to cook or clean and that this man was too good for me. *"Not this way,"* I said.

Finally, when God didn't seem to listen, I put out the fleece. Three times I asked for possible but highly improbable events. Three times the improbable happened.

I surrendered. We were engaged on July 28 and married on September 26.

We never know just what God has planned for us. But his ways are the right ways. Marriage was right for me. I've proved him time after time. So can you.

OCTOBER 22   COMFORT AND A SURPRISE

Read Psalm 68:6a.

Those first weeks and months after Mother died—before I met Cliff—were pretty lonely. Early in the new year our choral group was giving a concert in which I'd been scheduled to sing some solos.

"I can get someone else to sing if you don't feel like it just yet," our director said.

"I can do it," I replied.

My last number in the big Catholic Church on Chicago's South Side was "I Walked Today Where Jesus Walked." Nuns and church members greeted me after the performance, but best of all were the hugs and whispers from my fellow chorus members. I knew I had the support of friends. That was the way God helped me to begin that year on my own.

As my birthday approached, the mother of a friend said she'd bake a cake for me. But when the day came, she wasn't able to do it because she had to take her great-grandson to the clinic. I was feeling lonely when the telephone rang. It was my landlady inviting me down to meet the tenant whose flowers

279

in the window I so enjoyed. But when I got there, I discovered that was just an excuse. Somehow she'd found out that it was my birthday, and she didn't think I should be alone on that first one after Mother's death. It was a thoughtful and pleasant surprise.

When you are alone, God will have some surprises for you too!

OCTOBER 23   FEARS AND FAMILY

Read Isaiah 41:10.

The neighborhood where we had lived for many years was still a good one, but the Chicago Transit Authority had discontinued the elevated stop at our street. If I used the "L," I had to get off four long blocks before or after its previous station and wait for a slow streetcar on one of two dark corners.

We had moved to our small apartment when Mother began to have heart trouble. But there wasn't room enough for me to write at night. Nor could I practice singing in a large apartment building. So I began to look and pray for a larger apartment. I found a four-room place, with not only a bedroom but also a large dining room for my roll-away bed. And it was near transportation. I was still cautious, though, just as I'd always been, when coming home from a late concert or visit. I always walked swiftly and watchfully.

It wasn't until after Mother died that I realized that for most of my life, my fears actually had been for my mother and father. If something happened to me, who would care for them, pay their bills, love them? After they both become ill, I was the sole breadwinner. We had no family in Chicago. When we moved to Chicago, we had lost intimate family connections with the sisters and brothers of my parents in Missouri. None of them, except Uncle Marion, one of Daddy's brothers, were letter writers.

After Mother died, though I was alone, I discovered I was no longer afraid. Oh, I still watched the bushes and the alleys, but fear had left. That was a blessing. An even greater blessing came when God led me to my first big family through marriage.

Do you have a family? Try not to lose touch. Do you cherish them? Get along? Love one another? If not, try to mend the bridges. If you're alone, trust God to take care of you.

OCTOBER 24   PROTECTION

Read 2 Chronicles 18:31.

Most of us are careful these days. We don't know when a gun will shatter our windshield or someone will drag us into an alley or break into our homes. But God has many ways to protect us.

About two weeks after Mother and I moved into our new apartment, an eighteen-year-old girl from the neighborhood was found cut up in an old oil drum in Montrose Harbor. A few days later a woman was raped at a corner I had to pass each day. But, a strange thing happened to me.

I was always shy around dogs because of a confrontation I had had with one when I was about eight. So I shivered when a Doberman started to come out from between two houses and walk near me. Every morning he came out and walked either before, beside, or behind me, crossing the first big street beside me. At night, a fellow worker drove me to a northbound street, and I'd watch the bushes and the cars on the boulevard as I walked my four blocks.

In my imaginative way, I believe that dog was a guardian angel. I felt God had sent him so that any criminal would think he belonged to me and thus leave me alone.

Recently, while on a trip to another country where we had to use a different currency, a fellow traveler gave me a hint as to how never to bring my wallet out of my purse in an incorrect way, which would expose my credit cards to someone standing close by. It will prove a good tip to use at home too.

281

It's good advice to keep our eyes open, our wallets in our purses, and perhaps a dog by our side to walk with us. One woman I know even has a dummy dressed like a man in the car seat beside her. We can believe that God wants to protect us.

OCTOBER 25   REMEMBRANCE

Read Matthew 10:24-25.

Before I was twenty, I taught a Sunday school class of ten nine-year-old boys. The following year I was asked if I'd take a class of five twelve-year-old boys. "One of the boys asked for you," I was told. I agreed and taught them for the next three years.

There was Rich, who always managed to be the first to get from the opening exercise room to our classroom so that he could sit by the window and turn his back toward me. Harry was a very quiet boy, but he was the one who most often answered my questions. Wayne had a cleft palate and a hare-lip. He was the one, I later learned, who'd asked for me. Jay wanted to be a photographer. He was tall and thin and made all my pictures look like they were out of focus. Joe was my problem. If he was there, I'd go home almost pulling my hair out after trying to part two scuffling boys.

But I loved them. I tried to show it by taking them to out-side events and giving them good prizes for memorization contests—not like the bookmarks I used to receive.

Would you believe that three of them still keep in touch with me? My fighter gave up a good job to run a Christian camp. My picture-taker has been in charge of all the Chicago *Tribune* photographers. The one who asked for me discovered a doctor, through me, who made a prosthesis for him that enables him to speak clearly; the union asked him to teach apprentice printers. The boy who sat with his back to me didn't like having a "girl" teach his class. Now he is a preacher. He and his wife visited me this year. The quiet one is a Sunday school superintendent and heads a boys' club at his church.

Love the children or youth who are in your care. Compliment them. Keep them busy. You'll reap rewards.

OCTOBER 26   LEFT-HANDED? SO WHAT?

Read Judges 20:14-16.

I'm ambidextrous, but Mother tried to make me right-handed. I'll always believe she let me use one of her treasured collectible spoons only because I had to put it in my right hand to read the name of my town of birth. If that's right, it didn't work.

There's nothing wrong in being left-handed. I got to play baseball with the boys because I could switch-hit.

How many other things do some of us try to change in our children?

My husband appreciated his mother and took exceptionally good care of her until she died, but he never liked her criticism of his smoking. "She forgets I'm a grandfather," he'd sometimes say. Then one day, with a full carton on the closet shelf, Cliff quit, cold turkey, never to begin again. When I knew it was permanent, I said, "When I married you, your smoking was the only thing I didn't like about you. Now, what do I have to dislike?"

My youngest stepdaughter was fifteen when we married. She was 5'10" and weighed 225 pounds. Cliff kept trying to get her to diet and lose weight. I felt she ate because she missed her mother and was unhappy.

One day I said, "Cliff, I think you could lose her love if you keep nagging at her. She needs a motive. Then she'll change."

When she started working, she wanted her own apartment. Soon she and an overweight friend started going to a doctor. She shrank to 180 pounds and became proud and happy.

Motivation, not criticism, is what brings about change. Loving God and loving people will produce more change than any nagging and will teach us the difference between needed change and our own opinions.

OCTOBER 27   DEPENDABILITY AND TIMING

Read Psalm 89:15.

The day my husband died, he asked me to pray that it wouldn't be long. I did, and then Cliff prayed, "Lord, you know that I love you and am saved."

I called his best friend, because I knew they'd like to see each other one last time. Jim could then drive me home to get my bankbook and take me to the bank. I knew that Illinois clamped a lock on a person's bank accounts immediately after death. I didn't want to drive myself because it had been sleeting, snowing, and raining all day. What I didn't expect was how God's timing was so perfect.

Jim drove me to the Savings and Loan where I withdrew our money—and learned the bank would be closed the next day. We drove to another bank where I was going to open an account in my name, but we were five minutes too late. That was God at work too. Had I been able to open an account and deposit our money, we would not have made it back to the hospital before Cliff died. As a result, we were able to kiss and say "I love you" one last time.

That night I made an overseas phone call, trying to get my son-in-law home from his base in Spain. It so happened he was in Dayton, Ohio, and was scheduled to fly back to Spain the next day. Instead, he came to help me.

Everything froze that night, but Fran, Jim's wife, was able to get their car out of the garage and drive me to the station, where I caught a train to the Loop. At the bank there I talked to an officer who was a friend and who had the authority to return our money. He filled out the papers, showing that I needed the money for medical bills—and so I received our money there too.

I can assure you that God is not only dependable but also has perfect timing. If you've never tested him, try it. If you have, praise him along with me.

Read Psalm 68:3-6a.

Cliff died of cancer thirteen years after we were married. Three weeks later, I found myself unable to stop crying. I wept from 10:00 P.M. until 4:00 A.M. Suddenly, I got up and went to sit at our kitchen table. There I wrote the article that became my first nonfiction book. An agent, the friend of a friend, saw my article and told me I had the makings of a book.

I went to Florida to visit a sister-in-law and her husband and wrote the book in those three weeks. I sent the manuscript to a publisher and waited for the response. When the letter came from the editor, I left it on the kitchen counter for over six hours. If it was favorable, it could wait. If it wasn't, I didn't want to know too soon.

When I opened the envelope the first sentence said, "I've read your manuscript, and I like it."

You can bet I looked up at the ceiling, praising God and jumping around in glee like a ten-year-old. The book was in print nearly thirteen years—first in hardcover and then in paperback. Now it has been recycled into longer than usual meditations and is being considered by a publishing house.

Will I be able to jump up and down again? Why not? There are still new ideas to try, things that interested me as a child. There are still new roads to travel, new places to see.

And you—don't lock yourself up in closed doors with the shades down when life deals you a blow. Seek God's way for you. And be willing to venture out into new territory.

OCTOBER 29   **GOD'S WORD**

Read Psalm 119:9-11; John 14:26-27.

When I first moved to the town in which I now live, I took a survey to see how many churches continue to teach children Bible verses. I was flabbergasted by the results: 60 percent have no program, 39 percent leave it to the teachers (do the teachers know this?), and 1 percent leave it to the Bible in the pew.

I grew up in a church where Bible memorization was important. I learned that the Holy Spirit has the job of bringing Scripture to our remembrance when we need it most. He does his job.

I believe the meanings of scriptures are important and should be taught to children. Of course, some verses need more explanation than others. For example, I've never liked the Twenty-third Psalm as much as many do because, as a child, I didn't understand the phrase "I shall not want." Even as a kid, I knew I *did* want him.

When I taught Sunday school, I always held memorization contests. I prayed that my young people would find the verses a shield against temptation. Perhaps if more people helped our youth to learn and understand God's Word, young people would not turn to crime in such great numbers.

I enjoy reading some of the new Bible translations, which help to make some things clearer to me. I occasionally pick out a verse in one of them to memorize. I'll admit, though, that when our pastor uses a different translation for a known favorite of mine, I'll repeat it, silently, as I first learned it.

In my life of faith, the hidden Word and God's dependability in showing me its truth have been the ties that bind me closest to him. What about you?

OCTOBER 30   A MIND TO WORK

Read Nehemiah 4:1-6.

Have you read Nehemiah lately? If not, you're missing something special. It tells us how to prepare to accomplish something; how prayer is essential; how our mind-set is very important; how compatibly working together with our varied talents can bring fruition to our goal. Perhaps the verse I like best is the one that says, "So built we the wall . . . for the people had a mind to work" (4:6 KJV).

Some days while trying to write this month of meditations, my mind had a desire to work. The hours passed quickly. Other days I either hesitated or got bogged down in other things. Writing, like scrubbing the kitchen floor, doesn't always get going like a sled on an icy hill. Like other jobs, it can be hard, tedious work. At other times, I can't wait to get to my desk.

In any job, our mind either moves us or stunts our growth—even the jobs we do for God. So when I feel my lowest, I try to remember the words in Nehemiah 4:6 and get myself on the right track again. I'm glad that verse is in my memory bank so the Holy Spirit can bring it to me in my time of need. Maybe you will want to memorize it for future flashbacks.

OCTOBER 31   HEAVEN: I CAN HARDLY WAIT

Read John 14:1-3.

What can I say on this last day of October?

First, I'm glad God chose me. My life, with some of its difficult problems, might have made me an unhappy person, but God's presence has not only helped me through but also given me joy.

I'm glad God ordained me to bring forth fruit. I know I've failed. I haven't always pleased him in my fruit bearing, I'm sure, but I've tried.

I've asked many things of God: jobs, when I felt I needed a different one; money, when it was essential I have it; health, when loved ones and friends were ill; wisdom, when my parents were gone and when my husband died; directions, when my future was uncertain. There's been no failing on his part. Yet I must be honest—God, undoubtedly, has had some sad times when he has looked down at me. How wonderful that he forgives us!

As I look to the future, I know God still has good things in store for me. Especially heaven! In many ways I can hardly wait! What do I want to do in heaven?

To see my Savior, to hear heaven's music, to meet old friends and Bible characters I've loved. I have to ask David if he had red hair. I think he did. How does it feel to be "translated" as Enoch was? And I must tell James how I've loved his book and how it has molded my spirit.

How is my sweet mother? I'm sure my father will be able to stand on his feet and enfold me with strong arms. Did Ruby touch other Sunday school girls as she did me? I'll shout hello to Peter and blow a kiss to sweet, lovable John. I'll ask Andrew if he's the man I've pictured in my short stories. And I mustn't miss my mentor, Dad Crit.

I'll revel in the beautiful sights never seen before but dreamed of—sights that will be more beautiful than Lake Tipsoo guarded by tall, evergreen sentinels, with three-pointed Mt. Ranier covered with snow in the background. That is still my favorite scenic sight on earth. What will be my favorite sight in heaven?

I still believe God will have a tiny place in heaven that will smell like Saturday mornings at my house when I was a kid and mother was baking—a special place for me.

Crazy? Maybe so, but I have faith. Don't you? Think about it . . . and let us thank God together!

November
A Month of Gratitude
Marilyn Brown Oden

NOVEMBER 1   GRATITUDE FOR ALL GOD'S
CHILDREN

Read 2 Thessalonians 1:1-4, 11-12.

*I*f I were in charge of the world, what individual or group would be unsafe?" asked the Reverend Grace Imathiu from Kenya, who was leading a Bible study on the Holy Spirit.

Who would be unsafe if you or I were in charge of the world? Maybe we wouldn't classify anyone "unsafe," but what individual or group would we exclude from leadership or prominence? From social, political, or economic advantage? From comfort or healing? Who would be last in line?

Perhaps a softer way to ask this question is this: If you or I set the world's table, who would be unwelcome?

November—the month of thanksgiving, of gratitude—gives us a clue. This is a season when family and friends feast at the table together. When we set our own feast table, what individual or group is unwelcome? Those who hold different beliefs or values? Who have lighter or darker skin? Who are richer or poorer, older or younger? Though we are not in charge of the world, we are in charge of our own table—our list of those to invite and our secret list of those to exclude.

Paul says, "Your faith is growing abundantly, and the love of everyone of you for one another is increasing" (2 Thessalonians 1:3 NRSV). Our small contribution to make the world safe for all God's children begins by adding more and more leaves to our own table, increasing our love and living out our faith.

NOVEMBER 2   GRATITUDE FOR ALL GOD'S CHILDREN

Read Isaiah 2:1-5.

I was in Bosnia-Herzegovina during the NATO bombing in 1995. My husband, Bill, and I visited refugee centers sponsored by our denomination. We could hear shelling during the day and bombers flying overhead in the dark of night. With Isaiah, we longed for the day when it will be true that "neither shall they learn war any more" (Isaiah 2:4 NRSV).

In one refugee center, fifteen little boys and girls encircled me. We talked together with smiles, gestures, and gentle hugs—that universal language without words. As the sun began to dip behind the trees, a sentence from Amphilochius drifted to me from the fourth century A.D.: "Here am I with the children God has given me."

All of us are spiritual children of God. All of us are gifts to one another. Yet, we do not treat others like the children God has given us. We struggle against them for turf and power. We squabble about who gets credit for positive events and who gets the blame for negative ones. We hold prejudices and make assumptions about one another based on those prejudices. We fall into traps of dissension within the family, divisions in the neighborhood, divisiveness among colleagues—and even civil and world wars.

Wherever we are—around the table, at work or church, in traffic or a grocery line, or even in another country—we are with the child or children God has given us in *this* moment. We live out our faith by treating them as gifts.

NOVEMBER 3   GRATITUDE FOR COMMUNITY

Read Psalm 119:137-44.

The psalmist asks, "Give me understanding that I may live" (119:144 NRSV). Part of the understanding we seek is an understanding of others, for it is in community that our spirit is nurtured.

In his book *Soul Making,* Alan Jones tells us: "Spirituality rejoices in the interdependence of all things." It involves "the celebration of unity in unimaginable diversity." I experienced this celebration of unity in unimaginable diversity at an international church women's conference. The theme was "Come, Holy Spirit. Weave Us Together."

Five hundred women came together from fifty countries around the world—each one a colorful thread in the global tapestry. Simultaneously, in our own native tongues, we lifted our songs, prayers, and praise in celebration—every voice heard by the multilingual Holy One. In the name of the Christ, we were connected, one with another.

Jones defines *spirituality* as "the art of making connections." To connect is to remove our dividing walls. We throw up walls to protect ourselves from a real or perceived threat. Yet long after the threat is removed, the walls remain. We may not even remember why they were first built, but we are still afraid to remove them. Thus, we do not receive the gift of understanding. Our walls separate us from others, encroach on our spiritual growth, and divide our global community. "Something there is that doesn't love a wall," wrote Robert Frost in "Mending Wall." That "something" is our spiritual growth.

NOVEMBER 4   GRATITUDE FOR LIGHT

Read Luke 19:1-10.

"For the Son of Man came to seek out and to save the lost" (Luke 19:10 NRSV). Who are the lost? Sometimes it seems that the truly lost are those who judge another to be lost! They stand looking down their noses, self-righteously shaking their heads in judgment. But are "they" also "we"?

In the faithful community we speak the truth (as we see it), holding one another to accountability. But that truth must be spoken *in love*. If our motivation for confrontation is not purity of heart but egotism or ruffled feathers, we speak in judgment, not love. Love is the difference between the pointing finger and the tenderly clasped hand, between the glaring light of the inquest and the soft light of the candle.

A church women's conference closed late at night. We held our unlit candles as the auditorium lights dimmed, drowning us in darkness. Then one small candle took light from the Christ candle, and that little candle touched the wick of another, and that wick another. Each received the kiss of light from one sister and shared it with another until all five hundred of us held a flaming candle. Slowly we moved outside into the moonless night, singing "Weave Us Together," brightening the dark world with our little lights born of the Christ candle.

Who are the lost? All of us are lost to some degree. All of us stand in darkness at times. And all of us can offer light to another.

NOVEMBER 5   GRATITUDE FOR VISION

Read Habakkuk 1:1-4; 2:2-4.

I sat at a table under a sun umbrella on a warm Brazilian winter day. The air smelled of salt. Six-foot waves roared in, slapping the rocks and stirring the sand. The horizon was broken by skyscrapers to my left and mountains to my right. Between them the azure sea touched the sky. A family of three birds guarded the highest rock. And then, on the side of that rock, I noticed the graffiti—one swear word in bold black letters.

I thought of God's command to Habakkuk: "Write the

vision" (Habakkuk 2:2 NRSV). That gang had written their vision—a vision born of adversity and limited to one word that proclaimed their community. A gang gives its members companionship and a sense of identity and purpose. Within that community they know who is in charge, what to expect, and who their enemies are. But their vision fosters violence.

Habakkuk's words speak to us as members of the Christian community. Our community, like the gang's, gives us companionship and a sense of identity and purpose. But our vision is one born of love and peace and reconciliation. This vision is not painted graffiti on stone, but written daily with the work of our hands. It calls us to put feet on our fantasies and add deeds to our dreams, healing hearts and celebrating life.

NOVEMBER 6   GRATITUDE FOR LIFE

Read Psalm 150:1-6.

Today is my birthday. My birth, like yours, is amazing!

When I go back to the tenth generation beyond my parents, over two thousand women and men have been paired together into 1,024 specific couples who became my great-great-great/great-great-great/great-great-great-grandparents, scattered across different continents. I am here today only because the exact two people in every couple were attracted to each other, and all of those thousand-plus couples expressed their love physically during the month that they did! And then a particular son of half those unions loved a particular daughter of the other half, and expressed it when they did—and likewise their sons and daughters, and theirs, until the tenth generation, when my two sets of grandparents wed. And the only son of one and the second daughter of the other, born in different towns, found each other, married, and expressed their love in the moment that created me. Only then could I be here today—one who has received the gift of life! And so it is with you!

Once born, each of us who was physically able refused to settle for crawling and one day pulled ourselves to a standing position and began to try to walk. No matter how many times we fell down, we kept picking ourselves up and trying again. All of us!

God gave us not only the gift of life but also the gift of courage. "Let everything that breathes praise the LORD!" (Psalm 150:6 NRSV).

NOVEMBER 7   GRATITUDE FOR HOPE

Read Ephesians 1:11-23.

It hangs on my wall in the room where I work and reminds me of what real work, real patience, and real love are. It is a small piece of wood with "John 3:16" burned into the center and an intricate decorative border burned around the edge. Though of no financial value, it is a treasure to me—one I would save in the event of a fire.

My Czech friend made it. I met him when Bill and I visited a unique church near Prague. Its members—including the pastor, who is confined to a wheelchair—are a community of physically challenged Christians.

My friend has many physical excuses to live in hopelessness. Like his pastor, he lives and breathes and has his being in a wheelchair. His hands are gnarled and twisted as though useless. But those hands, hour after hour, day after day—one patient millimeter followed by another—wood-burned that treasured gift of love for us.

Paul prayed for the Ephesians, that "with the eyes of your heart enlightened, you may know what is the hope to which he has called you" (Ephesians 1:18 NRSV). That congregation of beautiful spirits enlightened the eyes of my heart so that I could see the hope to which the loving Christ has called us. When we face the impossible, our Lord brings hope to us, and with the birth of hope comes the possibility of achieving the impossible. Thanks be to God!

294

NOVEMBER 8   GRATITUDE FOR DIVERSITY

Read Psalm 104.

Recently I attended a seminar on how to lead workshops in multinational settings. The leader asked us to divide into groups of two or three and make a list of words we associate with diversity. The words were to begin with any one of the letters in *diversity*. When the groups completed the task and shared with the whole body, every one of the words was positive—such as *d*ynamic, *i*mportant, *v*alue, *e*nriching, *r*esponsible, *s*pirit, *i*nteresting, *t*otal, yeast. The words reflected the attitudes of the participants, but they were not what the leader wanted. Expecting the word *diversity* to arouse negative feelings, she had planned her follow-up lecture accordingly. But the Spirit had led us beyond the barriers.

As Christians, our worldview is not based on TV and newspapers. Owned by competitive megacorporations whose thundering call for profit stifles the whisper of honor and ethics, the media skew the news toward violence and destruction. (Perhaps that is because there is such a preponderance of good news that it isn't newsworthy!) Our faith calls us to look through the eyes of love, not fear, and recognize that grass-roots people across town and around the globe are all God's children with common hopes and concerns: security for family, dreams for children, safety to live full lives. With the psalmist we offer praise:

> O Lord, how manifold are your works!
> In wisdom you have made them all;
> the earth is full of your creatures.
> —Psalm 104:24 NRSV

NOVEMBER 9   GRATITUDE FOR UNIQUENESS

Read Luke 20:27-38.

I used to have a mental image of bishops' spouses that kept me at a distance. I was courteous but reserved with them. I don't know why. Perhaps I leaped to the conclusion that they would be judgmental. But then I became a bishop's spouse. And when I met the other spouses up close, I saw how distorted my view had been.

Persons married to bishops are the same unique human beings they would be otherwise. In my denomination they are male and female, liberal and conservative, employed for pay and employed for free. Some are clergy themselves; some are consultants; some are retreat leaders. Some are involved in education, some in the arts. Some raise money for worthy projects; some help network around the world. One has a Ph.D. Another is on a governor's task force. The traditional image of serious pious bishops' spouses is obsolete.

We all allow our images and stereotypes to steal life from members of groups we prejudge. We tend to see the deadening preconceived distortion we expect rather than the lively individual God gives us in the moment. What an opportunity we miss—both to be faithful and to enrich our lives! Luke tells us: "Now he is God not of the dead, but of the living; for to him all of them are alive" (Luke 20:38 NRSV). *All* of them!

NOVEMBER 10   GRATITUDE FOR RENEWAL

Read Haggai 2:1-9.

Like a one-eyed cyclops, the gaping hole stared down at me from high on the wall near the sanctuary rafters. This old Dallas church had once been filled with intergenerational families, but in recent decades the elders had died, their descendants had moved away, and the neighborhood had changed. Fear began to turn that community of faith into a corpse. In my mind I saw a tear fall from that single eye and heard the wall cry out, "Who is left among you that saw this house in its former glory?" (Haggai 2:3 NRSV).

But the basement witnessed to resurrection. Renovated for children's ministries, it was alive with their presence. Preschool children of all colors played and learned together, sang and laughed, drew and danced. I watched them gather for lunch around small tables, beginning with a prayer of thanks to God. Later in the day their bigger brothers and sisters also would come to the church for the after-school latchkey program. Through ministering to the neighborhood, that old urban church is coming alive again. Loving care has chased away fear.

When we went back upstairs, I stepped again into the sanctuary. It is farther down on the renovation list, for the worshiping congregation knows that sanctuary disrepair doesn't block God's presence. This time as I glanced at the gaping hole, I saw the smiling face of the Christ peeking through it.

NOVEMBER 11   GRATITUDE FOR VICTORY

Read Psalm 149.

> For the Lord takes pleasure in his people;
> he adorns the humble with victory.
> —Psalm 149:4 NRSV

Mary Pierce is one so adorned. Mary has invited many people to sit around her table. In the process, an urban neighborhood has been changed. Neighbors with community concerns sit beside city officials and inspectors, police officers, executives from a major foundation, and administrators from a school of theology.

There is nothing aggressive about Mary, nothing abrasive. She advocates bringing change by building a "ladies and gentlemen relationship." The people gathered round don't rise from her table feeling angry with one another; nor do they pat themselves on the back for a good discussion and better understanding. They rise to make a difference.

Working together they have painted over graffiti, picked up trash, rid the neighborhood of nearly two thousand tires by recycling them, and trimmed yards for senior citizens.

They saved their neighborhood fire station from closing, and it has become a state-of-the-art model station. They organized a cross-age, summer-activities program that keeps both youth and children busy, for the older ones oversee the younger ones.

Mary is humble herself, but proud of her community. She shows how people from diverse backgrounds can build relationships as they break bread together, no longer strangers to one another. When we offer our own table for this kind of feast, we brighten one small space in God's sacred world.

NOVEMBER 12 GRATITUDE FOR FAITHFULNESS

Read Psalm 145:1-5, 17-21.

Last year my husband, Bill, preached at a Sunday evening worship service in a church in Mikilov, Moravia.

The lively congregation prayed, testified to their faith, read scriptures, and listened to the preaching. But mostly, they sang—sang with joy in their voices and on their faces.

An older generation was notable, scattered across the front of the congregation. Less animated, they radiated a quiet strength. They had immigrated from Bulgaria during the years of World War II and the Communist takeover. Bill asked them if they would sing for us a Bulgarian hymn.

Shyly at first, the aged men and women began to sing. Their hymn was soulful and sad. Their eyes teared with memories of their homeland, for war had severed them from their roots, and they had never been able to return. Yet they were the ones who had brought the faith to Mikilov, Moravia, in Czechoslovakia half a century before.

"One generation shall laud your works to another, and shall declare your mighty acts," the psalmist proclaims (145:4 NRSV). In their stoic, steadfast way, these Christians from Bulgaria are a generation that lauded God's works to another generation and declared God's mighty acts.

A lost generation waits for us to be as faithful.

Read Psalm 122.

The dress-up celebration at the women's conference required native dress—striking fabrics of Africa, soft saris of India, long pastels of Asia, bold colors of South America, and nondescript attire of the West. Our customs and languages were as diverse as our dress, yet our faith united us.

Beforehand, each woman had written her name on a paper leaf. Now, as we sang together, those leaves in autumn reds and golds were hung on the barren branches of a tree, symbolizing that each of us *together* can bring new life to the world.

The plan, beautiful in the *thinking* stage, developed a problem in the *doing* stage. Because some branches were easier to reach, the leaves clumped together, and the tree began to lean. It ended up topsy-turvy and fragile.

Isn't that the way it is when diverse "tribes of the LORD" (Psalm 122:4 NRSV) work together? Inclusiveness is not neat and tidy. Not orderly. Not efficient. It is based more on hope, faith, and love than on achievement. It calls for perceptions from the spirit and visions from the heart. But no matter how lumpy and leaning the result, it is a source of wonder to the participants, evoking profound gratitude.

The Lord has many "tribes" who are "to give thanks." When we shape ourselves into a mosaic of gratitude—a mosaic complete because of the presence of each one and beautiful because of the pattern of the whole—we feel the jubilation of glorifying God.

NOVEMBER 14   GRATITUDE FOR CHALLENGE

Read 2 Thessalonians 2:1-5, 13-17.

There is a tendency to think that the idea of the equality of women is a relatively new development, one that the church fathers have resisted. But here is what one church father says. God lays down the same rules for both sexes. A woman "is endowed with reason on a par with man. She has the ability to think [and knows] what she ought to do. [She] knows as the [man] does what to avoid and what to look for. More than that, sometimes she is better than man at seeing what is useful, and she is a wise advisor." Those words came from Theodoret of the Greek Church, a church father writing in the fifth century!

Women have always been involved in shaping the world— at least the space around them. Historically, a few were involved overtly; many covertly through their influence upon husbands, fathers, sons.

A lot of responsibilities rest on our shoulders today— through our own choosing and our own actions. Surely it was simpler when Grandmom and Auntie lived in or nearby to help care for a sick child, cook and clean, wash and iron. Surely it was simpler before carpooling, commuting, and traffic jams. Surely it was simpler when the week was divided into routine days—such as wash on Monday, iron on Tuesday. Now each day is fragmented into hourly tasks and roles. It is not easy. But Paul reminds us that "our Lord Jesus Christ himself and God our Father" will "comfort [our] hearts and strengthen them in every good work and word" (2 Thessalonians 2:16-17 NRSV).

NOVEMBER 15   GRATITUDE FOR CHILDREN'S
                                    WISDOM

Read 2 Thessalonians 3:6-13.

A gray mist fell on this November Sunday morning. Rain dripped down the stained-glass window above the altar, like tears running down the cheeks of Jesus. The colors faded in the absence of sunlight, and voices too were subdued. The dark clouds seemed to hover just above the pews, pressing life's difficulties heavy upon us.

Those of us at the service were feeling smug about our own damp presence and judgmental of the others who had slept in. But mostly we were weary of doing our duty when that doesn't spare us adversity. A mood of Good Friday gloom shrouded this sabbath celebration of the Resurrection.

Then the Word came to us from a child during the children's sermon. The pastor asked the little ones gathered around her if they could remember any of the Ten Commandments. A little girl responded, "Thou shalt not whine."

Moses must have forgotten this one! Surely it was there. We can't praise God while we're whining. We can't hear the songs of the birds or the cries of the lonely; we can't taste fully the feast of life—not while we're whining.

Paul put it another way: "Brothers and sisters, do not be weary in doing what is right" (2 Thessalonians 3:13 NRSV). And he didn't add, "Unless, of course, you are experiencing adversity."

NOVEMBER 16   GRATITUDE FOR ADVERSITY

Read Isaiah 65:17-25.

Gratitude for adversity? Aren't those words contradictory? Isn't that expecting too much of us mortals?

We live in a given world. Not "given" as in "predetermination" but as in "gift." Our world is given us by God. We say with our words that we trust God. Yet we say with our lives that we do not. We live in anxiety about the next year, the next day, the next hour. Real trust in God leads to a response of *yes* to life—all of life—for life, like the world, is a gift.

Our *yes* does not mean that we are denying pain. We endure excruciating situations in which a part of us dies. Unable to bear the anguish, we go numb for three days or three months or three years. But our faith is a resurrection faith, and ultimately the stone is rolled away. Grief lingers to some degree, as does the scar from the wound. Yet the death of a part of us can birth another part of us. Through this awakening we experience the fullness of life. We die into deeper living—unless we choose to stay in the tomb after God rolls the stone away.

Isaiah reminds us that "before they call, I will answer, while they are yet speaking I will hear" (65:24 NRSV). Again and again God is with us in the tomb, and again and again God rolls the stone away.

NOVEMBER 17 GRATITUDE FOR MEMORIES

Read Daniel 7:1-3, 15-18.

She spoke to me through an interpreter, relating how horrible her life had become. And she was right. She was one of five hundred people in the twenty-seven rooms of a renovated school building in Travnik—one of the better refugee centers in Bosnia-Herzegovina. She and eighteen others lived together in an old classroom crowded with sleeping pallets and their few remaining possessions—the ones they were able to carry on their backs when they fled for their lives. The women and little ones knew that their missing husbands, sons, and fathers were doomed to be in one of the secret mass graves carved into the countryside where the trees watched and wept.

These refugees had lived in nice village homes before neighbor turned against neighbor, manipulated by the leadership of all three factions (Muslim Bosnians, Orthodox Serbs, and Catholic Croats). There were no innocents—each faction's leaders misused religion for political power.

Now, here she was—a refugee mourning lost loved ones, alone, with eighteen strangers for roommates and a tiny remnant of her cherished mementos. Like Daniel, she could say, "My spirit was troubled within me, and the visions of my head terrified me" (7:15 NRSV). Her face creased in anguish. She begged me to help her.

I listened. Powerless. Precious memories were the only good part of her present life.

Read Psalm 118.

Living next door to the woman we read about yesterday, and in the very same situation, was another refugee displaced by the war in Bosnia-Herzegovina. She too had fled from a nice home in a beautiful village. She too was living in a crowded classroom with strangers. She too had only a tiny remnant of her cherished mementos. She too was mourning her lost loved ones.

She was setting three little plates of food on a small table for three young children. In the turmoil of the country, they may or may not have been her own children but, regardless, she was their mother figure. As I passed by the open door of her room, she looked up at me and smiled.

She *smiled*.

The children saw her smile, and they too smiled at me.

This woman embodies the best of our gender. She was bringing happiness and peace to her tiny space, as horrible as it was. And the children God had given her in the moment, who had suffered so much, who now lived in the atmosphere she painted for them, felt safe and were able to smile at a stranger.

This courageous Bosnian woman "was pushed hard, so that [she] was falling" (Psalm 118:13 NRSV), but she was able to live out her faith and say, "This is the day that the LORD has made; let us rejoice and be glad in it" (Psalm 118:24 NRSV). The image of her smiling face continues to be for me a contemporary image of the face of Christ.

NOVEMBER 19   GRATITUDE FOR THE HEALER

Read Luke 6:20-31.

He bent to fix the toilet in my room at the retreat center, his jean jacket hanging loose over his head by the hood. He chatted while he worked, then turned to me, continuing his monologue. His bright blue eyes dominated his face framed by graying sandy hair.

"Talk about physical abuse!" he said as he raised his palm, fingers spread, holding back the invisible pain. "You haven't seen nothing until you've experienced mental abuse with the tongue! My mother called me a dummy from the time I was old enough to know the word 'til I was eighteen or nineteen years old. Then I went to college. And I learned I wasn't a dummy."

No, he wasn't a "dummy." But neither was he healed of the wounds inflicted so long ago.

"Love your enemies," Jesus said, "do good to those who hate you, bless those who curse you, pray for those who abuse you" (Luke 6:27-28 NRSV). That seems impossible. Yet loving our enemies can break their power over us; doing good to those who hate us can keep evil from producing evil; blessing those who curse us can free us from their curse; and praying for those who abuse us can heal our hearts.

I can't begin to imagine the inner strength required to pray for an abusive parent. But I can pray that one day he'll be able to do that. And then the Healer will hear and heal his broken heart.

NOVEMBER 20   GRATITUDE FOR IN-LAWS

Read Luke 21:5-19.

Today is the birthday of my daughter-in-love, Angela, the wife of my older son and the mother of Chelsea, Sarah, and Graham. One of my favorite pictures shows the two of us sitting together beside a fountain; it catches our comfortable joy in each other's presence.

In Luke Jesus warns us of conflict in the world: "Nation will rise against nation, and kingdom against kingdom" (21:10 NRSV). Our culture would set mother-in-law against daughter-in-law, and daughter-in-law against mother-in-law.

Cartoons, TV sitcoms, and jokes implant an expectation that in-law relationships result in conflict rather than support—especially conflict between daughters-in-law and mothers-in-law. How easily these expectations become a self-fulfilling prophecy! I cringe at my own early misperceptions about my husband's dear mother.

The bridge toward an authentic, loving relationship feels slippery at times on both sides. Continuing toward each other takes a lot of swallowed words and patient listening. If we are concerned about meeting the other halfway (and only halfway), we may never get together. What difference does it make who goes the farthest? What matters is getting within soul-hugging distance, undergirding each other with love and support, and truly adopting each other into our heart of hearts.

Today I send a hug on angel's wings to Angela, a hug filled with deep love and gratitude.

NOVEMBER 21   GRATITUDE FOR FREEDOM

Read Isaiah 12.

We sat beside each other, drinking coffee and eating cookies. Her deep brown eyes looked directly into mine. She, my Kairos sponsoree, was serving a life sentence in a Louisiana women's prison. I didn't ask why, and she didn't say. She'd been there since her children were small. Grown now, they live in a northern state where they were reared by their grandmother.

The bars surrounding my Kairos friend are visible. Ours outside of prison are invisible but no less real. We gradually imprison ourselves as we surrender our inner resources and succumb to pressures around us, as we grow bitter and cynical in the face of life's adversities, as we begin to look at ourselves as victims and relinquish our own responsibilities. A judge sentenced her. We sentence ourselves.

"I will trust," Isaiah says,"and will not be afraid,/for the

LORD GOD is my strength and my might" (12:2 NRSV). My Kairos friend does not forget this. She wakes up each morning behind bars and marshals her inner resources through prayer and Scripture reading. She is paying dearly—but without bitterness and cynicism—for the worst thing she ever did in her life. Taking responsibility for herself, she blames no one else. Her outer world is a prison, but her inner world is free.

We too can remove the invisible bars around our inner lives by remembering to trust the Holy One and not be afraid, for God strengthens and sustains us.

NOVEMBER 22   GRATITUDE FOR SABBATH
                                              WORSHIP

Read Psalm 63.

Weekly we come together in worship as the people of God, to celebrate the Resurrection. Like the psalmist, we too can say, "In the shadow of your wings I sing for joy" (63:7 NRSV).

Sometimes we come to worship with our souls in darkness, aware of the shadow of death—worried about marriage, children, friendships, health, money, pressures from a job or lack of one, loneliness, emptiness, addictions, monotonous routines and ruts. We slip into the sanctuary with our souls empty and groaning.

Yet, with our weekly rhythm of celebrating resurrection comes the joy of anticipation and confidence. We pray and praise, hear the Word, offer our gifts and receive God's grace, confess and feel compassion for others (and ourselves), repent and are renewed. As we sit in the pews, we feel the awakening of our dead souls. In the shadow of God's wings we sing for joy, and in the light of God's love we are sent forth.

We come to worship disheveled. We leave dedicated to share the good news by the way we live out our lives in our home world and our work world.

And wonder of wonders, next week we can come again!

NOVEMBER 23   GRATITUDE FOR CELEBRATION

Read Psalm 100.

To celebrate is to praise, to honor, to commemorate, to proclaim. When we think of celebration, we think of birthdays, anniversaries, and holidays. For Christians, there are also celebrations when we come together for special events. "Worship the LORD with gladness," the psalmist tells us, "come into his presence with singing" (100:2 NRSV). This verse seems to set the tone not only for weekly worship but also for special services.

For me, the word *celebration* is epitomized by a worship service I attended in Rio de Janeiro. Thousands of Christians from all over Brazil came together, many riding all night on buses. The participants in a global church conference were their guests. The Word was preached and sung and danced. Great choirs offered vibrant anthems. During a lively hymn about the Holy Spirit, children ran around the huge arena, flying kites with colorful tails that waved above the crowd. All of us—rich beside poor, old beside young, our nationality beside another—became renewed, rejuvenated, recommitted.

When we come into God's presence with singing and we worship the Lord with gladness, it is as if we awake from a deep sleep. The stone is rolled away, and we step into the light of the Son. In that light we can blossom into a beautiful garden for God.

NOVEMBER 24   GRATITUDE FOR OPPORTUNITIES

Read Jeremiah 23:1-7.

Recently I visited my denomination's mission home in San Antonio, Texas, now in its second century of service. It is directed by a layman. One program focuses on multiply challenged deaf persons, training them for jobs and teaching them how to live independently. All of the staff know sign language; some are deaf persons themselves.

During my tour, one of the teenage clients took it upon herself to join us in a leadership role. Petite, with dark hair and a bright smile, her denim dress spotless, she signed that she wanted us to see the dorm—specifically, her room. When we became sidetracked, she rounded us up in her charming way and turned us toward her goal. The smell of cleanser told us she had just cleaned her room. Her beaming face told us she was proud that she could do it. Soon she would be able to move into a transitional apartment complex.

God "will raise up shepherds over them who will shepherd them," Jeremiah says, "and they shall not fear any longer, or be dismayed" (23:4 NRSV). This teenager shepherded us as she had been shepherded at the home: with joy and determination and an eagerness to share. Her world is not one of sounds, but it is one of smiles, for she is not afraid or dismayed.

I wonder how often we miss shepherding opportunities, for not all the shepherds God raises up are clergy.

NOVEMBER 25   GRATITUDE FOR ACTION

Read Luke 23:33-43.

"The people stood looking on, and their rulers jeered at him," writes Luke about the crucifixion of Jesus (23:35 NEB). How easy it is for us to look on while others jeer at someone. We remain silent, not wanting them to turn their jeering on us. That "jeering" can range from public harassment to a private conversation that belittles an absent one. Even if we don't add some form of jeering ourselves, our silent presence can be interpreted as tacit approval. Indeed, we may desire that interpretation in order to protect ourselves from the disagreeableness of disagreement! We stand guilty time and again of the sin of omission.

You know the parable of the snowstorm and the tree. Snowflakes, one at a time, come to rest on a branch of a massive tree. Each snowflake is so tiny and weightless that it makes no impact on the tree. Soon thousands of them are thick on the limb. Then one more minuscule snowflake falls, and the tree limb breaks.

The parable causes us to ponder whether our tiny weightless snowflake of silent omission will be the one that finally breaks part of another's life—this child of God given us in the moment—when a word of support or a gesture of kindness might have nurtured and sustained.

NOVEMBER 26 GRATITUDE FOR CHOICES

Read Philippians 4:4-9.

We have many choices around the Thanksgiving Day feast table—garden salad or cranberry salad, candied yams or mashed potatoes, pumpkin pie or mincemeat pie, maybe even ham or turkey. Or, more than likely, we forget choices and just eat it all!

We also have a choice about what we say to other people—something kind or aggressive, straightforward or passive; something that soothes or leaves a stinging residue; something that brightens the flame of faith, hope, and charity or whooshes it out with a whisper. Or perhaps we forget we have choices and our words go unleashed.

We have a choice about what we do each day—feeding our minds with junk food or with nutrients, deepening our relationships or pretending two monologues equal dialogue, venturing on a holistic spiritual journey or settling for pseudo-faith. Or perhaps, unaware of choices, we bump along the same ruts year after year.

We have a choice about our thoughts, which affect our attitudes. We can focus on lies, dishonor, injustice, corruption—on what is disagreeable, worthless, insignificant, and reprehensible. But that is not what Paul taught: "Finally, beloved, whatever is true, whatever is honorable, whatever is just, whatever is pure, whatever is pleasing, whatever is commendable, if there is any excellence and if there is anything worthy of praise, think about these things" (Philippians 4:8 NRSV).

On this Thanksgiving Day, as we feast with family and friends, may we feast also on holy thoughts.

NOVEMBER 27   GRATITUDE FOR THE SAINTS

Read Colossians 1:11-20.

A meeting in a sanctuary opened with prayer, and I leaned my chin on the tip of my left-hand forefinger. When I reopened my eyes, still looking down, the small, unremarkable engagement diamond with my wedding band did a remarkable thing—it reflected a section of the stained-glass window above the altar. Just a few inches from my eyes was a blue-robed Christ with outstretched arms. I moved my finger slightly and saw the word *hold* reflected in red. Searching the distant window, I finally found *Behold*. It seemed magical that something so tiny as my ring could mirror the original work so beautifully that the reflection was brighter and more detailed than the images in the distant window.

Something of that idea may be what Paul had in mind when he wrote, "May you be prepared to endure everything with patience, while joyfully giving thanks to the Father, who has enabled you to share in the inheritance of the saints in the light" (Colossians 1:11-12 NRSV). The saints stand distant from us in the long-ago past, but we share their inheritance; we see their reflection in others' lives. This reflection can go unnoticed if we are too preoccupied to pray, too practical to pursue mystery, or too hurried for patience.

The reflection can teach us of a Christ with outstretched arms, inclusive of all. It can teach us to "hold" one another in loving support. When we do this, we share in the inheritance of the saints in the light.

Read Luke 1:67-79.

My friend from Pakistan told me about a boy named Sala-mat, which means "peace." He was wrongly accused of a crime and sentenced to death, for he was of a minority reli-gion rather than of the faith of the State. At first letters and pleas made no difference, but as they piled high and the sit-uation drew attention from the international community, the boy finally was exiled instead of executed.

From prison he flew far away to a strange home in a foreign land. His new family would love him and treat him well. But he would not be able to see his parents or his old home, hear his old language on the street, see his old friends, or be with the Pakistani people who had worked so hard to save his life. And so the people ask, "When will Salamat [meaning peace] fly back to Pakistan?"

And we too ask a question. When will *salamat*/peace fly into our own lives and communities and nation and hemi-sphere?

> By the tender mercy of our God,
>   the dawn from on high will break upon us,
> to give light to those who sit in darkness and in
>   the shadow of death,
>   to guide our feet into the way of peace.
>   —Luke 1:78-79 NRSV

We wait for that dawn, and we help bring it about by guid-ing our feet and our words into the way of peace.

NOVEMBER 29   GRATITUDE FOR SIMPLICITY

Read Matthew 24:36-44.

Jesus reminds us that "if the owner of the house had known in what part of the night the thief was coming, he would have stayed awake and would not have let his house be broken into" (Matthew 24:43 NRSV). Our spiritual house gets broken into because we do not keep awake. We nod off spiritually for days or months or years, which affects all the other dimensions of our lives, including our relationships with others.

A priest once asked Mother Teresa how to live faithfully. She told him to spend an hour a day in adoration of the Lord and not to do anything he knew was wrong. Mother Teresa's words are simple, like the faithful presence of her life. But what an impact that kind of wakefulness could make!

The things around us would change if we began the morning by centering ourselves in the Lord and spent the rest of the day not doing anything that we know is wrong—not at home, not at work, not at church. No matter how tempting. Not to get something we want. Not to gain power. Not even to make a few more dollars.

We wouldn't change the whole world. But our wakefulness would bring grace to our own small space within it. And, after all, the world is merely a combination of small spaces.

NOVEMBER 30   GRATITUDE FOR JOY

Read Psalm 89:14-18.

The psalmist sings, "Happy are the people who know the festal shout"! (89:15 NRSV). During November, we have pondered gratitude for many aspects of life, and we come to the end of this month knowing the festal shout.

We know it early in the morning when we sit in solitude at the table of the Lord. We know it around the feast table with family and friends. We know it when we carry our table into the world, welcoming others, serving them, and offering a hospitality of the heart wherever we find ourselves.

The festal shout is a silent shout of the soul. Saint Augustine suggested:

No words are needed to make [our] joy heard. It is the song of a soul overflowing with joy. . . . We find ourselves in this state of jubilation when we are glorifying God and we feel incapable of speaking of [God]—when for example we are considering the whole creation which makes itself available for us to know and to act in. The soul then asks: "Who has made all this? And who has put me here?"

And we can do no other than exult in our Lord's name!

In the light of the Lord's countenance, reflecting Christ's love by loving God's children given us in the moment, we respond in gratitude for the joyful gift of life, dancing our faith into the future!

December
Unexpected Light
Donna Schaper

God's strategy of unexpected light is one we all know well. Our personal experience tells us that God most often arrives unexpectedly—not on cue, not by command, not even by the most earnest prayers. God comes when God will, not when we will.

Gladness leaps to joy when we least expect it. I get to the end of my tunnel and begin to give up. But I see a light deep down there, and so I keep going. I often describe the God I know as living at the bottom of my stomach—in the place below fear. I rarely expect to be met in the midst of so much trouble, trouble that often derives from exclusion of God in the first place. But I am met. The light I expect may or may not arrive, but the light I don't expect always does. God surprises me in joy and in sorrow.

Sending a baby as Messiah was not what the Jews were expecting. Something grander would have communicated the Messiah to them.

God's sending Jesus as a baby did three things: It disarmed

their great expectations, it let them feel good about their own smallness, and it surprised them. Some even may have had their warm responses to a baby leap to a larger joy, the joy we know now as Christmas—Emmanuel, God, surprisingly with us, coming to a dark world with an unexpected light.

Thank you, God, for your ever-surprising gift of Jesus.

DECEMBER 2   "LET THERE BE LIGHT"

There are at least two different meanings for the word *light*. One comes from a candle; the other is the opposite of *heavy*. As women, we reach for both. We want what lets us see, and we want what contrasts heaviness. We want to be people of the light step, people free from hurry and its anxiety. We want to be lighthearted. We also want to be well lit; we want sparkle in our eyes, and we want to see that sparkle in others as well. We want an inner glow.

We want to "let" there be light! Spiritual light is like the light of creation. It doesn't come from our action, such as turning on a switch, as much as it comes from God's action, such as creating us out of nothing. God had a surplus energy in creation. First, we weren't. Then we were. Light was let to be.

One kind of light enables the other: When we can see deeply enough into our lives, we see that God's action "let" our action become possible. First God made us; then we made electricity.

I find great peace in knowing that I did not create myself. I was made. I am not self-generated, nor do my days need to be.

Keep us, O God, from turning ourselves on and off. Let us remember that we were handmade, by you.

DECEMBER 3   PRAYING AT HOME

Our homes are places where we can pray. There we light candles. There we find our way to peace. Maybe we kneel at the side of our bed before we sleep, or count sheep and give God thanks for every one of them. Maybe we pray in the morning—outside, facing east, turning to the light.

How we pray doesn't really matter. The way we manage the blessing of our homes with prayer is what is important. The peace is what matters. Marge Piercy describes the rhythm of prayer as coming through the great doors of night into the "clean quiet room of Sabbath."

Prayer is the practice of the presence of God. It involves Sabbath and morning and evening rituals. These things are best done in the home, not in temple or at church. They make the days good.

Lift up the light of your countenance on us, O God, in the light of dawn and the light of the Sabbath.

DECEMBER 4   THE BROKEN LIGHT

In 1896, Thomas Alva Edison, the great inventor, presented the first incandescent lightbulb ever made to an admiring crowd at Princeton University. The hundreds of people present in the great hall had invested in his invention. They were shareholders.

Edison had invited an eleven-year-old boy to carry the first lightbulb forward on a velvet tray. The boy made it up the first steps to the podium, and he made it up the second set of stairs. On the third little rise, he tripped and fell. In front of the entire assembly, he broke the first incandescent lightbulb.

Edison must have been very upset, but he did not show it. He simply invited the entire crowd to come back one week from that day—at the same time, to the same place. When that day came, the same boy carried a new lightbulb on a velvet tray. He made it up the first set of stairs. He made it up the second set of stairs. He even made it up the last little rise, and there he presented the first lightbulb to a roaring, cheering crowd.

What was the crowd actually cheering? Not only the

lightbulb. They also were cheering a great inventor who knew how to forgive. Edison had learned how to start over and over again. He knew the presence of God.

God is with us when we are "good" and when we drop things, at home or in public. Prayer attends both good and bad, both in and out.

God, be with us in the broken light.

DECEMBER 5   BEING INCARNATION

What statement best describes you and your activities this Christmas season?

I . . .

—— love Christmas preparation.
—— will fly to be with family for Christmas.
—— will entertain more than twenty people during the season.
—— will participate in a Christmas Eve service.
—— am maintaining a daily Advent devotional discipline.
—— have more than four grandkids.
—— have children at home who still get excited about Christmas morning.
—— have kids who still get excited about Jesus!
—— will share a joy with friends.
—— have written my Christmas cards already!
—— have seen an example of love being shown recently.
—— will vacation during the week between Christmas and New Year's Day.

These were some of the responses given to the opening question at an Advent gathering recently. Each of these can include the Spirit of God, if the door is open to God's partnership. God let Jesus carry his Spirit to earth; this permission is what we call the Incarnation. We have that permission every day in every way.

The Benedictines will tell you that you may wash dishes to the glory of God. You may wash hands spiritually. You may enjoy heaven on earth.

God's strategy to "ransom captive Israel" is incarnation. Here's the double meaning: Earth and heaven are one, in God.

Such is the point of Advent: incarnation-overlap. The sacred and the profane are the bread in the sandwich; Jesus is the meat. We are connected to Christmas trees and holly as well as to matters that are much more, and perhaps much less, holy.

O God, let the holy be comfortable to us as it comes among us.

DECEMBER 6   TIPPING THE BALANCE

*The wrong we do is made worse by the good we leave undone.**

What tips the balance between good and evil? Forgiveness tips it. Not giving up tips it. Falling down seven times and getting up eight tips it. I know because I've been forgiven. I've been allowed by the grace of God to go on. My major impediment has been looking back after being forgiven—when I could have looked forward. I got stuck in my sin: God did not.

In winter, when the earth tilts away from the light, we have lots of chances to miss what is really going on. What is really going on is Advent and its preparation for the way of forgiveness. God is sending Jesus to earth. Jesus is one sign of our absolute forgiveness.

Jesus was clearly brilliant, with a remarkable and poetic, metaphoric mind. He was not ascetic but world affirming. He was an ecstatic, and he practiced the presence of God. He was a healer filled with the Spirit of God. Jesus taught the wisdom of forgiveness—that we are free also to be filled with the Spirit of God. That Spirit tips the balance for good. We may stop leaving any more good undone.

O God, with hearts open to your love, with hands outstretched to one another, and with whole selves willing to accept the cost and joy of being Christ's disciples, let us accept your forgiveness.

*From a confession written by Peter Heinrichs, pastor of South Church, Springfield, Massachusetts.

DECEMBER 7 ADVENT SPOTTING

The World Trade Center, New York City

Her appointment was on the top floor.
She went back down.
She has paid $14.00 an hour
To park the car.

To the attendant:
"When do you arrive at work?"
"7:00 A.M."
"When do you get off?"
"5:00 P.M."
"When do you take lunch?"
"We don't get lunch."
"How much are you paid?"
"Seven dollars an hour."

"By the way, lady,
when you are way up there,
can you see us down here?"

Labor asks questions.
"Lady, can you see us down here?"
She could.

Cookies

She bought store-bought rolled cookies.
She makes them for her children.
She finds a song in her heart.
She sits down
With her children and eats the cookies.
They weren't homemade.
But they were good.

If we want to find Advent, all we have to do is look around us, right where we are, and see what we can see. I wrote these poems after hearing two friends tell their stories. These two friends practiced the art of Advent spotting. They looked where they were. They saw what they saw. They did what they could. They found God nearby.

Advent promises God is near. Advent delivers on its promises.

Open our eyes, Lord, that we may truly see.

DECEMBER 8   **HOPELESS HOMELESS**

Think of how their feet hurt.
Think of the cold.
Think of the boredom.
Think of their stuff, of carrying it all on their backs.
Think of their closetlessness.
Think of their lost children.
Think of no telephone.
Think of no mail.
Think of shampoo.
Think of coffee.
Think of Jesus.
He bore it all by refusing to bear it.

Some things you must always be unable to bear. Some things you must never stop refusing to bear. Injustice and outrage

321

and dishonor and shame. No matter how young you are or how old you have got. Not for kudos and not for cash; your picture in the paper nor money in the bank either. Just refuse to bear them.

—William Faulkner, "Intruder in the Dust"

Come, Holy Spirit, with homes for all. Come soon.

DECEMBER 9   THROWN OUT

I once read a story about a famous actor who ducked into a four-star hotel to escape a sudden downpour. An assistant manager spotted him but did not recognize him. After announcing that the hotel had had a rash of room thefts, he asked the actor to leave. A small argument ensued, after which the actor was promptly thrown out. He said that he never again set foot in that hotel for fear of being taken again for a petty thief.

Have you ever been thrown out? Or made to feel unwelcome? Or told you didn't belong? Have you been made to feel less than someone else? If so, you are ready for Advent. Our God had no room in the inn. Our God came to earth as an outsider. Be an outsider today in honor of God's choice to have no home.

Get thrown out of a nice store or restaurant or hotel—or imagine such an experience! It will help you know God.

God is not the one who keeps us from getting thrown out of places. We are the ones who live to keep God from getting thrown out.

Today I will be an outsider, God, in honor of your choice to come to our world as an outsider.

DECEMBER 10   "AS QUIET AS BETHLEHEM"

Poet Thomas Merton wrote that the full moon is "as quiet as Bethlehem." Even if I can't always hear the great quiet of Bethlehem, I know it's there. Advent's music may be absent for me, but I can remember times when it was there. I also can look forward to its return. If things get really noisy, I can sneak out for quiet in the night.

One of the gifts of insomnia is 3:00 A.M.—when it is "dead" quiet. In those moments the quietness draws me close to peace—toward the great quiet of Bethlehem. If you're not lucky enough to have insomnia during Advent, set your alarm clock for 3:00 A.M. Alarm clocks are very important in Advent—and can't go off often enough in any case. Wake up, they say, wake up—and prepare for the great quiet of Bethlehem.

Quiet us, O God. Quiet us deeply.

DECEMBER 11   SITTING IN DARKNESS

The people which sat in darkness saw great light.
—Matthew 4:16 KJV

Let us sit in darkness sometime today before we light a candle. Then we'll be acquainted with the darkness enough to know the light. Many of us know just how bad things are for some people. We know about the children who are going to bed hungry, or alone, after having been beaten. We know about the parents who long ago ran out of energy for these children—and how much they yearn for the return of love to their hearts. We know our own dark prisons and acknowledge the dark times we have already endured. The dark has much truth in it—perhaps too much. But the dark is not phony; it is real. Walk first in darkness to see a great light.

When we have let our hearts touch the great sadness that the world knows, and that we know, let us light a candle. That candle is the promise of God to be with us in Jesus. The presence is as real as the darkness. The presence is real, not just in the candle but also in the act of lighting it. We made the decision for the light. There is no end to the decisions we can make for the light.

But first we must walk in the darkness. Then we may reach for a light.

Let the light shine in the darkness, O God. Put our hands on a match so that we can be a partner in incarnation.

DECEMBER 12 "FEAR NOT, FOR BEHOLD . . ."

There is no point in our fear. If we fear not, just as the Christmas angel tells us in Luke 2:10-12, we can become light and let the heavy go. I think often of the comment made by one of Handel's great sponsors. She said that she could not bear the sight of him seated next to, but not playing, his harpsichord after he went blind. "His light was not spent but overplied," she said. Many of us are spent. The weight of our work catches up with us—and vision means nothing more than great longing for the empty afternoon of a snowy day.

Wanting "more vision" may actually be greed, the kind that leads us so inexorably to the "too-muchness" of our time. What most of us need is less, not more, of just about everything. We are longing for the time that is light to carry, as opposed to heavy. We want the deep rest of Sabbath time.

If this Sabbath works, grace will pay a visit. The afternoon will open up into God's time. The first step is to leave our fear at the door, to take the angel's advice. Fear not. Then we can come into the quiet room God has made for us.

Let us get to our empty afternoon earlier today, O God. Give us enough light for today, and every day, along the way. Give us habitual light.

DECEMBER 13 "COME, THOU LONG-EXPECTED JESUS"

Living by long expectation is living by habitual light. Automatically lighting a candle in the evening lets us sit and remember that there is no reason to be afraid. We have our "later" now. We have our lightness now. We have our light now.

The theme of Advent is Jesus' coming as unexpected light. Jesus, the Messiah, is often described as the "long expected One." In our daily meditation, we make a habit of long expectation. The strategy of God was to surprise the world with the Messiah—almost to sneak up on us with the good news, hoping that maybe we could hear it that way. Trumpets and crowns might obscure it. Something simple, small, and common in experience, such as a baby, might not frighten us as much as a flashier Messiah would. God's strategy is unexpected light—to make the light come out of a place where we least expect it, so that we can surely comprehend it and not be afraid of its power to change and complete our lives.

Encourage us, O God, in the habit of deep waiting, wherein we mark time by lighting candles and looking deeply into their glow.

DECEMBER 14   GOD'S LIGHT STILL SHINES

You are the light of the world.   *—Matthew 5:14 NRSV*

God's light is for the people who don't make it, who never get beyond what has been done to them. Bad things have happened to us. Bad things have happened to children. Innocent people have been harmed. Old ladies have been knocked over in parking lots. But still, God is the light of the world. Today, we remember that evil is not in charge. We acknowledge that *God is in charge.*

Some of us have stopped watching the news for fear that another set of frightened eyes will tell us another fire story or crime story or child-rape story. Others have stopped listening to our aging parents' arthritis stories. Others have tuned out our own arthritis or bursitis or-itis-itis. We have made decisions for the dark and not looked up for a long time.

God's light still shines. It makes its appearance even to those who don't look up to see it. We could look around today and peek, just to make sure we're not missing something! We could read the story of God's adventure in Jesus and see if there is anything there for us. Or we could tell someone else that we are looking for the light and wonder if we could borrow some of theirs. The light is there, even when we can't see it.

Lift up our eyes, Lord. Let us risk seeing the light—your light, and ours.

DECEMBER 15   LIGHT AND THE ALIENATED

A light to lighten the Gentiles. . . .   —*Luke 2:32 KJV*

If we can get beyond this left-brain/right-brain stuff and beyond being a liberal or a conservative, we begin to develop peripheral vision. We begin to understand the Gentiles—the outsiders—and the Gentile within us. Advent tells us that Gentiles don't disappear; rather, they/we lighten up. We see our opponent in ourselves and ourself in our opponent.

When it comes to enemies, everybody has a few. Each of us has our own fears and our own paranoias. We have reason not to trust everyone we know. We have reason not to trust ourselves.

When Jesus comes to lighten even the Gentiles, he is addressing these alienated parts and persons. He is encompassing our fears and our paranoias. He puts his great arms all the way around them. Nothing stays untouched by the light. Grace accepts the things we can't accept—both within us and outside of us. Even those who have hurt us, violated us, stolen our dignity—even these Gentiles—get the love of God. The good news is, in a way, that we no longer have to forgive them. God does. We don't have to keep them at arm's length—or, for that matter, get too close. God has taken care of what we can't manage. We walk in the same light as our enemies do.

Open our hearts, O God, to the Gentile, the Samaritan, the one who snubbed us, the one who violated us. Like a door finally opened, then rush in with your light. Take fear from our doorstep.

DECEMBER 16   INTO THE CLUTTER

"It came upon the midnight clear . . ." we sing. So little is clear—so much is fuzzy. Advent can bring us to clarity. The process is the lifting of one layer of confusion and clutter at a time, so that we may see. Like cleaning out a closet that has been allowed to fill up for years, spiritual clarity is the removal of layer after layer of what the Berenstein bears call "messy buildup." When cleaning closets, we put aside all that is unnecessary. We give away what we can no longer use. We throw things away and kiss them good-bye on their way to the dump.

Spiritual clarity is as often ignored as spring cleaning. We almost fear it, so large is the task. The daily habit of devotions can confront the size of the task. Every day we can do a little. At that pace, any project, inner or outer, is possible.

Advent gives a focus both to history and to personal life—both, not one or the other. It says that God came down, into this clutter, into this mess, into these closets where we hide what we don't want to know. God is here, at the very center. We just have to peel the layers back and get to the focus. We don't have to be afraid of what might be there, on the deep inside. It will not be empty. There will be Jesus, incarnate as Messiah.

Show us, O God, how we use confusion to avoid spiritual clarity. Give us a deeper appreciation of our layered complexity, and from deep within it, let us see the center of history, the center of our life.

DECEMBER 17   A SHELTER

Ulysses, a forty-year-old African-American male and former journalist, entered the ministry as a second career.

One balmy night early in his internship he went to the door of his church upon hearing what he thought were firecrackers. He entered the church vestibule only to be grabbed by a woman and dragged out to the street where another woman lay bleeding. She had been shot in the head by a drive-by shooter. Her two children, ages four and seven, were leaning over her yelling, "Mommy, Mommy, wake up, Mommy!" It was clear that she was already dead.

Ulysses put his arms around the children and called out the name of God. He felt like a shelter, he said, a useless shelter, but there was nothing to do but to sit there and hold on to the children. The police came. The ambulance came. The reporters came.

It was when the reporters came that Ulysses remembered who he used to be: an observer. Now—as he sat there in the middle of the street sheltering two children who were not his own—now he was no longer a reporter. He had become something else, like a shelter—maybe even a minister.

Help me, O God, to be a shelter for those in need.

**DECEMBER 18   A PRAYER FROM THE STAINED-
GLASS WORKSHOP**

Sometimes, O God, you move into my life so surreptitiously that I don't even know you are coming. I remember the time you found me in the stained-glass workshop. It was early morning. The stained-glass repairers were already there, making colors, patching broken glass, and letting beauty find its way to light. You brought tears to my eyes. I repair stained glass for a living too—I repair broken churches. You let me know the depth of my grief that day. You let me acknowledge how much beauty and color is already gone. Help me bring it back. Help the stained-glass repairers bring it back. Help the street workers bring it back.

Help the youth group leaders bring it back. Let us help you bring it back.

I remember the yellow there that they had spent two years perfecting. It was to match a certain fourteenth-century alabaster. Thank you for making such a beautiful yellow. Help me to get my yellow right. Let me be patient in learning my skill and my art and my yellow.

O God, I know that not all the glass is broken, not all the lives are broken. Most of the stories, in fact, are unbreakable—made of stronger stuff. But enough glass is broken, enough color has already disappeared from our lives. Help us, O God. Don't break us, but help us put things together.

Use us for color, for light, and let us be headed straight for both. Let us today be a part of their restoration.

In the name of sparkling light, Amen.

DECEMBER 19   WHY LEARN TO PRAY?

One morning by the oddest of chances, I saw a Paris street sweeper on the steps of the great cathedral Sacre Coeur, which overlooks the entire city of Paris. He was sweeping the broken wine bottles and empty potato chip bags off the steps of the cathedral. They appear every night as the product of youths who enjoy the city lights.

All day long the faithful go in and out of the cathedral. At night the revelers arrive. They leave a mess.

At one point, between steps, he leaned on his shaggy broom and closed his eyes. Surely he was praying for strength to do the rest of the steps. Why clean the cathedral? Because the people who want to pray will soon be there.

We pray by hoping for the triumph of our "day selves" and our "dawn selves" over our "night selves," because there is a little bit of litter in each one of us—and a little bit of the saint also. We each have a part of us that is night and a part that is day, a part that is worship and a part that is revelry.

Why learn to pray? Because we want our "day selves," our

"saint selves," our "worshiping selves" to come out a little ahead of the other parts.

Why pray without ceasing? Because the night will come. The bottles will break on the steps of Sacre Coeur (which means sacred heart). We will have nothing to do with their mess, and their shards, but to pray them off the steps.

Why learn to pray? Because dawn will follow night. Because joy will come in the morning. Because prayer can happen anywhere, even between steps at the back end of a broom.

Lord, teach us to pray your way, not ours.

DECEMBER 20   BEING LIGHT

Thy whole body shall be full of light.
—Matthew 6:22 KJV

We come to a clearing in the great forest of our days. There is a glow; it is from God. We can meditate our way to the clearing today. Then we can see the rest of our day from its perspective.

In meditation, we may not see what we planned to see. We may find that the person at the center of the clearing is a friend, holding a flashlight; or a long-lost relative, who is stringing lights on a Christmas tree; or a kitten with glowing eyes; or a wolf, strangely gentle. Meditation is fun because it doesn't announce its destination until we arrive.

Meditation is often "grabby." It wants something "spiritual" for us. And surely it delivers. But one of the great zany ironies of life is that we get only what we give away. If we become the light in someone else's clearing, we may find more light in our own. I like to come into another's life, almost unannounced, and really connect to the script the other person is reading. I like to be that person's light. It makes me more confident that I will find my own.

O God, let light shine for me and from me.

The "flap" in the O. J. Simpson trial about who could wear an angel lapel pin or angel earrings tells us more than we want to know about the theology of the American middle class. To say that it is slightly pagan is to underestimate it. I prefer to call it "folk" religion. I believe the gospel can be served by folk wisdom as well as by professional wisdom.

Folk religion is more prevalent than we believe. According to one survey, 53 percent of Americans "believe" in angels; 92 percent of Southerners believe that the devil's power is equal to that of God. Louis Harris used his own pagan polling religion to get those figures.

The simple things that people want from church should not be belittled. They are comfort—like a bowl of mashed potatoes. They are small things. One day on a long car trip I heard "Someone to Watch over Me" by Ella Fitzgerald on the radio. I cried and cried and cried. I told the mountains I wanted someone to watch over me. I am sure an angel came into the car and drove the rest of the way with me. Or might have. Or did. Can't be quite sure anymore. But the story "preached." I no longer mock others' "paganism," particularly as I begin to understand how much of it I have myself.

The biographer of Henry Ward Beecher records that Mr. Beecher said, "A text is like a gate; some ministers swing back and forth on it; I push it open and go in." Beecher also said, "Do not prove things too much," and "No knowledge is really knowledge until you can use it without knowing it." These admonitions tell me that we have to get out of our own way in lots of things. Maybe all we have to do is wait for the angel of the Lord.

Today I wait for your presence, your message, O God, however it may come.

People come to church on Sundays, after they have been in charge of their week, looking for "someone to watch over me." They know they're in trouble—if not for sin, then for the weight of carrying themselves all the time. Religion exists to manage "extra-dependence" well. Extra-dependence is the mature part of dependency. Whereas interdependence is the area of doing, of work, of roles well played, of law, extra-dependence is the area of being, of play, of essence, of grace. Lloyd Ogilvie advises us, "Let God love you." Lean on the everlasting arms.

Think of a child and a mother at a park. The child circles the mother. The child goes farther and farther away from the mother but touches base as part of the circle he or she makes.

We are like that with God. Worship is touching base. Those who don't worship don't touch base. They die of their trouble, of the sheer weight of carrying it.

John Wesley said that the true catholic spirit involves asking the right questions of one another. We can avoid trouble by getting to the right question. He said, "I ask not of you, whether you allow baptism and the Lord's supper at all? Let all these things stand by; we will talk of them, if need be, at a more convenient season; my only question at present is this, 'Is thine heart right, as my heart is with thy heart?' "

Athletes might call worship "being in the zone." Will we be in the zone this week—sometime, if not all the time? Will we let God love us? Will our hearts be right? These are the things that matter, in Advent and year-round.

O God, help us to get our hearts right, today and every day.

DECEMBER 23   THE PLASTIC, PARTICIPATORY
CRÈCHE

The most popular nativity scene in one Minneapolis church is a set of large, nonbreakable figures made in Germany. Children are invited to move the figures and to talk to them. Most do!

Salvation has the nature of a child, said Paul Tillich. The best thing about children is that they don't get stranded too far away from their own experience. We may think it is cute that they talk to the crèche, but they don't.

George Eliot's Silas Marner said that the little child came to link him to the world once again. This old miser knew that children aren't just cute; they have a purpose.

What is the purpose of a child? To link us to the crèche and the meaning of its story—the story of God's coming to be with us.

One of the meanings of its story is that we have the power to act. We can become children, and like them, we can move right into the crèche and its drama. We can be different. Because God is with us, we do not have to live with reactive negatives; we can be proactively positive. Note the difference:

Reactive Language	Proactive Language
There's nothing I can do	Let's look at our alternatives
That's just the way I am	I can choose a different approach
He makes me so mad	I can control my own feelings
I have to do that	I will choose an appropriate response
I can't	I choose
I must	I prefer
If only	I will

Move into the crèche today, and speak as the crèche has taught you.

O God, give us words straight from the crèche, words of possibility and hope. Let us use them even if we sound cute.

A two-ton truckload of turnips arrived at my church in New York one year, the day before Christmas. Brad Reeve, a local farmer, donated them to our soup kitchen. A lot of people would have liked to have left it right there. Send Mr. Reeve a nice, gracious note—thanking him for the turnips, or the delivery of the turnips, for the dumping out of the turnips on church property—and hope that he never does anything like that again.

When the truckload of turnips arrived, the word spread around town. One of the regular clients of the soup kitchen, a man who often showed up un-inebriated, that day showed up inebriated. For him, Christmas Eve started early and ended much—too much—later. He took one look at the enormous pile of turnips and said, "Oh, man, they said you had food over here. All you got is turnips!"

His comment reminded me of a typical supper at our house. "They said you had food in here. All you got is peas!"

We have to tell our children that what we've got is good. There's a wonderful poem called "Jacob" that ends, ". . . all angels /Travel under assumed names."

All angels travel under assumed names. Sometimes they come as peas, other days as turnips. The angels are not going to switch their habit. Their habit is not to be habitual. Their regularity is the way they come in irregular ways. Their orthodoxy is their unorthodoxy. We must teach our children that all angels travel under assumed names.

I don't care if you like turnips or not, or whether habit has grown a thick crust on your skin. What I do care about is marvel. We just have to have some people around who can marvel. Everybody doesn't have to marvel all the time. Some people are legitimate when they say, "*They* said you have food over here; all you got is turnips!" Some people are correct when they inquire as to who allowed someone to dump a load of turnips on the church lawn. Children are right about some of the meals we serve them.

Some of us also have to be open to marvel at the strange gifts that come our way.

Open our eyes and our hearts to wonder, O God.

DECEMBER 25   MOOD SWINGS

Unto us a child is born.   —*Isaiah 9:6 KJV*

Christmas is a conundrum because it moves toward peace and excitement simultaneously. We want both the big orchestra and the serenity of quiet. We want the party to end at just the right moment, long before we are exhausted but not until we've had enough fun.

What happens in the middle of these emotions is Christmas. We should expect some "mood swings." We actually want these mood swings. We come to the holidays to swing our moods, to take them out for a dance, to give them a whirl on the floor.

Oddly, our best perspective on the season comes from those whose life is dominated by larger seasons than Christmas. Oklahoma City teenagers. People with AIDS. Mothers with new babies. Anything larger than Christmas enlarges it too—and makes its mood swing.

Today we may know all the moods of Christmas—the joy, the sorrow, the ups and the downs. Let us wait with hope for each one.

O God, you have promised that unto us, all things will come. We praise you that unto us a child is born.

DECEMBER 26   "LET NOTHING YOU DISMAY"

Instead of anticipating these mood swings from high to low—rarely middle—many people get lost in the dance. We lack the art of ritual—because ritual puts its arms around highs and lows and enjoys them. Ritual double twists. It dips on purpose. It holds our hand. It leads the dance. Ritual predicts difficulty and transforms it into holiday.

Lots of people become dismayed at this time of the year. *Dismay* means being overwhelmed. *Dismay* means too much of everything right in the middle of the time when things are supposed to be so right. That's why the carol "God Rest Ye, Merry Gentlemen" has it so right. "Rest" and "merry"—not either, but both. The song also tells us to let nothing dismay us. What is happening in the ups and downs is supposed to happen. Give it a rhythm. Dance it.

Can we dance even if we have a lot more HO HO HO than "Dough" RE MI? Of course. Sufficiency and Christmas are permanent enemies. Thus it will always be that the money will run out before the end of the month. Let it be. "Let nothing you dismay." Dance!

Bring us back from dismay, O God, to fullness of time right where we are.

DECEMBER 27   "JOY TO THE WORLD"

It is still the season of what Eugene Petersen calls "the big nouns": *joy, glory,* and *peace.* It also is the time of the great verbs: *to forgive, to save, to love.* Let them be. Their very greatness is their refusal to be manipulated, bought, bowed, packaged, or carried. They will come when they will come. All we dare trust is that they will be there.

We still may be waiting for Christmas long after the tree is down. We may have to wait longer than we are able. Advent waiting doesn't stop just because Christmas comes. The light has arrived, but we may not quite see it. Yet one day we may stand surprised at the edge of a stable. That will be our Christmas. Or we may find insomnia gifting us with the time to light the candle we didn't think we had all day. Or we may just pray for the light to come to a darkened world.

Lord, let there be light—and let it reflect well on the big words.

Children are not supposed to be afraid. And mothers are not supposed to be afraid. And fathers are not supposed to be afraid. But some children have awful nightmares; and some mothers know the table is too thinly laid—sometimes even when it has a lot of food on it; and some fathers drive on tires so thin and brakes so worn that they know they get where they're going safely because of angels, not wheels.

This is why we like the Christmas story so much, because it counsels us not to fear. "Fear not, for behold!" The power of the story is that it guarantees that there is no reason to be afraid. Sometimes we are more impressed by the problems of the world than by the power of God. We think that everything depends on us—a thought guaranteed to make us depressed. But in this season we remember that everything is up to God. There are modern-day "Herods" chasing children everywhere (see Matthew 2:16), but they are not going to catch them. Finally they will be stopped, by the power of God.

There are "Herods" hurting for what remains of the child in us too. Our adult souls get slowly bent out of shape by their too-eager embrace of the dishtowel and broom, their love affair with the ratchet wrench, their assumption that if we only have enough stuff surrounding us we will be protected against the "Herods." John Updike thought of America as a "vast conspiracy to make people happy." God knows, we work at it. Wouldn't it be fun not to work at it for a while—to give up all the effort of making others and ourselves happy and just *be* it or *do* it? Dishtowels folded and put away, us in the living room eating popcorn that we don't have to clean up later.

The modern Herods have killed the modern children with the conspiracy to make them happy, filling their hearts with the distortion that things and effort produce happiness. It is as if we looked in a mirror and saw ourselves in a funny shape—a bent-out-of-shape circus clown crying that we are empty inside and need cultural filling.

The truth is the opposite of this distortion. What is good about us is what is inside, what is God-given, what exists despite effort or wealth. "Be not afraid." What the angel meant was to evoke that inner strength against outer distortion. Angels wipe out fear by recasting the mirror of ourselves. The Spirit recasts the mirror.

The Spirit says, "Fear not, for behold . . ." there is *enough*.

Thank you, O God, for filling us with your Spirit.

DECEMBER 29   KILLING THE CHILDREN

What if someone is trying to kill the child within us? Or the children in our cities? What if we are bothered by troubles at work or at school or in our wider family? God gives you the resources you need to make peace in all these places. The larger the trouble, the larger the peace—and the more brilliantly it will shine in the place of the previous darkness. "Let nothing you dismay."

Every Christmas I make a pilgrimage to New York City to see the big tree at Rockefeller Center with all its lights. I can't help myself. One year I barely could afford to go, and I was having a little pity party about how I couldn't buy anything, not even a hot dog or a soda. I had just the money for the train in and out.

As I left the city—a relatively rich but momentarily poor person in the world's terms—I realized that Grand Central Station was filled with song. I thought maybe I was a little crazy. More than the usual number of homeless people were in the station that night. They seemed to be lined up everywhere. Their genuine poverty only humiliated my felt poverty even further. Lo and behold, there *was* music in the station—it was the entire Yale University Glee Club, singing a concert for the homeless.

My inner child was not killed—it was just not listening deeply enough.

Lord, let our inner child live. Let us learn to listen.

In his book *The Long Walk,* Slavomir Rawicz, a Polish prisoner of war, tells the story of being picked up by Stalin's army in 1944 and walking several thousand miles across Siberia in a chained line of three thousand men. Talk about standing in line! He was a nobleman who simply had been in the wrong place at the wrong time. The story of how he and six other men escaped and walked back across Siberia, through two winters, to safety in India, is an inspiring one.

They spent one Christmas Eve on their chained way north. Men were dying as they walked. A German man who had been keeping track of the days began to sing Christmas carols. The rest were surprised to know it was Christmas Eve. They made him stop singing. They couldn't bear the sound of beauty on their walk.

After Christmas, as they were still walking, Russian aboriginals, riding on reindeers, came to their line. They whispered, "We know you people. We have seen you before. For hundreds of years, bad Russians have tried to steal the wealth of the North Country by marching people like you here. Our ancestors told us to put food and pelts out on our door for you. The food and pelts will be there when you escape. Look for them."

When the seven men escaped, they made it because of the shoes they had made of the pelts, the fire they had made with the matches, and the food they had eaten before they were able to hunt.

Whenever I feel as if I am spending my whole life standing in line, I remember the story of their great escape. If they could get out of Siberia, I can get out of the grocery store! There is no need to fear for the light. We have matches in our pockets.

O God, point us to the matches, everywhere, waiting for us to strike them.

339

If you have been wondering why New Year's resolutions are often high on the joke circuit, wonder no more. Glenna Salsbury gets to the root of our perennial failure to become who we want to become in her book *The Art of the Fresh Start: How to Make and Keep Your New Year's Resolutions for a Lifetime.* She roots our resolves in our fears and anxieties. But fear can't motivate us, and thus every time we even think of our resolve, we become more afraid.

By a series of practical suggestions, she shows how to root our resolves in our hopes and in calmness. From there we can become who we want to be.

Lots of aphorisms come to mind. The first is from the apostle Paul, whom Salsbury quotes frequently, if not always naming him. (Is she afraid her Christian "slip" will show?) "The good that I would do, I do not. And the evil that I would not do, I do" (see Romans 7:15). Another aphorism that rings true to her work is more current. "Would that I didn't know now what I didn't know then." Salsbury shows the deep complexity which every human being is. She gets to the bottom of our inability to be our best selves and then, with very practical advice, moves us to the place we can either simply *be*—without becoming "better"—or *become,* slowly and carefully, who we want to be.

I think of these lines from Robert Browning's *Rabbi Ben Ezra:*

> What I aspired to be,
> And was not,
> comforts me.

That phrase helps me to keep my resolutions!

O God, we follow your light, with resolve, into the new year.